DATE			

DREAMS:
A Key to Self-Knowledge

I believe it to be true that dreams are
The true interpreters of our inclinations,
But there is art required
To sort and understand them.

Montaigne

Imagination imitates and competes with reality;
It leads either to success or failure.

DREAMS:
A Key to Self-Knowledge

Zygmunt A. Piotrowski, Ph.D.
with Albert M. Biele, M.D.

LEA LAWRENCE ERLBAUM ASSOCIATES, PUBLISHERS
1986 Hillsdale, New Jersey   London

Lawrence Erlbaum Associates, Inc., Publishers
365 Broadway
Hillsdale, New Jersey 07642

563 71548

Library of Congress Cataloging-in-Publication Data

Piotrowski, Zygmunt A. L., 1904–1985
  Dreams: key to self-knowledge.

  Bibliography: p.
  Includes indexes.
  1. Dreams.   I. Biele, Albert M.   II. Title.
BF1078.P58   154.6′34   86-1435
ISBN 0-89859-691-2

TO HALINA

*without whose presence
this book would not have been written*

PERSONALITY ASSESSMENT

A series of volumes edited by:
Charles D. Spielberger and James N. Butcher

PIOTROWSKI • *Dreams: A Key to Self-Knowledge*

Contents

PART III   FREUD AND PDS

PART IV   APPLICATION OF THE PDS

Acknowledgment

Generous financial aid from the Benjamin A. and Evelyn P. Strouse Foundation is gratefully acknowledged. Special appreciation is expressed to Dr. Lisa Okoniewski for her editorial assistance.

Zygmunt A. Piotrowski (1904–1985), Ph.D., and Doctor of Science h. c. (Hahnemann), was Clinical Professor of Psychology at Hahnemann University; Member, American Board of Professional Psychology; Professor of Psychiatry and Human Behavior, Thomas Jefferson University; Adjunct Professor of Psychology, Temple University; Consultant to the Veterans Administration; former President of the Rorschach Institute; author of Perceptanalysis, etc.

The late Albert M. Biele, M. D., was Clinical Professor of Psychiatry Thomas Jefferson University.

1 INTRODUCTION

1 Introduction

The *Perceptanalytic Dream System (PDS)* differs from other systems of dream interpretation in several ways. What makes PDS most unlike other systems is perhaps its basic postulates: (a) that sleep dreams be evaluated as if they were events observed consciously in overt, empirical reality; (b) that sleep dreams offer descriptions of dreamers' intrapsychic conflicts (somewhat different at different times) pertaining to the roles dreamers play in interpersonal relationships that matter at the time. The term *role* connotes not only overt behavior, conscious and unconscious in varying degrees, but also internal, subjective attitudes, feelings, self-evaluations, impulses, inhibitions, anxieties, pleasures, depressions, and their numerous varieties, conscious and unconscious (Piotrowski, 1972).

Also, PDS has a unique origin — a case of sheer serendipity.

On the first dry, sunlit, beautiful day of the spring of 1969, six men emerged from an overlong and uninspiring conference conducted in a windowless room. It was time for lunch, and we were suddenly in a jolly mood. As we settled around a circular table, Dr. Albert M. Biele followed his habit of reading aloud the dreams of patients he had in psychotherapy. Before anyone could groan or say a word, we heard a dream report. Although serious cogitation was far from our minds, we did take turns explaining the dream. Given in jest, however, our interpretations were extravagant. Finally my turn came. All the "clever" ideas I was going to use had been preempted. Before I knew what I was doing, I was interpreting the patient's dream according to my *Thematic Apperception Test (TAT) rules*. These rules had been written 20 years earlier and were published in 1950 in the *Psychoanaltyic Review;* their application to a long, verbatim TAT record was demonstrated two years later in the same journal (Piotrowski, 1950, 1952a, 1952b). When I finished, Dr. Biele said in earnest, "That's what the patient has been telling me for the last four months. Would you like to hear his recent dream, which he brought this morning?" And off he went. This time I applied TAT rules with great care and heard "Right again." At this moment a great discomfort overwhelmed me. How was it possible, I asked myself, that TAT rules apply also to dreams and do so even more successfully? TAT pictures are interpreted consciously and deliberately, giving subjects the opportunity to improve, suppress, or greatly change spontaneous associations to stimulus pictures and thus to dissemble genuine ideas and inclinations. Dreamers, on the other hand, produce visual imagery unconsciously. Moreover, dreamers are asleep and are not in any active interpersonal contact. Yet, while typically mistaking dream events for empirical reality, dreamers do not get confused and disoriented (although psychotics do in some of their dreams). Excluding anxiety-producing nightmares that wake dreamers, dreams rarely interrupt sleep; apparently people prefer to rest during the night without disturbance (Piotrowski, 1982).

TAT rules need only minor changes to be made suitable for the interpretation of dreams. Furthermore, they yield more abundant and valid information when used with dreams. Therefore, the difference in the parts of conscious and unconscious mentation during the production of TAT stories and sleep dreams seems irrelevant. What becomes important is the similarities. One is that, in creating dream events or in making up TAT stories, individuals imagine people intertwined in diverse relationships with one another but not with themselves; all overt action takes place only in the visual imagination. Subjects are observers, not actual participants in the social activities that take place before their mental eyes. As observers, they need not feel responsible for what is happening; therefore, they cannot be proved wrong or guilty. In both situations the stimuli are indefinite and equivocal — day residuals in dreams, ambiguous pictures in the TAT. With the TAT, many different reactions are obtained from a large sample of subjects. However, an individual gives only some of those responses, very many of which are equally plausible. Including all visuomotor details of dreams, each dream is unique, like a fingerprint; dreamers unwittingly reveal their preferences, antipathies, and anticipations. When asleep and physically inert, dreamers receive no significant sensory impressions (or, when some impressions penetrate, dreamers wake up or incorporate them into their dreams without affecting the validity of the dreams). Experiencing nothing inconsistent with their spontaneous imagery, dreamers find it easy to mistake dream imagery for actual sensorimotor impressions. This illusion allows people to react in dreams very much in the way they behave mentally in daily psychosocial relations (Piotrowski, 1980).

Dreams are remarkably truthful because they have an efficient way of obviating repression without complicating and confusing dream messages.

Whenever mental content disturbs dreamers, and they wish to avoid becoming aware of its implications, they can and do unconsciously attribute the disquieting content to dream figures other than themselves. Fundamental PDS premises are that dreamers ascribe traits to themselves in their dreams and that they believe these traits are their own, genuine characteristics. When dreamers ascribe traits to figures other than themselves, particularly to strikingly different ones ("animate inanimate" objects or forces, for example), they can easily disown or dissent the traits and thereby eliminate much tension. Because a positive but far from perfect correlation exists between the *assent–dissent* dimension and the *conscious–unconscious* dimension, the diversity of dream figures (humans, animals, natural forces, animate inanimate objects) provides a multipoint scale of degrees of the unconscious (Piotrowski, 1977). There is no doubt that unconscious motivation influences our intentions, perceptions, and activities. Moreover, such motivation may be very consistent and pervasive, making people pursue goals of which they are unaware and do so even when they want to do something different. In sleep dreams there is usually a rational element. It manifests itself in the logical and physical sequence of cause-and-effect actions from the beginning to the end of dreams. (This observation does not apply to psychotic dreams.) An outstanding example is the dreams of Hervey (1867/1964). He dreamed about his frustrated suicide. Of course, he was not in any danger of dying in his safe and comfortable bed as he tried to see his death in a dream. However, his unconscious would not entertain even the thought of a fictitious death. By contrast, Hervey succeeded in his deliberate attempt to sleep-dream about pleasant, life-asserting situations.

Dreams serve an important psychobiological function. They help to formulate and dramatize intrapsychic conflicts (Piotrowski, 1971). When we wish to stop being tormented by frustrations and troubles, we look for the causes. The unconscious helps us in this search through dreams. The most frequent theme of sleep dreams is frustration. Typically, we are ready to board a train but miss it by a few seconds, or we are looking for a particular street but get lost in the city. As dreams disclose intrapsychic conflicts, our being late or getting lost is our own doing. To create such dreams unconsciously, reasoning in terms of cause-and-effect relations happens both in our conscious and unconscious mental states. However, because the relations between cause and effect and also between consideration of the effect and its conjectured cause are abstract, and because the language of sleep dreams is concrete (visuomotor), the causal connection in dreams is shown as a temporal sequence of antecedent (cause) and sequel (effect). Subjects explaining TAT pictures also speak of antecedents and sequels. Dreams of nonpsychotics at times show the dreamers and other dream figures in situations and environments in which they have never been or are most unlikely ever to be, but the environmental situations are not bizarre or, in the opinion of the dreamers, physically impossible (for example, children may see their deceased mothers in dreams). Dreamers must have an idea of what they should do to get out of their difficulties, or have an idea of how a conflict will end when they do not have the mental or physical strength to resolve personal difficulties. Nightmares are dreams in which dreamers struggle with intrapsychic conflicts but have no idea of a solution. In deteriorated old age or severe illnesses that greatly reduce mental and physical resources, struggle with intrapsychic conflicts ceases, and dreams end.

The conscious–unconscious dimension is avoided in the PDS for purely methodological reasons, specifically because of the impossibility of obtaining reliable and valid measures of the degrees to which conscious and unconscious determine action tendencies and overt actions. The more dissented an intent is, the greater the likelihood that it is controlled or inhibited consciously or unconsciously. Strength and degree of incompatibility move the conscious and assented intents (or motives) to curb the dissented ones. The very appearance in sleep dreams of the most dissented, destructive, hostile intents seems to require assented, weak, frightened personality traits; this is seen most frequently in dreams preceding a psychotic breakdown. The effect of unconscious mental processes is demonstrated by the very existence of night dreams that are unconsciously produced in sleep. Awareness of dream events proves that the conscious also has a part in sleep dreams. As individuals work through dreams in therapy by unwittingly revealing evidence for the interpretation of their dreams, the intermingling of the conscious and unconscious becomes even more noticeable. Sleep dreams are not overrated when they are called the "royal road to the unconscious." They reveal dreamers' psychodynamics directly and correctly, provided they are generated spontaneously. Moreover, they do this in concrete detail, not in verbal generalizations. We have to remember, of course, that no single dream reveals the "whole" personality of anyone; it tells primarily about what bothers the dreamer at the time. This is why dreams have a sober mood or are depressing or frightening. If they were fulfillments of desires, we would expect them to be diffused with joy and self-confidence.

Psychotherapy or self-analysis is an excellent method of verifying the proposition that dreams concern dreamers' intrapsychic conflicts, which are stressful to a low or high degree. When individuals have a series of successive dreams pertaining to the same conflict, we can observe how the course of treatment or the dreamers' personality changes are accurately reflected in the successive dreams and sometimes even precede the dreamers' manifest psychological changes, good or bad; the series of dreams with the same basic theme is usually interspersed with other dreams.

A dream should be treated as a logical unit. It should not be chopped up into parts (verbs, nouns, singled-out scenes, persons, and so forth) that are to be analyzed separately from other parts. Its full message is contained in the entire dream. Of particular importance are the first and last dream scenes. A comparison of the last with the first discloses the quality and purposes of the different interacting intentions and actions. The intermittent scenes between the beginning of the dream and its end display the mental processes that unify the elements of the dream into a meaningful unit. In this manner, dreamers offer their intrapsychic processes to direct inspection.

There are no serial-free associations and no latent dreams in PDS. Concepts of PDS are empirical in the sense that concepts correspond to definite things that manifest themselves in the external or internal life of dreamers. No auxiliary theoretical concepts, which have no empirical denotation, are used; everything is verifiable by empirical evidence. Theoretical concepts that do not refer to clearly described and accurately delimited actual, empirical phenomena serve to fill in the gaps in explanations of the interrelations among investigated phenomena (Piotrowski, 1982). "Ether" is a theoretical concept. It is not perceptible. It was introduced into physics as a theoretical crutch to "explain" the possibility of the propagation of light. Theoretical concepts may have educational value. Sometimes they suggest novel experimental methods. Occasionally, eliminating a theoretical concept opens gates to new scientific conquests. Personology changed thoroughly after the introduction of "unconscious motivation," that is, after the notion that the relationship between natural parents and their children leaves a unique and lasting impression upon the children was discarded.

The psychobiological significance of sleep dreams is attested by their universality. Dreams begin as unconscious processes while dreamers are out of effective touch with the surrounding environment. Dreams indicate unconscious intrapsychic conflicts. When struggle causes sufficient stress, dreaming becomes conscious, although dreamers do not wake up unless intense anxiety is stirred. Dreamers then watch the action as if they are inactive and only indirectly involved observers. Verbal reasoning (a critical evaluation of the meaning of observed dream events) is incompatible with sleep. Thus, the language of dreams themselves is visuomotor. In the visual imagery of dreams, individuals disclose their experiences and intents, the degrees to which they assent or dissent their attitudes and behavior toward others, and their feelings about themselves.

Although PDS is clear and simple, it calls for unfamiliar thinking on the part of the dream analyst. A beginner's frequent tendency is to assume that dreams disclose actions that dreamers consciously or unconsciously anticipate performing in waking life. This assumption implies a wrong conception of dreams. The fundamental PDS postulate is that dreams display correctly and directly intrapsychic conflicts; these conflicts influence overt psychosocial behavior — but to many different degrees and in a great variety of ways. In estimating the bearing dreams have on dreamers' overt psychosocial behavior, we must consider at least two facts: There are many slips between the cup and the lip, between actions and words; when dreamers appear in their own dreams as figures, they assign to themselves only those traits that they genuinely believe to be their true, real traits. Therefore, it is highly probable that these assented traits appear in the dreamers' manifest behavior. Traits assigned to dream figures that are unlike the dreamers are dissented to various degrees and therefore appear less frequently in dreamers' overt behavior.

According to the intra-individual Axiom A, dream figures dramatize distinct quasi-autonomous function units of the dreamers' personalities. Axiom B is interpersonal; it postulates that the distinct traits that dreamers assign to separate figures in their dreams reflect the dreamers' feelings, thoughts, and intentions regarding the type of person (male, female, old, young, active, inactive, and so forth) the figures represent. From the axiom pair A and B, it follows that in our dreams we attribute to figures other than our own those traits of which we are not aware of possessing or of which we authentically doubt or deny possessing. At first sight, this conclusion astonishes some people. It seems to go too far in assigning assented personal traits to dreamers' selves and in assigning dissented (and usually undesirable) traits to others in dreams. However, this negative reaction occurs when people forget that dreams express intrapsychic processes and not overt, concrete behavior and attitudes.

Intrapsychic events produced unconsciously in dreams are nonetheless apperceived consciously and can be reported in public, verbal language by dreamers; this seems the most fascinating aspect of dreams. This process is possible because verbal thoughts and visual imagery relate to the same reality, despite differences between visual and verbal languages.

Over 50 definitions of personality have been published. PDS identifies "personality" as the roles individuals assume, consciously or unconsciously, in relationships, intra-individually (in mentation) and interpersonally (in overt behavior); specifically, "personality" connotes individuals' psychosocial relationships and behavior as well as mentation (intents, affects, perceptions, thoughts, and self-centered feelings) related to interpersonal roles. PDS conclusions are empirically verifiable and do not directly concern themselves with etiological theories of the origin of any aspect of personality.

Many of the personological terms and conceptual definitions used in this book can be found in Piotrowski (1977, 1979). These terms and definitions were formulated with the aim of making them reliably demonstrable in empirical reality. Pursuit of this aim led to the adaptation of Das' definition and classification of emotions in perceptanalysis: "Emotion is a desire to associate with, or dissociate from, other persons with the intent of a voluntary or forcible continuance or discontinuance of exchange of pleasures and/or pains" (Das, 1953). The term *emotion* indicates desires. Emotional acting requires more than mere desires. The definition clearly discriminates between positive and negative emotions. Positive emotions prompt individuals to associate with others, whereas negative emotions induce them to avoid others. Love is an example of a strong emotion, and liking is a mild emotion, but both are positive. Analogously, hatred also exemplifies a strong emotion and dislike a weak emotion, but both are negative. The adapted Das definitions are helpful generally in their reliable applicability and specifically in the interpretation of dreams, which are silent (no speech); affective attitudes must be deduced mainly from the movements of dream figures.

Besides interpersonal emotions, which draw individuals toward or pull them away from others, there are intra-individual feelings. *Feelings* are those affects and preoccupations that center around individuals themselves. People feel good and bad about themselves, optimistic and enterprising, discouraged and depressed, fearless and anxious (fearing the unknown), spontaneous and procrastinating, and so forth. In all these states of feeling, our attention, thoughts, and affects focus on how we feel. Feelings and emotions together constitute the class of affects.

Each intent, thought, and action tendency is expressed in visuomotor imagery during sleep dreams. By studying this imagery, we can gain valid knowledge of our intrapsychic dynamics; we can learn of any existing dissonances between our conscious, social, public self and our internal forces. As a rule, however, cognizance of the intrapsychic processes that interfere with effective conscious functioning escapes us. Dream interpretations help to remove the blinders from our eyes.

2 Brief Historical Review of Dream Interpretation

In the study of dreams two basic problems must be addressed. These problems have different histories. They require separate methods of investigation and pursue different goals. The psychologically more important and practically more useful goal is determining the meaning of dream content. Does this content offer unknown information, the conscious knowledge of which can relevantly help dreamers to change behavior to make their lives more secure? Since its beginning, humanity has tried numerous means and invented many rituals to accomplish this desirable end. The purpose of the second basic problem is to discover the causes of dreaming and the determinants of specific dream contents. Which factors external to the process of dreaming and emanating from the dreamers' physical surroundings or from physiological processes of the body influence the content of dreams? When and how do these factors work? This second line of inquiry has undergone tremendous changes in the last decades, thanks to the discovery of Aserinsky (Aserinsky & Kleitman, 1953) that the movements of sleepers' eyeballs indicate that they are dreaming. It is interesting that the connection between dreams and eye movement in sleep has been considered by hunters and country people to be a sign of dreaming in dogs for a long time. Humans sometimes discover human traits in animals but less frequently animal traits in humans, especially when the traits concern mental life. However, inquiries regarding the significance of dream content show relevant insight into and grasp of the meaning of dreams beginning in antiquity. At the same time, fanciful and unsound symbolic interpretations were also advanced, particularly of the concrete nouns or of the objects to which those nouns referred. The capricious method of interpreting dream symbols has been by far the more popular one.

The first written mention of a dream was carved on a stela in Babylon circa 3000 B.C. This monument commemorates a statesman for his outstanding achievements. The text reveals that the man had been God-fearing and that his dream confirmed it. Unfortunately the stela, now in the British Museum, does not reproduce the dream or its analysis. At the time, Babylon was a theocracy, and its priests were naturally interested in a prominent man's religious beliefs. The practice of consulting dreams before making a decision in important matters, private or public, was maintained late into the 16th century A.D. Numerous individuals continue doing so in their private lives even today.

Dreaming is not an abnormal activity, but it is so sensitive to what occurs in the body that it frequently reveals severe personality changes that have taken place or that are imminent as a result of physical disease, particularly of the brain. This had been recognized already in the 5th century B.C. by Hippocrates. The great advances in neuropsychiatry and biochemistry, made possible by highly sensitive and reliable detection devices, have enabled scientists to study the body processes that accompany dreaming. Since Aserinsky and Kleitman (1953) proved that eye movements are much better indicators of dreaming states and nondreaming sleep states than whole-body movements are, the physiology of dreaming has become an object of intensive research. This book attempts to contribute to the understanding of grossly psychopathological dreams that are not apprehensible without knowledge of underlying organogenic disorders.

The universal interest in dreams is prompted by the basic need for security. This need engenders the desire for knowledge of the future. Thus, by far the most frequent use of dreams has been prognostication of future events. People want to know whether a wish will be fulfilled or a disaster prevented. As early as old Babylonian times, priests were professional soothsayers who based their predictions on analyses of clients' dreams. The whole life of Babylonians was arranged in harmony with dream interpretations. This practice was maintained by many up to the 17th century in Europe. The famous Egyptian dreambook was written in the 2nd millennium B.C. and has been republished and translated into many languages, finding readers even today. Antiphon, a Greek in the 4th century B.C., wrote the first large, dictionary-like dreambook for practical, professional interpretations. He stated clearly that dreams are not created by supernatural powers but by natural conditions and that natural connections exist between peoples' futures and the content of their dreams. The first entirely preserved dreambook is of Artemidorus, a Greek physician who lived in Rome in the 2nd century A.D. The book includes material from the Egyptian version.

The ancient Greeks made great advances in the investigation of dreams. Plato (429–347 B.C.) noted that even good men dream of uncontrolled and violent actions, including sexual aggression. These actions are not performed by good men in waking states but are openly acted out by criminals without guilt. He deduced that normal people have antisocial inclinations motivated by aggressive and sexual desires. Freud identified these inclinations as basic instincts. Plato remarked further that dreams contain visual memories of earliest childhood, memories that are long forgotten in waking life. Democritus (5th century B.C.) stated that dreams are not products of immaterial soul (as Plato taught) but originate as a result of penetration of visual impressions of the material environment; these impressions influence our imagination, which explains why dream imagery is similar to perceptions of reality. Aristotle (384–322 B.C.), too, recognized the psychological nature of dreams and denied their supernatural origin. He stated emphatically that dreams can predict future events. His idea was that dreams result from sense organ movements that, in turn, produce images. Aristotle admitted that sometimes dreams can be of limited prognostic value and that prognosis must have a natural basis (a disturbing physical illness, for example); Hippocrates discovered earlier that onset of physical diseases affecting the brain can be revealed by the patient's dreams.

Hippocrates was "the father of medicine." He was also named "the first psychoanalyst" by Brill (1936), who translated Freud's *Interpretation of Dreams*. Hippocrates was the first to separate medicine from philosophy and theology. He was as rational and empirical about dreams as he was about diseases and their causes. His dream criterion of a nonpsychogenic illness affecting mental functioning was a dream in which the dreamer's past experiences were represented in an illogical and unreal manner. The more abnormal the dream events were, the more urgent he considered the need for therapy. Healthy people (in other words, nonpsychotics) realistically re-experience their past in dreams, and reports of their dreams do not violate standards of logic and reality. Hippocrates was born on the island of Kos, within sight of the Asia Minor coast. On this island was a famous temple of Aesculapius, the Greek god of medicine. The temple was a healing place, the equivalent of a medical school. Hippocrates belonged to the Aesculapians and probably was introduced by them into the arts of dream interpretation and of using dreams as therapeutic devices. In many parts of the world and in many different epochs, incubation has been used as a means of healing. It was practiced also in Kos; there were about 300 Aesculapian healing centers in Greece alone at the time. In these places patients would be assigned a room with a bed. In the evening a priest would tell the patients that they were to sleep and dream and that in the morning the priest would return to ask the patients about their dreams. In the morning, the priest not only listened to the dream reports but made the patients actually act out all the roles they had performed in their night dreams, as actors on a stage; the priest would assume the role of other characters from the same dreams. The obvious purpose was to make the dreamers more conscious of their intrapsychic inconsistencies and to make them experience these incompatibilities and roles intensively. This method and its variants have been revived in recent times, and good results have been claimed. During all periods of time, the interpretation and the therapeutic use of dreams were rational and psychological (in a minority of people) and irrational and superstitious (in the majority). So it was in Greece. The disastrous Peloponnesian war affected freedom of speech and writing. The clearheaded Hippocrates was cautious when he wrote about dreams. He said that he was concerned only with little, less important dreams, dreams originating not with gods but with mortals. He left interpretation of "great" dreams to others. As a physician, Hippocrates was interested in how diseases of the body or mind influence dream content. His thesis that illnesses change dreams is significant. He saw a basic problem that is still largely unsolved. How can some dreams (and these are not rare) reveal a physical illness and particularly a debilitating psychological condition before any noticeable outward signs appear?

Artemidorus, the Greek 2nd century A.D. physician in Rome, wrote perhaps the most popular dreambook in history. He used all literary sources known in his time. His dreambook has been translated into many languages and has been republished continually for at least 16 centuries. It is astonishing how much faith was put in the prognostic value of dreams. Some of the most important decisions of individuals and even of states were made in accordance with the interpretation of dreams. Artemidorus could not discourage this practice but tried to warn against uncritical acceptance of interpretations. He advised dream analysts to study the personality traits of dreamers to avoid mistakes in the interpretation of their dreams. He emphasized a modern point: Dreams are products of the mind and are not exclusively results of external sensory impressions. However, he also made a politically cautious note that possibly dreams were messages from gods. A century earlier, Cicero considered it impossible that divine powers created human dreams. Cicero thought that if gods wished to reveal something to humans, they would rather communicate with people who were wide awake and who could hear well than with sleepers who snored. Empirical verification, he added, was required to determine whether dreams had any predictive value. Imperial Rome was dangerous to prominent and simple folks alike. Disasters and loss of life threatened frequently. Cicero, a republican, was murdered by political enemies. One of his dreams, which he interpreted himself, made him follow the wrong strongman.

On his way to Rome to fight Pompey for rule over the Empire, Caesar stopped at the Rubicon river. It was the psychological and administrative frontier of Italy. Crossing the river would mean an irreversible challenge to the older man, Pompey. During the night before the announced crossing, Caesar had a disturbing, incestuous dream. Later he decided to cancel the order to march but his chief of staff pleaded that the troops were rested and eager and that instead of being a bad omen, the dream was a good sign. The chief argued that just as Caesar possessed his mother in his dream, so he would possess Italy, which was the "mother" of them all. He persuaded Caesar, and the crossing took place as planned. In pre-Christian times, a dream of incest with mother was believed to be favorable, predicting among other things a happy return from war. Interpretation of objects or animals seen in dreams seems capricious. Mackenzie identified the meaning of the snake in four cultures. To the Assyrians, seizing a snake meant that the dreamer would be protected by an angel. The Egyptians thought that seeing a snake in a dream indicated that a dispute would be settled. According to the Greeks, a snake signified sickness and enmity; and a powerful snake, a severe illness. The Jews were reassured by dream snakes because it meant that the dreamers' livelihoods were assured: Bitten dreamers' livelihoods would be doubled; dreamers who killed snakes would lose their livelihoods (Mackenzie, 1965). A French, 19th-century dreambook affirms that dreaming of a skin disease such as pimples or scabies means getting money and that the amount of riches increases with the severity of the illness. Viewing feces in dreams as symbols of gold is an old tradition. So is the occasional custom of assigning to verbs occurring in dreams meanings that are opposite of the meanings ascribed to the verbs in standard dictionaries. This is still done today, especially by psychoanalysts. Throughout the ages people have disagreed least about sex symbols. There have always been many of them in all cultures and languages, but agreement regarding their specific meanings has been relatively highest. Two facts appear to explain this: Sexual behavior is conditioned by human anatomy and biology, which are the same everywhere; sexual functions are inevitably essential to our origin.

The discovery of the unconscious made it possible for the first time to examine systematically the curious and unique psychological state of dreaming. This state consists of conscious observations of involuntarily and unconsciously produced imagery arising while dreamers are asleep and unaware of physical stimuli emanating from the immediate physical environment. The idea of unconscious motivation radically changed and enriched the psychology of personality. Although speculative theories of the unconscious existed in India, Greece, and Europe during the Middle Ages, they were mystical or physical theories. In 1714 Leibniz proposed the first purely psychological conception of the unconscious. By unconscious he meant originally the subliminal perceptions that play an important part in human mental life (Ellenberger, 1970). But Leibniz also included dreams in the unconscious — separation and solution of problems during sleep, responsive perceptions, operation of an unconscious censor, appetitive acts, inclinations, sentiments, and recovery of a sense of self-identity on waking. Leibniz noted that we are unconscious of these realities unless we conceptualize them. The concept of the unconscious is fertile in explaining experience, he asserted, but its main role is maintaining the fullness and reasonableness of individuals (Loemker, 1972). Important for the development of future empirical psychology is Leibniz's elaboration of his predecessors' ideas and his concept of purposiveness of action and value, purposiveness that no human logic alone can reveal by rational deduction. "Uncertainties can be dealt with only through a logic of probabilities; emergence of pragmatic conceptions of verification result from a reliance on experience and on the recognition that possibilities outreach actualities and thus involve uncertainty." Leibniz laid the theoretical foundations of psychotherapy by pointing out that, whereas logic alone (consciously directed reasoning) cannot disclose the "reasons of the heart," it can assist materially in "the ordering of those reasons" of affects and intentions; Leibniz identified intention with will (Loemker, 1972). Shortly before, La Rochefoucauld's maxim appeared in print: "The heart has its reasons which reason does not know" (1665), which is a terse definition of the unconscious.

Many diverse and great changes from the 17th century on were conducive to an interest in the individual human being and individual differences: exploration of the world and of the diverse peoples and their customs; growth of the merchant and manufacturing class, which increasingly challenged the unquestioned power position of the gentry; diversification of religious beliefs and moral codes; increased knowledge of personal habits and of behavior of many different people; more frequent communication between people. Theories and experimental investigations multiplied. Many separate scientific disciplines were developing. The person who knew everything that was to be known disappeared. The era of the specialist began and extended, naturally, to dream interpretation. Times were cruel and warlike, and economic crises were frequent. A very large proportion of the population was ill at all times; few people reached old age. All these conditions taken together contributed to the growth of psychopathological states and behavior.

The Discovery of the Unconscious: The History and Evolution of Dynamic Psychiatry (Ellenberger, 1970), is a consummate, extensive, balanced text. The book deals in part with dreams and their use in therapy; for example, the section entitled "Healing through gratification of frustrations" describes the importance 17th-century Native Americans attached to the gratification of individuals' wishes as expressed in their dreams. The period covered is from antiquity through the present. At the beginning of the introduction, the author explains:

> This book is intended to be a history of dynamic psychiatry based on a scientific methodology, with a detailed and objective survey of the great dynamic psychiatric systems, notably those of Janet, Freud, Adler and Jung. An interpretation of facts and systems is proposed, on the basis of an evaluation of the socioeconomic, political, and cultural background, as well as the personality of the

pioneers, their environment, and the role of certain patients. The starting point of my study came about through reflection on the contrast between the evolution of dynamic psychiatry and that of other sciences. No branch of knowledge has undergone so many metamorphoses as dynamic psychiatry: from primitive healing to magnetism, magnetism to hypnotism, hypnotism to psychoanalysis and the newer dynamic schools. Furthermore, these various trends have gone through repeated waves of rejection and acceptance.

Ellenberger collected a great deal of information that helps to explain how and why the founders of dynamic psychiatry created their systems. Besides providing biographical information, this book illustrates the varied experiences that shape thinkers' intellectual creations.

A comprehensive, thorough, systematic book devoted exclusively to the science of dreams was published by Siebenthal (1953). Very methodical, the book concerns the methods and technical details of dream interpretation and covers 1,309 bibliographical references in four languages. Siebenthal did not present problems and results of the new science of the brain physiology of dreams. The physiological concomitants of dreaming, the results of Hall's (1953) statistical study of the content of more than 10,000 dreams and other details associated with dreaming, were reported in *The New World of Dreams,* edited by Woods and Greenhouse (1974). This anthology also contains innumerable dreams with comments. The information in these three very different books is immense and cannot be recapitulated here. Instead it seems advantageous to note that all these volumes clearly imply that dream thoughts are very similar to waking thoughts and that they concern conflicts of ungratified wishes.

Wallace (1967) reported on dream theory and dream rituals of the 17th- and 18th-century Native Americans belonging to the Seneca nation. These people had a sophisticated theory of dreams. Wallace wrote:

> It would be fair to say that (their) understanding of psychodynamics was greatly superior to that of the most enlightened Europeans of the time. However, the use they made of the dream contents sometimes led to gruesome consequences. They firmly believed that the fulfillment of dream wishes of any member of the tribe must take priority over other priorities. Any dream which involved others beside the dreamer was presented to the elders. The imitation of the dream in waking life became a serious matter when the dream wishes revealed in it were of the Supernatural being who appeared in the dream. Frustration of the wishes of the Supernatural was dangerous for he might not merely abandon or directly cause the death of the dreamer, but bring about disaster to the whole society or even cause the end of the world.

Wallace concluded that the desire for freedom — intrapsychic and social — had inspired the dream theory:

The culture of dreams may be regarded as a necessary escape valve. Iroquois men were, in their daily affairs, brave, active, self-reliant, and autonomous; they cringed to no one and begged for nothing. But no man can balance forever on such a pinnacle of masculinity, where asking and being given are unknown. Iroquois men dreamed, and without shame they received the fruits of their dreams, and their souls were satisfied. . . . 'The Iroquois have only a single divinity — wrote Father Fremin — the dream. To it they render their submission, and follow all its orders with the utmost exactness' (Wallace, 1958). . . Men had frank dreams of sex with women other than their wives. Often there were dreams in which objects of monetary value were demanded and obtained. In all cases the tribal council saw to it that dreamers got what they wanted. Even cruel and ghastly dreams had been carried out in reality. These included suicide dreams in which dreamers saw themselves tortured and burnt alive. The dreamers insisted that everything be done to them as it was done in their dreams. However, it appears that the dreamers could interrupt the proceedings by saying that they were satisfied and that their dreams required nothing further . . . The Iroquois (Huron and Seneca) theory of dreams was basically psychoanalytic. In 1649, Father Ragueneau, a Jesuit, described this theory in language that might have been used by Freud himself: 'They believe that our soul makes these natural desires known by means of dreams, which are its language. Accordingly, when these desires are accomplished it is satisfied. But, on the contrary, if it be not granted what it desires, it becomes angry, and not only does not give its body the good and the happiness that it wished to procure for it, but often it also revolts against the body, causing various diseases, and even death.' (Wallace, 1972, p. 61)

The Iroquois had a remarkable psychological insight. They differentiated between conscious and unconscious parts of the mind. They recognized the great force of unconscious desires, and were aware that the frustration of these desires could cause mental and physical (psychosomatic) illness. They understood that these desires were expressed in symbolic form, by dreams, and that the individual could not always properly interpret his dreams himself. They distinguished between the manifest and the latent content of dreams, and used what resembles a free association technique to unravel the latent meaning; other members of the tribe participated in this process of unraveling. The whole village tried to grant the dreamer his every wish, for according to their beliefs, any frustration was a threat to life not only of the individual but of the whole community. They assumed that the same desires, actions and frustrations ruled the three different realities thought to exist: waking life, dream life, and the world of supernatural spirits. These spirits controlled human lives if they so desired. They were angered and offended, as humans were, but they could revenge themselves on the humans mercilessly (Wallace, 1972). Thus, while believing in psychosomatic determinism, the Iroquois felt exposed to unpredictable grave danger because of the capricious and cruel mood swings of the supernatural spirits.

An uncommon and inventive investigator of dreams was Hervey (1822–1892), a specialist in Chinese language, culture, and history at the Collège de France. He started recording his dreams at the age of 13 and drew colored pictures of some of them. Dreams were his hobby, which he pursued vigorously. He gave lectures on his views before serious scientific societies in Paris and published articles in learned journals. His book *Les Rêves et les Moyens de les Diriger* (1867) appeared anonymously. It was reprinted in Paris (1964) with Hervey's name on the title page; a 50-page informative and evaluating introduction with many pertinent bibliographical references and biographical information preceded the text. Hervey had rich and diversified intellectual and social lives. He was quoted, always briefly but in important contexts, by leading writers on dreams. The quotes were practically always secondhand, because Hervey's anonymous book was very hard to obtain.

Hervey thought that dreams should be written down immediately after awaking and preferably also illustrated, for otherwise they are quickly forgotten or significantly changed. Furthermore, he took note that the habit of immediately recording dreams stimulates additional dreaming. Contemporary statistical investigations confirm Hervey's conclusions about immediate recording; after more than six waking minutes, memory of sleep dreams becomes distorted, and some important dream elements are forgotten. Hervey, an independent and innovative thinker, was a dispassionate polemist who argued clearly and fairly. His cherished purpose was to develop a method of deliberately changing sleep dream events, in desired and specific ways.

To achieve this purpose, Hervey used the following technique. While falling asleep, in a drowsy and hypnagogic state, he thought intensely of the visuomotor image of the event he wished to see in his forthcoming deep sleep dream. The consciously projected image was to replace the negative and unpleasant element which had appeared during a previous occurrence of the same sleep dream. It took Hervey about a month of persistent trying to experience the desired changed version of the original sleep dream in a recurrence of the dream dealing with the same problem. One must persevere, noted Hervey. For example, he cited his success with migraine headaches, by substituting a pleasant experience for the previous painful headaches, in the same dream scene. Hervey reported results of his technique with 42 dreams. Success was complete in 23 instances; in 13, it was "mixed"; in 4, new images but quite different from the intended one appeared; in 1 instance, the intended image appeared only in the moment of awaking; and in 1 case the effort caused awaking from the dream.

Hervey also investigated the possibility of deliberately creating disastrous and life-threatening sleep dreams. For example, in a dream he attempted to see his own suicide by jumping from a great height. Paris then was being rebuilt with tall houses along new broad avenues. In a dream, Hervey saw himself walk on one of those avenues. He noticed an open window on the top floor of a building. As it happens in dreams, in the next instance he saw himself standing on the sill of the window. And he jumped. There was again a sudden change of scene: Hervey found himself in a square in front of a church. There were many people around, all looking in one direction. Hervey inquired what had happened and was told that a man had just jumped from the church tower and had killed himself. Another time he wanted to commit a dream suicide by jumping from a cliff on the French side of the English channel. He managed to leap from the rock, but before he hit the water, a balloon appeared, and its gondola scooped him up gently to deposit him on firm soil. In these dreams, he always noticed that time elapsed between the instant he jumped and the instant he reached the bottom — time enough for many things to happen, considering the speed with which dream events take place. The situation is different when people attempting to commit suicide cut their throats or shoot themselves; the fatal result occurs instantly after the initiation of the attempt at suicide. Once, when Hervey was trying to dream about cutting his throat, he was defeated by the sight of the razor at his throat. He was also inhibited — albeit in a different way — when he intended to dream of shooting himself. Hervey owned a pair of dueling pistols that he kept in a special case in a drawer containing all sorts of things. When, in the dream, he had removed the pistol case from the drawer, he noticed some old photographs. One of them made him think of the past, and, in the dream, he forgot about the pistols. To think of something in a dream is to "see" it, and absence of thought means absence of imagery. This is one of Hervey's fundamental theses. In his attempts to dream his self-destruction, he dramatized the early phase of the intended action in visuomotor images, but he was unable to achieve the ultimate purpose of the intended action. Obviously Hervey's unconscious desire was to live, not to die. In each of these dreams, he decidedly evaded his actual suicide and thus confirmed in advance the statement in PDS that dreamers attribute to themselves, when they appear in their own dreams, only their assented traits. Suicide, the opposite of life, was dissented and not dramatized. Hervey wanted to experience his death only in fantasy and not in reality. He assented the thrill of facing mortal danger but also successfully escaping it. Some of his other dreams reveal this trait more directly. In his book, Hervey reports and at least briefly interprets hundreds of his own dreams.

Hervey's experimental bent is manifested conspicuously in his unusual experiments with the conditioning of dreams, about half a century before Pavlov conditioned the salivary reflexes of dogs. During a carnival season, there were quite a few private dancing parties. Hervey liked to attend these parties at which he usually saw most of the same people and the same orchestra. He made an agreement with the orchestra leader: When Hervey would dance with the young lady in blue, the orchestra would play *valse bleue,* and when he would dance with the young lady in pink, the orchestra would play *valse rose.* This was done throughout the season. In his bedroom, Hervey adjusted a music box so that it would play at a volume that he would notice subliminally but that would not wake him. The selected valses were sufficiently different for easy identification. His assistant would select one tune or the other at random, having made certain that Hervey was asleep before playing it. Hervey did not know ahead of time which music would be played during a particular night or whether music would be played at all. The subliminal music evoked the dream image of the correct young lady. The scenery, however, was not always that of the ballroom, and the partner was not always wearing her ball costume; he "saw" them involved in diverse events. Thus, the conditioned connection was between the tune and the person. Similar experiments with olfactory stimuli (perfumes) were less successful. He explained his inability to dream about his own suicide through another thesis, namely, that we never dream anything not experienced in waking life. According to his own data, this thesis applies to verbs, that is, to expression of desires and actions in dreams but not to inanimate objects (for example, clothes or locations). Hervey, speaking of repetitive dreams, said that their images, uniform in structure but undergoing mild variations in details, reveal the same subjective problems (idée fixe) that worry dreamers. Dreams display active frustration of active intentions; this frustration is displayed before conscious dreamers. Hervey's fundamental principle is: To think of something while asleep is to dream about it; to dream of something is to have an image of it. Dreams are thoughts, and reasoning in sleep dreams is the same as in waking states. According to Hervey, however, we base our dream judgments on incoherent illusions because of inadequate intellectual contact with the empirical world. His explanation of symbols in dreams is remarkable; he emphasized that the same object "seen" by different dreamers may have different meanings and that an object seen by an individual in more than one dream may also have different meanings. Waking persons and dreamers concentrate on a particular feature of an object, disregarding all others. An orange has form, color, taste, size, and so forth. The mind can "abstract" or "detach" just one characteristic at a time. This abstraction applies also to mental attributes. Perhaps this is why people known to us sometimes behave out of character in our dreams. PDS explains symbolism in the same manner. Actually, this should not be surprising, for in normal thinking and in science, the same mental process is frequently used but not stated. In India a religious image represents one or another divine attribute. The image is not an idol but merely an aid used in meditation; the supreme divinity is "formless" and thus cannot be represented by an image.

Among Christians reigns the same custom. For example, Rome has a church of St. Mary of Peace, another of St. Mary of Victory, a third of St. Mary of the People, and a fourth of the Holy Name St. Mary. Each of these churches is dedicated to the same St. Mary.

By quoting some of his predecessors and their results and by confirming their findings, Hervey emphasized the importance of dreams in the early diagnosis of severe diseases, especially organic brain disorders. He advocated the use of dreams in medicine. Of course the need for psychological diagnostic aids has drastically diminished in view of the remarkable development of biochemical and electronic techniques. Nonetheless, Hervey's interest in the diagnostic and therapeutic application of dreams testifies to his sagacity. This does not weaken his insistence that the "movements of the brain fibers" do not determine the content of dream events, the course of which, "except for some occasional causes, is controlled by psychological affinities" that is, by desires or intentions. To say this during a period of philosophical materialism, when anything mental was viewed by the learned world as a mere epiphenomenon of organic brain processes, was daring. Modern neurology does not believe that organic defects correlate perfectly with loss of functions. Among other beliefs, Hervey was certain that there was no night sleep without a dream, a fact confirmed by modern techniques.

Hervey's most fostered idea was to develop means of conscious and effective control over dream content to achieve beneficial mental states. He was convinced he had discovered "the means of control" and believed in its efficacy as a result of experiments performed on himself (and by friends on themselves once they had mastered his technique). He lectured to psychologists and physicians about it. Three conditions must be met to obtain mastery of dreams. First, while sleeping, dreamers must maintain consciousness of their dreams. This habit, Hervey claimed, can be acquired easily by keeping records of dreams and persistent training. Second, dreamers must associate waking sensory perceptions with dream elements in such a way that the recalled sensorimotor images, consciously controlled during the dreams, blend with the dream content. Third, associated memory images must be used to influence dream pictures according to dreamers' wills. Hervey defined *will* as directed desire, which, he said, never fails to exert its influence when people are conscious that they dream. Because thinking about something means dreaming about it, dreamers can deliberately think of altering the development of their dreams in a desired manner. Taken separately, original dream content, associated visuomotor memories, and the blending of the two are not unusual. Combining the three psychological elements, however, gives surprising results. Suppose people dream of wishing to do something, but they are so slow in their dreams that they miss their chances. Following Hervey's instructions, they would recall similar frustrating situations they had experienced in waking life. They would then blend the two situations and imagine a different course of dream events. They would be relieved and would gain increased self-confidence because of their success. Hervey reported a number of his lucid personal dreams, those dreams over which voluntary control of some aspects of dream events is maintained. He illustrated his procedure and analyzed the mental process by which dream events could be directed toward desirable endings. Attaining this mastery over dream events, however, is easier said than done; Hervey attempted many times to dream in sleep only what he had planned in detail ahead of time but succeeded merely in part and after weeks of determined trials. In the end, Hervey reported success in influencing the endings of his dreams and the subsequent improvement of his state of mind. Disciplined self-training is necessary in this self-therapeutic method. Hervey noted that acquiring the skills to have lucid dreams and to guide them in desired directions takes time. In view of the high degree of consciousness in these 'lucid' dreams, we wonder how deep and intense the conflict between impulses and counter-impulses is, to be able to appear in lucid dreams without waking dreamers or to occur only in sleep dreams during which people are not aware that they dream and are not capable of assessing the significance and implications of dream events. In deep dreams, powerful emotions, mainly anxiety, are sometimes experienced but cannot be changed consciously and in a specific and desirable manner. By all appearances Hervey developed a technique of influencing unconscious habits through conscious alteration of dream endings, a technique that usually allows frustrations and inhibitions to be vented. Ullman and Zimmerman (1979) wrote:

> What does it mean when, in a dream, you realize you're dreaming? That is referred to as 'lucid' dreaming . . . In any dream the setting is always involuntary; we do not will the opening scene. We experience it initially as an audience of one, witnessing the images that are thrust upon us. As the dream progresses, more and more voluntary and volitional elements enter the picture. We are in the dream actively or as a spectator; we are acting as well as reacting to what is taking place. As we become more and more aware of our own role in the dream, we may suddenly experience the awareness that it is all a dream. Some lucid dreamers are able to take the next step and begin to shape the subsequent course of the dream (but) the element of control occurs only within certain limits . . . A dream dealing with an unresolved problem does not 'come true,' but it is true as a symbolic depiction of a real-life situation.

This is also the basic PDS thesis.

Ullman had an intensive and diversified clinical and experimental research experience with all kinds of dreamers and dreams, normal, paranormal and pathological. Together with his associate (Ullman & Zimmerman, 1979) he formulated the psychological function of dreams, thus: "Dreams urge us to face the issues that restrict and discourage us, or that limit our inventiveness. They remind us of our responsibility we all have to free our emotional life." Their book contains a brief history of dreams and summarizes what is known about dreams nowadays. Delaney (1979) advocates initiating and deliberately trying to direct our dreams toward a dissolution of conflicts, employing incubation. This means literally sitting on eggs, warming them, and thus bring them to full development; figuratively, it signifies that by a covert (unconscious) process dreams can make visually explicit the implications of the dreamers ambivalences and inhibitions which are unknown to them or are vaguely perceived by the dreamers. Giving insight, dreams can promote dreamers' efforts to resolve their conflicts. Incubating dreams by the phrase-focusing technique is simple. Before falling asleep, the prospective dreamer asks himself a question that puzzles him and that he wishes the dream to clarify, e.g., "What does really happen between me and my mate?" or "How can I be more productive?" or "Why am I afraid of heights?" Both books contain many analyzed dreams to exemplify the procedures presented by them.

Three illiterate societies existing before World War II are known to have routinely practiced dream interpretation similar to Hervey's. Families living on the Malayan peninsula, for example, discussed their night dreams during breakfasts. When a boy had a nightmare in which a tiger threatened to kill him, his father quietly explained that, in a future dream of the same kind, the boy should not wake up in terror but should make a stand and frighten the tiger away. Anthropologists have described the tribe as confident and peaceful.

From about 1880 until the present, a great deal has been written about sleep dreams in which dreamers cannot critically evaluate and voluntarily modify parts of their dreams. Writers on the subject have complemented rather than contradicted one another. In *Interpretation of Dreams* (1900), Freud introduced the idea of making serial-free associations with elements of a manifest dream. Dream interpretation had begun to change into systematic analysis. Systematic analysis enables the therapist to hold the dreamer's unconscious on a leash, albeit a loose one. Free associations and rapport with therapists help dreamers to recall experiences that are pertinent to therapists' fitting interpretations of dreams.

No therapy is more effective than that of dreamers' gaining sudden insights that their dreams uncannily throw a convincing, yet different, light on relationships or actions that they have previously misinterpreted. Encouraging patients to free-associate has been used since the 18th century with hypnotized subjects manifesting conversion hysteria and multiple personalities. Other important and enduring findings were that the first years of life exert powerful and lasting influences on future personality development and that early life experiences are reflected in dreams. At one time Freud went so far as to consider ungratified infantile sexual wishes to be the ultimate causes of dreams. His etiology of dreams was preconceived. Five years before *Interpretation of Dreams,* Breuer and Freud published *Studies on Hysteria* (1895), in which they explained the origin of conversion hysteria symptoms. Freud assumed that the manifest dream and conversion symptoms were equally disingenuous and were results of the identical psychodynamic processes. Therefore, the meaning of a manifest dream must be uncovered through the same methods used to uncover the meaning of conversion symptoms. Freud felt backed in this false belief by his earlier principles that the sexual instinct is basic and that it affects both physical and mental processes. Freud believed that he had founded his dream theory on an objective, real, physical, biological force — a condition required by the 19th-century, materialistic–philosophical orientation. His formulation, however, overlooks the great functional difference between manifest sleep dreams and hysteria symptoms, especially conversion. Dreams clarify intrapsychic conflicts and help dreamers face these conflicts with greater realism, whereas hysteria traits make the patients unaware of their real intrapsychic conflicts and divert their conscious attention toward symptoms and away from real inhibitions and disorders. Dreams connect and unite quasi-autonomous affectomotor parts of the personality, whereas hysteria dissociation disconnects and disunites the forces of personality.

Remarkable acumen was shown by a 19th-century writer, Nietzsche (1844–1900), who made many lasting contributions to dynamic personology. His work is summarized by Ellenberger (1970). One of Nietzsche's writings on sleep dreams describes their main function; it was written about 1880 but published posthumously (Nietzsche, 1965): "Our entire dreaming discloses the possible causes of all our motives: this is because one becomes aware of a (personal intrapsychic) condition only when one has become aware of the pertinent causal nexus of that condition" (v. 3, p. 804). This sounds like a formula for successful Freudian psychotherapy. Nietzsche did not believe that human psychology had changed essentially during the last thousands of years. He concluded that "in dreams we repeat the (intrapsychic) impediments ("pensum") of earlier humanity" (v. 1, p. 454). This brings to mind the Jungian concept of archetypes. Nietzsche was a perspicacious personologist, as demonstrated by these sample ideas quoted by Ellenberger: "Oblivion is not a mere force of inertia. It is an active, and in the strictest sense, a positive capacity for inhibition . . . The degree and quality of a person's sexuality finds its way into the topmost reaches of his spirit . . . Everyone is farthest to himself; the unconscious is the essential part of the individual, consciousness being a more or less fantastic commentary on an unconscious, perhaps unknowable, but felt text." Nietzsche also recognized the strength of aggressive as well as sexual drives. In fact, he attributed the uppermost significance to the drive for power (i.e., domination or assurance of personal security). Explaining that inhibition was a result of opposition of mutually exclusive drives or intentions, he had no need for a special censor.

Ellenberger reported that the role of frustrated wishes in the etiology of disease has been known from time immemorial. Western, 19th-century psychiatry did not attribute officially any significant role in the origin of disease to frustrated wishes. In some illiterate or sophisticated societies, psychosomatic illnesses have always been acknowledged. Freud's work, together with that of Janet, Charcot, Bleuler, Jung, and others (see Ellenberger's description of lives and work), has exercised a powerful influence in bringing to light psychogenic or psychosomatic illnesses.

PDS most closely resembles Jungian principles. According to Jung (1961):

> Salvation (personality improvement) lies in our ability to bring the unconscious urges to consciousness with the aid of warning dreams. These dreams show that there is something in us which does not merely submit passively to the influence of the unconscious, but on the contrary rushes eagerly to meet it. (p. 245)

Both the conscious and unconscious undergo changes, and to Jung and to Freud, dreams were the most productive means of investigating the unconscious; dreams can also be used quite effectively in psychotherapy. Jung shared the belief that dreams can be predictive. In writing about his experiences Jung (1974) narrated a fitting example in which a colleague

> always teased Jung about his dream interpretations. The man whom he met one day in the street called out to Jung: "How are things going? Still interpreting dreams? By the way, I've had another idiotic dream. Does that mean something too?" This was the man's dream: "I am climbing a high mountain over steep snowcovered slopes. I climb higher and higher, and it is marvelous weather. The higher I climb, the better I feel. I think, if only I could go on climbing like this forever! When I reach the summit my happiness and elation are so great that I feel I could mount right up into space. And I discover that I can actually do so. I mount upwards on empty air, and awake in sheer ecstasy." (p. 98)

Jung knew that the man could not give up mountaineering but implored him to take two guides when he was to go again. "Incorrigible!" cried out the man and left laughing. Jung never saw him again. Three months later the alpinist went on a climb with a younger friend, but without guides. Another climber's guide saw the man literally step into the air while descending a rock face. The man fell on the head of his friend, and both perished. This was "ecstasies with a vengeance." Jung interpreted the dream report as if it were a description of a real, empirical event. In real life, people cannot move upward by treading the air; when they step on empty air over a precipice, they are hurled down. Verbs are veridical, according to PDS Rule 2; treading air is a fully assented personality trait, according to Rule 2. Besides, affects felt during dreaming were energizing. Therefore, action indicated by dream verbs was likely to be realized as an unconsciously motivated fatal "accident" or as a consciously performed suicide. Jung stressed the point that psychotherapists should habitually analyze their own dreams in order to get to know their own unconscious forces, and familiarize themselves with the great effort needed to integrate the conscious and unconscious forces. This self-analysis, with the aid of personal dreams, is a necessary preparation for leading others in their endeavor to remove intrapsychic conflicts and in improving personality integration. However, the therapist must interpret his patients' dreams as manifestations of the patients' personalities and not as creations of his own. "The greatest mistake an analyst can make is to assume that his patient has a psychology similar to his own" (Jung, 1954, par. 498). Jung emphasized the importance of dreams' visuomotor elements as valid manifestations of dreamers' psychosocial forces. "I learned how helpful it can be, from the therapeutic point of view, to find the particular images which lie behind emotions" (Jung, 1961, p. 177). Lastly, an advice: "We would do better to inquire not why this dream, but what its purpose is" (Jung, 1961, p. 103).

The art and science of interpreting dreams has a 5,000 year history, during which it became part of the art of government from antiquity to the 17th century. However, a large survey of classified dream contents did not exist until recently. Hall and Van de Castle (1966) published a survey containing 10,000 dreams of contemporary Americans. Among the highlights of this publication are (rare in literature) reports on series of successive dreams of individuals that relate to the same main topic. Hall endorses the basic ideas of Freud regarding the most powerful and lasting psychodynamic motivating forces. However, Hall (1966) differs distinctly from Freud in his definition of dream symbols and in his conviction that sleep dreams are veridical: "Symbols of dreams are there to express something, not to hide it." Quite the contrary, ". . . man wants to express his thoughts as clearly as possible in objective terms; he wants to convey meaning with precision and economy. He wants to clothe his conceptions in the most appropriate garments. And, perhaps, although of this we are not certain, he wants to garnish his ideas with beauty and taste. For these reasons, the language of dreams uses symbols" (p. 108).

Hall said that dreams do not duplicate the workaday world and that dreams are about people who are associated in some way with the dreamers' personal conflicts. The most frequent conflict manifested in dreams involves the relationships among three people — the dreamer, a man, and a woman. Such emotional triangles, Hall commented, are commonplace in life and fiction and influence intents and action. By contrast, ordinary waking pursuits such as working, buying, and selling rarely, if ever, cause intrapsychic conflicts and virtually do not appear in dreams; even drinking and eating are infrequent. Dreamers' being energetic is in the service of pleasure. However, say Hall and Van de Castle (1966),

> happy dreams do not necessarily reflect a happy disposition . . . dreams do not have much to say about the joys and accomplishments of man. This cannot be accounted for by the kind of people whose dreams have been studied. Our informants are not neurotic people. They are not social misfits or psychiatric pa-

tients. They are on the whole an accomplished, capable group of people who have had more than their share of successes and gratifications in life.

Yet, these normal and successful people dream about conflicts concerning them, as indicated by the fact that "the chief character in almost every dream is the dreamer himself; he is an active participant in many of the events that take place, and when he is not participating, he is observing what others are doing." In fact, unpleasant dreams are much more numerous than pleasant ones. These facts agree with the conception that dreamers use visual images to express intrapsychic conflicts and plans concerning these conflicts. The most important thinkers on dreams agree that conflicts play the decisive and greatest role in dream production.

Foulkes (1978) wrote the first formal sign language for transcribing dream reports into a language of abstract symbols. His *Scoring System of Latent Structure (SSLS)* "attempts to reconcile two levels of analysis – a comprehensive and lengthy enumeration of content categories not unlike that of Hall and Van de Castle (1966) and a brief set of rating scales yielding one overall score per dream per scale" (p. 197). Four basic "interactive relationships" are discriminated: moving toward, moving from, moving against, and creating (the first three relationships are signified by arrows; the fourth by a little circle with an arrow that begins at the center of the circle, pierces the circumference, and points outward). Three "associative relationships" indicate actions through which relationships are made, broken, or turned hostile (p. 201). Numerous other symbols signify many noun varieties. Each of these abstract transcriptions, however, misses some data. Foulkes' SSLS is rather extensive, especially in recording what is of primary significance: dreamers' intentions; qualifications of dreamers' attitudes; movements, on the dream stage, of dream figures. Foulkes follows Freud theoretically and uses both the manifest dream and postdream associations. In Foulkes (1978), he wrote:

> The would-be user of SSLS must be sensitive, at the time associations are generated, to its analytic requirements. There must be pressure for clarity and fullness of expression. On hearing the free associations, the user must visualize their conformity to the requirements of SSLS' translation, path and structural transformation. (p. 297)

Following these instructions, SSLS specialists process much more than unconsciously produced sleep dreams; they include in the process extensive, conscious, waking associations, which outnumber the elements of the manifest dream. There is, in effect, a world of difference between visuomotor manifest dream imagery and conscious, waking-life memories associated with manifest dream reports. It is no wonder that Foulkes (1978) remarked somewhat wearily at the end of his SSLS transcript of Freud's Botanical-Monograph dream and Freud's post-dream associations to the dream:

Shouldn't there be revealed one, or, at most a few simple motives which underlie all of the dream text? . . . What is one to do with all these motives (indicated
in the dream plus the associations)? . . . With respect to the *kind* of motive
structures revealed by SSLS's analysis of 'Botanical Monograph', there also
may be some feeling of disappointment. Is there, after all, enough *depth* to
them? (p. 296–7).

Freud (1900) dreamed: "I had written a monograph on a certain plant. The
book lay before me and I was at the moment turning over a folded colored
plate. Bound up in each copy there was a dried specimen of the plant, as
though it had been taken from a herbarium" (p. 169). There is affective
"depth" in this dream, but it is in the dream proper—in the manifest dream
and not in the postdream associations in which thoughts and affects related
to thoughts are dissipated. At the time of his dream, Freud was in his forties
and had a burning ambition to astound the world with his theories. He was
already an author of note. In the monograph of his dream, he described
"turning over" a colored plate of a plant. Copies of the book all contained
dried, dead specimens of the plant, which is colorful when it blooms. The
only color to appear in the dream was on the plate; somehow Freud did not
have to unfold the inanimate plate to get a good look at the color. The weak,
colorless remnants of the flower had been taken from a herbarium, a kind of
mausoleum for flowers. Thus, remnants of the living flower, once colorful,
were dead. The color in the dream was artificially produced. Furthermore,
unfolding and viewing the colorful reproduction of the living plant would
have required special effort. Freud did not want to see even a deliberately
made copy of the real flower. In real life, he saw a colorless, shriveled, dead
specimen and held no hope of finding the living flower: All copies of the
book had dried specimens. The dream was created by a superior man, a studi-
ous writer, a lover of books; at the time of the dream, however, Freud was
discouraged and depressed. Another interpretation of his dream is possible,
based on the symbolic meaning of the concrete noun *plant*. Freud said the
plant was a cyclamen. This low-growing, pretty, nodding flower blooms
early, in the "youth" of the year, and has bulbous roots. A "Freudian" interpretation (from which Freud was deliberately abstaining during postdream
associations) could be made plausible. Reinforcing this interpretation is
Freud's reluctance to unfold the colored plate and to have a look at the color.
Freud turned the plate over "folded," consigning it to the past, as it were. Of
course, the plate was not relegated to the past with firm conviction and a
sense of finality—the colored plate, after all, played a prominent role in the
dream.

These two interpretations have one theme in common: There is no greater
pain than that in recalling a happy past from a vantage point of wretched-
ness. Freud was living then in relative isolation, and life was not particularly
cheerful. He suffered from cardiac distress and many minor ailments and

was engrossed with his self-analysis, the foundation of his psychoanalytic system. In addition, he labored at what was to become his chief work, *The Interpretation of Dreams*. Finally, he had to face the negative attitudes of important colleagues (Jones, 1953–1957; Schur, 1972). During the period in which he experienced and interpreted his dream, Botanical Monograph, Freud wrote a letter to Jung with whom he was then on the best of terms:

> I would like . . . to tell you . . . of my many years of honorable but painful isolation which started after I had had my first glimpse into the new world; of my closest friends' lack of interest and understanding; of the anxious periods when I myself believed I had been mistaken, and wondered how I could still turn to advantage a bungled life for the sake of my family. (Schur, 1972, p. 88)

Vande Kemp's (1981) scrutiny of dream interpretation and etiology from 1860 to 1910 in the United States, Canada, and the British Islands disclosed that:

> When psychology emerged as an independent discipline and solidified as a profession during the latter decades of the 19th century, it had unequivocally fallen heir to the study of dreams . . . The literature of the popular culture concentrated on premonitory dreams which literally came true, the telepathic and clairvoyant dreams which transcended time and space, and dreams which gave a prominent role to death (p. 88). A significant portion of the literature was directed at verifying the presence of imagery in dreams. As a result, writers were able to conclude that dream imagery (hallucination) was far more common than dream perception (illusion) casting doubt on the earlier associationist assertion that dreams were always produced by external stimulation. (p. 95–96)

Here *hallucination* is a visual or other kind of perception of something that dreamers do not or could not perceive earlier in rational, waking life; dreamers' sensory perception of something that had actually been perceived earlier — in a rational, waking state — is called an *illusion*. The relationship of dreams to reality "was a major focus of 19th century dream literature." However, the nature of perceived reality was disputed in metaphysical concepts. Clymer (1888) gave a toxicological explanation; by blaming "brain persons" for dreams, he introduced the concept that mind-altering drugs influenced dreams. That dreamers were apprehending realities not accessible to the waking mind, was asserted by Melinand (1898). The notion of subconscious mentation had become commonplace by the 1870s.

Vande Kemp concluded:

> By 1910, a number of views of the unconscious were in competition, all of them emerging in the dream literature. William James' (1912) 'fringe of conscious-

ness' was a locus of ideas outside of personal attention (p. 101). . . . Probably most prevalent was the view of the unconscious as the storehouse of memories (p. 102). In fact, much contemporary dream interpretation implies that the dream, though an autistic phenomenon, . . . offer(s) a means for integrating our personal, private selves with a public one. Currently we have the Jungian emphasis on the compensatory function of dreams, with the injunction that dreams be regarded as *real,* rather than merely symbolic experiences. (p. 103)

Vande Kemp (1981) also remarked that scientific "investigations which did take place and which are currently in progress, seldom concentrated on the questions which interested the dreamers themselves, and are answered primarily outside the mainstream of the profession" (p. 103).

Dreams have always aroused great interest in all countries on all continents. By far the main assumption of dream interpreters has been that dreams pertain to dreamers' capacities for handling intrapsychic difficulties. Frequently, however, the significance of dreams is not limited to intrapsychic conflicts; it can involve any type of conflict experienced in objective, conscious, waking, everyday reality or in relationships between humans and supranatural powers. Reasonable and realistic interpretations (the minority of interpretations) have existed side by side with arbitrary and fanciful interpretations (the majority). Since the 18th century, interpretive methods have gradually become more reliable and valid, stressing more the psychodynamic significance of dreams (for understanding dreamers' intentions, emotional attitudes, and assessments of their personality functioning in general). Emphasis on the psychodynamic significance of dreams has become possible as a result of the increase in humane (noncondemnatory) interest in psychopathology in general and in serious mental conditions, hypnotic states, multiple personality studies, and dissociative states in particular. Cases have been followed over time in attempts to observe changes in patients (there is no substitute for long follow-ups in personality investigations). Moreover, the study of deviants from average or so-called normal people is fruitful, because the phenomena to be studied occur with greater intensity, frequency, and variability in deviants than in normal people. The sound health practices of healthy people are based on knowledge gained from successful care of the sick. Great novelists describing mental aberrations and criminal behavior and specialists studying mental disorders have taught us more about the laws of normal, healthy functioning than have all the studies of healthy people. The reason for this state of affairs is methodological: Researchers find more to study and learn when investigating those who have a mixed and diversified life than when investigating those who are predictable. Dreams can become important in assessment and prognosis if they are studied on an empirical, rational basis. Even in the most superstitious times, certain people have known this.

3 Dreams of the Mind-Disordered

The sharpest minds in ancient Greece described dreaming as thinking in sleep. In Babylon thousands of years earlier, however, dreaming had already been viewed as thinking; dreams were believed to convey messages to dreamers. If dreams are conceptualized as thinking, the question is raised as to whether schizophrenic thought disorders are apparent in dreams of schizophrenics. It is well known that some, but not all, dreams of these mentally disturbed individuals display illogicality or serious defects in the sense of reality. Boss (1938) collected 620 dreams from 150 schizophrenics and 200 dreams from organic psychotics. He found that one-third of the schizophrenic dreams were no different in form or content from those of nonpsychotics.

Boss cited a woman who was in the fourth year of her schizophrenia; she dreamed that a cow was to be slaughtered and wanted to go to the aid of the mooing animal but got stuck in the mud in front of the barn door. A nursemaid appeared in the dream and laughed at the patient, who woke up agitated and in great fear (p. 465). Boss remarked that he could easily quote many nonpsychotic people whose dreams resemble this patient's. When Axiom B of the PDS is applied to dream events, they might amuse people. However, when Axiom A is applied, dreams might sadden people. Remembering that all dream figures represent dreamers themselves according to Axiom A, we notice that moods or affects of dreamers are not homogeneous. The fourth-year schizophrenic was anxiously agitated and at the same time amused to the point of laughter (she was the nursemaid figure too). Her assented trait was self-preservation (she was as passive and helpless as the cow). However, her efforts to save herself from impending death were futile. Her desire to help the cow which represented her dissented self in the dream, according to Axiom A, resulted only in a weak, vain start and a display of her incompetence. The most dissented traits were indicated by the cow, which differed from the woman to a degree much greater than that between the nursemaid and the woman. These traits included constriction, helpless passivity, and plaintful wailing and were her only active reactions to her threatened destruction. Thus, the ineffectual desire to end her helpless passivity and anxiety was conspicuously frustrated by the patient's incompetence. This suggests that she was given a poor prognosis despite residual resistance against hebephrenic psychotic dissolution. Because both her call for help and her attempt to help were feeble, the patient seems to have had some energy left — enough for a laugh at herself; the lack of homogeneity of affects facilitated the tragicomic derision.

This patient deteriorated over the years; in the twelfth year after the onset of her psychosis, she degenerated in morals and habits. She had the following dream, recounted in Boss (1938): "A crouching woman raised her legs and a man mounted her (to fornicate). Suddenly I slipped inside that woman and my father was pulled into that man who had advanced upon me and did many filthy sexual things with me" (p. 466). The fundamental postulate of PDS is that dream events should be interpreted as if they were empirical events perceived consciously in waking life. From this viewpoint, the patient's dream is unrealistic. People cannot slip physically inside other people and, in addition, carry out personal intentions while inside these bodies that become protective shells. Yet the patient developed her dream as if all the activities were biologically and physically realizable. She did not joke; she was earnest. At first the dreamer was rather restrained, indicated in the dream by the fact that it was another woman, and not the dreamer herself, who tempted the man. Besides, the woman crouched, which is a flexed, shrunk posture, and at the same time, raised (opened?) her legs, which is an extended and counter-gravity movement. This reveals an ambivalent attitude, partly compliant and withdrawing, and partly assertive. However, the ambivalence was reduced abruptly: "Suddenly I slipped inside that woman and my father was pulled into that man." By means of magic, the patient had an imaginary, physically impossible incestuous sexual intercourse. Even on an imaginary level the desire remains dissented more than it is assented. Father and daughter are disguised and unrecognizable. The desire is there, but the inhibitory counterforces frustrate its gratification, and, furthermore, the sense of reality is too defective. The patient condemned the intercourse in words only, and not in the far more revealing and valid visuomotor imagery ("filthy sexual things"); there is no evidence that she physically struggled against the incestuous encounter in the dream. Clinically speaking, she disguised her incestuous wishes during the dream.

Boss also described five dreams of a paranoid schizophrenic. Five years before the onset of psychosis, the patient had a repetitive dream:

Lost in a desert, he roamed around thirsty. Finally, he noticed a ravine in the distance and heard the murmur of water. However, each time he approached the ravine, a large bear appeared and threatened to devour him (p. 468). The dream expressed the patient's inability to stop the process of deterioration. The inner force that frustrated his attempts at recovery — his reaching the life-sustaining water — was represented by a large bear, that is, by a powerful and implicitly destructive, dehumanized force (Axiom A). The prognosis, therefore, is assessed as unfavorable. A bear is a powerful but lonely and rather nonaggressive creature until provoked; the dreamer strongly dissented his tendency to assume this "bear personality." Nothing in this prepsychotic dream is physically unrealistic. The patient was a military officer used to forging ahead, and he was a woman's man. Shortly before the appearance of his paranoid ideas, he had dreams about his school teachers, who then mistreated and quarrelled with him once he began receiving help. After the onset of the manifest psychosis, the patient claimed to establish direct contact with Christ. He dreamed that he was in heaven being received with great ceremonies as the spiritual brother of Christ. A year later, he saw in a dream God the Father with a lightning sword. He was allowed to touch this sword with his hand; he felt his belly open, and a new Son of God grew out of him. Many angels surrounded him and sang "You are the Supreme Power and the Mother of God." Two years after the onset of psychosis, the patient dreamed that he was Hercules and that all the male nurses at the hospital danced around and kissed him (p. 468). Narcissistic and homosexual tendencies gradually increased with time. Before the onset of the illness, the homosexual desire was completely repressed. This dream lends itself easily to a psychoanalytical interpretation that rests on premises much unlike those of PDS. The two interpretations are not contradictory; each stresses a different set of traits and uses very different validating criteria.

Boss described two types of dreams that only schizophrenics have. In the first type, weird dream scenes, pale and volatile, follow one another with uncanny and unpleasant speed; dreamers try to retain and remember the scenes but do not succeed; he feels under pressure. The second type is the opposite of the first. Dream imagery is banal (for example, a bed pillow), but it is perceived with uncommon clarity and distinctness. Typically, schizophrenic dreamers see a shadowy, unsubstantial world. Boss suggested that the creators of such dreams are afraid of reality. When schizophrenics deteriorate, they become increasingly incapable of consciously and deliberately submitting their ideas to be critically evaluated for reality and appropriateness. Dream images, which glide by at a fast and uncontrollable rate, cannot be remembered, and therefore, do not perform the function of orienting and preparing these people for adequate handling of reality. When dream imagery is extraordinarily salient, the visual component is so strong that it captivates perceptual attention and stifles thinking. In both types of Boss' pathognomonic, schizophrenic dreams, then, serious thinking malfunctions occur.

Several writers have noted the value of collecting dreams over the years to observe changes in dreamers' psychoses. Both improvement and deterioration are revealed in a long series of dreams, even when the personality changes are clinically inconspicuous. A series of dreams of a schizophrenic will reveal increased affective coldness and rigidity and decreased capacity for adaptation to people and situations; chronic cases gradually become more noticeably passive and do not try any longer to change. The disintegration of personality leads to Bleuler's (1950/1911) autism (incapacity to appreciate reality for what it is; thinking unmindfully of empirical reality, regardless of whether thoughts violate reality). In other words, autistic people live in their fantasies and are oblivious to the real world. Because fantasies originate with sensory experiences of the world, however, autistic thinking, unless extreme, appears only as distorted, exaggerated mentation. What sets autistic people apart, warned Bleuler, is the intensity and extensiveness of thought disorders.

Only in schizophrenics' thinking can the most diverse and incompatible ideas exist side by side without influencing one another, with the result being that the process of thinking becomes incoherent and inconsistent (Bleuler, 1950/1911). This can be observed even in dreams of incipient patients: Goal of thought is not kept firmly in mind for a sufficiently long time; consequently, looseness of association can develop. In early cases, precise thinking may suddenly alternate with vague, delusory ideas. Bleuler stressed that disturbance of association is primary in schizophrenia; it involves blocking, systematic splitting, and a decrease in the number of logical affinities. In hysteria and under hypnosis, splitting is secondary. It is not an effect of a primary disorder of association and thinking (resulting from a pathological change in the brain) but rather is a direct effect of psychogenic processes such as neurotic repression or reaction to a hypnotist's instruction.

During a long-term investigation of personality changes in mild schizophrenics (Piotrowski & Efron, 1966), a small group of patients became chronic, deteriorated residents of mental hospitals. These patients attracted attention because of their superior intelligence, education, and one, persisting delusion. The two patients seen most frequently over a long period of time were first admissions who were studied for four months in a university psychiatric hospital as in-patients. Discharged as nonschizophrenic psychoneurotics, both knew the difference between the terms *delusion* and *illusion*. During numerous hours of interviews, they seemed to know that their obsessive fears were rather illusory and disquieting.

One of these patients was a custom tailor who owned his own establishment. His clientele consisted of wealthy, elegant women, and he was successful in his occupation. Because all fittings and changes were done by his female assistants, the patient never touched the clients. One day, during a fitting, a window was open; the patient heard male voices in the backyard. Suddenly the patient was shocked by what he took to be a remark by a man (whom for physical reasons he could not have seen had he tried). The soft-spoken, polite, quiet patient heard himself addressed in what he called a "vulgar" voice that suggested "loudly" to him that the tailor would rather have a boy for amorous purposes. The other patient was a chief accountant in a large corporation. He had the delusion that fleas were crawling on his hands. He felt compelled to drop them with great care into wastepaper baskets.

Initially, both men experienced their symptoms about once a week, but gradually they exhibited them with ever greater frequency. Both were greatly embarrassed and anxious. The fear that others might notice their intermittent anxiety states and symptoms prompted them to seek professional help. Both agreed that their symptoms were illusory. Both returned to the hospital and requested hospitalization within 10 months (at somewhat different times). Both became permanent residents of the same public hospital. I saw one 15 times in 12 years and the other 7 times over the same period. Both patients were deteriorating. As their personalities regressed, they complained of their symptoms much more frequently. The man with the auditory hallucination wrote letters to the hospital directors and requested to be housed in a building "without noises." The other man silently picked up his delusional fleas all the time, except when he was eating or sleeping. He also performed the "service" for others who were near him and who talked to him. At the last visits, I was no longer able to have a meaningful conversation with these two patients.

Other schizophrenics had, during follow-up years, intermittent periods of semiotic blackout, or self-monitoring and self-evaluation (SMSE): They suddenly lost their ability to comprehend what was being said, as if they were deaf. Mild cases realized that others were speaking to them, but they could not make out the words that were enunciated and could not grasp the meaning of what was said even when they had heard something that they thought was articulate speech. Semiotic blackouts did not last long when psychosis was incipient or mild. Interviews conducted over the years revealed that these blackouts had become gradually more frequent and longer if patients' mental, conceptual, realistic thinking had worsened as a result of progressive exacerbation of the disease process; damage to conceptual, abstract thinking seemed irreversible. However, the deteriorating process could stop, as Bleuler (1950/1911) noted, at any level of deviation from normal, healthy functioning. When schizophrenia is mild, semiotic blackouts are rather rare and brief and may not be noticed by others. If mild schizophrenics say or do something odd, psychoneurotic conflicts are likely to be blamed for the odd-ity. Semiotic blackouts and their increased frequency (a result of progressive severity of psychosis) can be observed in sleep dreams and in waking states.

Disintegration or looseness of association is considered to be the basic schizophrenic disturbance that is particularly noticeable when it appears in the absence of affective stress. Bleuler (1950/1911) described "disturbance of association as primary insofar as it involves a diminution of leveling of the number of affinities" (p. 350) or of dynamic interconnections — logical, af-fective, motor. The expected and natural development of thoughts, affects, and actions is cut short or mixed with incompatible details, resulting in the blending of sound, realistic, and meaningfully interconnected ideas with unrealistic, irrelevant, and physically impossible pseudoconcepts.

A sleep dream of a very bright young woman manifests disintegration with loss of the sense of empirical reality. This lack of realism means that the woman imagined in detail scenes that closely resembled known reality, but that could not actually exist physically; this is different from and betrays a dereism more severe than that involved in dreamers' making up physically possible scenes with which they are not familiar. The woman's dream pre-ceded an acute onset of unquestioned schizophrenia by a few weeks. She had a position for which she was prepared by appropriate graduate university training. Boss (1938) reported her dream:

> I walked in a long corridor that had no doors and no windows. It was not straight; there were many irregular turns. The lighting in each section was dif-ferent. Sometimes it was dark, sometimes bright, and sometimes dim in some hallways. At one turn I was startled. There was a strong, healthy looking elderly man standing there, unhurried and relaxed. His feet were slightly apart. He looked attractive. He watched me with a peculiar smile. The scene changed all of a sudden. We were now in some kind of large hall, immersed in a reddish, orangey fog. I could barely make things out. I noticed there were no walls, just a murky fog. A low roof was kind of floating in it. I got very frightened. I could not understand it. How was it possible? The scene changed again and I was alone in a dark cave-like room. There was some kind of light on the opposite wall. I approached it and noticed a mirror. I felt trapped and felt panicky. I saw a face in the mirror. I did not recognize it. It seemed to change and I saw it was my own face. It was distorted. I couldn't help looking at it. Pieces of my head were breaking off and disappearing. I screamed and woke up in terror. (p. 484)

The woman's alienation and depersonalization from the world increased with each scene. At the end she "saw" parts of her head disappearing and si-multaneously watched the process, as if spellbound. She was at the same time a physically and mentally preserved observer of herself and a fatally disintegrating and disappearing person. The reason for her de-personalization was a defective functioning of her brain. She experienced the process of dementia in the dream: First she felt entrapped, then she panicked, then she felt depersonalized ("I did not recognize [my face]"), and finally, when she recognized her face, she had already begun her terrifying breakdown. She experienced an incomprehensible destructive process, and she herself was deteriorating; her condition changed gradually from bad to desperate. In the beginning she felt entrapped but actively looked for a way out; in the end her activity was limited to a visual examination of her head. Such an evolution of dream events toward increasing restriction with a simultaneous personality disintegration is always an unfavorable prognostic sign. It should also be noted that a consequential psychogenic sexual shock decomposed the dreamer mentally. The unexpected sight of the imperturbable, healthy man who "watched [her] with a peculiar smile" was a crucial moment in the dream. She had been immured in the corridor, but after having been "startled" by the elderly man, she suddenly found herself in a large hall without walls and with a floating roof. A "murky fog" replaced the walls. The brighter and darker lights in the corridor had been replaced by fog. The dreamer wondered how such a change could be possible. Anxiety overwhelmed her. The enormous expansion of the space in which she could not move and in which she "could barely make things out" terrified her instead of relieving her after the constriction in the passageway. The shaded, "murky" red and orange indicate preoccupation with violent aggressiveness. These affective changes in the middle section of the dream appeared with strikingly unrealistic notions regarding empirical reality: a building without walls, "just a murky fog," a floating roof. The roof was unstable, had no visible means of support. The dreamer could not "understand it." The dream revealed a "reality breakdown" of which the patient was fully aware. In the opening part of the dream, the patient walked inside a passageway with no windows or doors. If the inside of a structure is taken as a symbol of the mental life inside a human being, then we can look at this patient's walk in the irregular corridor as her conducting a survey of her self. First, her self is closed to the world, has no outlets, and cannot go to the outside world. The thought of an unexpected or impulsive encounter with an elderly man (father figure?) shocked her intellectually and affectively. In the closing part of the dream, the patient was defeated in her attempts to find a way out of her appalling psychosis; she was surrounded by the walls of a dark, cave-like room, resigned and inactive except for her witnessing with intense fear her progressive intellectual deterioration (the crumbling head). According to Axiom A, the man in the dream was the bearer of the patient's dissented traits. These traits were desirable, except his/her smiling "peculiarly" at an older person of the opposite sex. The young woman's dissent meant that she did not consider strength, health, relaxation, as well as being self-confidently unperturbed and attractive, to be her personal attributes. A comparison of her former condition with her present one struck terror into her.

Boss (1938) reported that when a male schizophrenic had a death dream, and an attempt was made to discuss the dream with him, the patient was unable to produce free associations or to relate any feeling that the dream might prove true. Moreover, the death dreams of schizophrenics who subsequently improved and the death dreams of nonpsychotics almost always ended in nightmares in which the felt terror of impending death stopped dreaming and woke the dreamers. In other words, death was avoided just in time. In these good-prognosis dreams, figures other than the dreamers play influential roles. Bad-prognosis schizophrenics usually died in their dreams, lonely and in strange surroundings. A chronic, massively hallucinating female catatonic who exerted great willpower in her performance of steady, routine work had a repetitive dream for years (Boss, 1938):

> I see a deer-like animal with its belly ripped open which runs through many wards, but always returns and passes in front of me. Each time when it races near me, it has become skinnier. It braces itself up every time and darts off again. The last times when I sometimes see it, it is only a skeleton, and yet it rises upon its hind legs every time. (p. 485)

The patient said that the deer was her own tormented and sick self. The repeated mobilization of effort and the unchangeable performances in the dream were the patient's own daily, waking-life, activities. The deer, the carrier of her strongly dissented traits, revealed the patient's hopeless struggle for imminent improvement (Axiom A).

Boss (1938) pointed out that schizophrenic dreams are quite different when patients' mental disorders improve. Dreams also change during remissions, when symptoms decrease in intensity and frequency, or during quiet periods between acute episodes. At these times, concrete reality usually reappears in dreams, which then resemble the wishful dreams of children or of demented organics. Seventy-two of Boss' schizophrenics improved strikingly. In these cases, regardless of treatment, the degree of normalization of dreams did not match clinical improvement. Boss added that the change in dreams was a better and more reliable measure of post-treatment improvement than was clinical assessment. In no case was a complete restitution of normal personality functioning made. Schizophrenic dreams, then, are of great practical and theoretical value and assistance in the care of the patients. However, it is not easy to elicit dreams from these patients. But schizophrenics, like cerebral organic patients, dream more in the incipient and wild states of their diseases than when they deteriorate or grow old. Dreams gradually taper off in number with progressing illnesses.

Both schizophrenics and organics produce many endoscopic dreams in which the dream imagination visualizes defects or disintegration of the dreamer's body. The two groups' dreams' however, differ conspicuously.

Boss (1938) reproduced a traumatic Korsakov psychotic's dream that conspicuously brings out this difference. Before his disease, the patient lived according to a highly moral code. In the dream, he was sitting with his little daughter in a restaurant. Suddenly the daughter became a young woman surrounded by many admiring men. However, she loved only the dreamer. They drank champagne and went with erotic intentions to a special room (p. 487). This dream was followed by another in which the dreamer participated in a hunt. "Without intention," his male companions turned toward him in pursuit and aimed their rifles at him. Finally he got tired and had to lie on the ground. At this point, the others burst into laughter and said that all they had intended to do was to scare him; then they started masturbating one another (p. 487). The events in the two dreams are not typical of normal social or family life, but they are not impossible events. Dream settings were realistic, many normal-looking people appeared in each dream, and the dreams lacked spontaneously disintegrating bodies of the dreamer or of any other dream figure. Nonetheless, 70% of the dreams reported by Boss' 200 organics were similar to the brief, simple, harmless, wish-fulfilling or anxious dreams of small children with adult psychophysiological desires. Often hospitalized organics dreamed that they were children again in their parental homes. Boss (1938) reported an example: "Last night my mother appeared in the dream. She was very loving towards me, and we promised each other always to remain together" (p. 489). An anxious patient with senility dreamed that he saw his son go to war. The son did not return. The old man took his revolver, went to the forest, and aimed the gun at his temple. He pulled the trigger, but the report of the gun woke him up, and he survived. A demented paralytic had just one repetitive dream. He heard his mother tell him not to lose confidence; "it will be better again" (p. 489). Organic psychotics "see" the environment in greater concrete detail than do schizophrenics. Dream figures appear far more normal; their own dream behavior is ineffective, limited, and immature, but rarely ghoulish, murderous, or demoniacal. The sense of empirical reality is much better preserved than in schizophrenic dreams; frequently even small details are realistically seen, and dream events are not weird or evanescent. Both groups of patients reveal, in their dreams, their awareness and experience of reality.

As a consultant to cancer patients, Dr. Albert Biele collected dreams from six terminal cases, all of whom died within two months after their recorded dreams, and also from one man who survived his carcinoma after radical surgery. In keeping with established procedure, the author (ZAP) blind-interpreted the dreams. First reading of the recorded dream was disconcerting because the dream was so clear and realistic that it did not appear to be a dream. When asked about it, Dr. Biele explained that he, too, had felt compelled to ask the patient several times whether she had the dream while asleep or whether she were relating her past. Another remarkable feature of the dream was its comparison of a happy past with an awful present, impending death. This feature marked the dreams of the six terminal cases. Of course, the number of cases is too small to claim that the feature characterizes dreams of all cancer patients facing inevitable death.

The following dream was the first of the series collected by Dr. Biele. It was a repetitive dream of a 55-year-old, married woman with two grown-up daughters:

> The whole family is there and I am in the midst of it all, and I'm cooking and setting the table and being very efficient. Everything is turning out so well, but suddenly I remember that I can't walk and I can't do this. That frightens me. I dreamt that I had made this beautiful cherry pie and I was getting ready to sit down when I thought: "How could I make this pie? I can't get around in the walker and I can't manage the kitchen very well." So that is the dream that bothers me the most.

Asked what she felt in the dream, she replied: "Well, I'm worried about not being able to walk because I want to get home and back into a routine." The patient's joy in life was keeping home for her family. She loved to prepare evening dinners, which were happy and cheerful when the appreciative family gathered around her culinary creations. She was aware of her family's discomfort when they visited her in the hospital to try, without conviction, to cheer her up. Conversation was difficult. The patient had been suffering from cancer with multiple metastases. This dream was classical. Other dreams of the same patient were not repetitive; although they also dealt with the acceptance of the inevitable consequences of her fatal illness, they revealed her reluctance in facing a dire end. In another of her dreams, a Chinese grandfather lost a skill of which he had been proud. The theme of the long dream (here abbreviated) was as follows:

> The elderly gentleman discovered that he had lost his special paper and tools which he used to make figurines. He was quite depressed about it. We tried to cheer him up but we couldn't. So we told him that he could probably make a Chinese home with the sliding walls. We told him we would try to find the material for him, and he was very happy. I think I woke up then.

Applying Axiom A (all dream figures represent the dreamer), we see that the dreamer, on a decidedly dissenting level (the gentleman differed from the dreamer in sex, age, ethnic background, and preferred life occupation), lost the capacity to create artistic objects that had brought him renown. To dissent a trait means to believe it does not exist any longer. On an assented level, the patient and the unidentified "we" "would try to find" new material that the gentleman could use to make something other than the figurines that made him famous. The woman, too, was renowned for her arts (cooking and homekeeping). Making Chinese homes requires less skill than making artistic paper dolls does. The well-meaning but nondescript (thus hinting at a secret) individuals "tried" to cheer up the grandfather "but we couldn't." Then they told him they would try to "find" the material for making Chinese toy houses, and he was "very happy." However, the Chinese grandfather was the bearer of the non-Chinese female dreamer's dissented traits (Axiom A). Therefore, happiness cannot be considered a genuine trait of the dreamer herself. Besides, to try (to find the material) does not always end in success. The patient faced bravely the destructive effects of her illness and still attempted, albeit unconvincingly, to delay the worst.

Another patient, a 69-year-old, single woman with Hodgkin's disease, had to have her spleen removed; she died seven days later because of bilateral pulmonary embolism. She was a former singer and teacher of singing. She had the following dream several days before the operation:

> I dreamt that I was coaching a scene from the third act of Carmen. This is something that I had done in my life before and that I am not continuing to do at the present time. Carmen and the smugglers were all around, in their quarters, waiting for the great haul and they had great hopes for their future. Carmen was sitting beside them, brooding, playing with her deck of cards alone. And the music changed from this light, gay, hopeful future for these smugglers to something very slow very dramatic, very weepy; and Carmen throws her card: La Mort! I can't sing it now. I don't have to translate: "Death!" She throws another card to another chord of music and there it was again: "Death!" And I said to the girl that I was coaching, to Carmen, I said: "I want that weep, I want that cry in your voice to break, and then put it together and sustain it." And we got the results.

The variant in this dream is that the woman being coached — women are carriers of traits dissented less than those attributed to men in a woman's dream — repeated the dreamer's past success, whereas the dreamer herself abstained from singing. During a subsequent interview with Dr. Biele, the patient said: "I was satisfied particularly with the role of Carmen. The dream clung to me and it frightened me because I felt that it was, oh, I repeat the word 'ominous,' I felt that something tragic was going to happen. And that one note, 'La Mort,' was in my mind." She indicated the weakness of her hopes for a good future by not ascribing the hopeful expectations to herself in the dream. Instead she ascribed hopeful expectations to the male smugglers, bearers of her dissents or doubts. These doubts were strengthened by her assigning the fearful expectation of impending death to Carmen, a figure much closer to her than the highwaymen.

A 51-year-old, married man with children was admitted to the hospital with weakness and shortness of breath. Three years earlier he had had radical surgery for carcinoma of the bowel. This time in the hospital, he developed a rapid heart rate and became confused. He had an atrial flutter that resisted treatment. It was felt that this "was a terminal event notwithstanding the carcinoma of the colon with metastases to the sacral plexus." The patient and Dr. Biele had the following conversation:

PATIENT: The dream was like, in the form of these, the old-fashioned leeches that the doctors used to use. Like, doctors injected a snake into my thigh to get the poison out of my system, you know. But the real, the terrible fight that I had was to make sure . . . I figured this was a snake that had to come out of my system, otherwise I would be doomed forever. I mean it's just like that. So I remembered that much of it. And I wrote it down on a piece of paper so that I wouldn't forget it.

DR. BIELE: Could you give me more details?

PATIENT: The only thing I remember is it was a group of people giving me this particular thing, you know, like a leech. Is that the right word? A leech or whatever it was that was inside of me. But the main thing of it was that the snake was so slippery getting it out, or whatever it was, something of the nature. I didn't know whether it was the back of the snake or what.

DR. BIELE: You mean?

PATIENT: Yes, they were putting it inside of me. I thought it was me who was to get it once its job was done. It was so slippery getting it out. And I couldn't quite get a hold of it and that was the problem. I was grasping for weak.

DR. BIELE: Where did the dream take place?

PATIENT: I have no idea. I just felt that I was in a bed and I was fighting to get a hold of it. That was my main problem. I finally did get hold of it and got rid of it. I felt a lot better.

Inserting a snake into a thigh to suck up poison in the body is an odd idea. The patient's model was the ancient practice of using leeches for bleeding patients. At the time of the dream the patient was in intensive care. In the dream, "doctors injected a snake into [his] thigh," but he assumed the difficult, all-important role (as he described it) of removing the snake and the "poison" from his body; he did it well and "felt a lot better." His firm determination to heal, to try his best to achieve this goal by his own effort, albeit with the assistance of the doctors, is striking. He survived. On leaving the hospital, the patient went back to his regular job, which he performed conscientiously for three years. He died on the job, of heart failure, not of cancer. He was a skilled machine operator and a stoic.

Terminal cancer patients slowly but inexorably approach death. Therefore their mental preoccupations must, at least at times, be different from those of other persons. Not all their dreams compare their active and harmless pasts with their wretched and painful presents. All characteristic terminal dreams, however, disclose the dreamers' despair and their awareness of their fates. Pathognomonic terminal dreams center around the dramatic decline of dreamers' personalities; these dreams appear as if they were conscious, waking descriptions of irreversible deterioration. We should note that not all terminal cases dream only the characteristic dream; if, however, they produce a dream that contrasts their premorbid condition with the final state of their illness, they are surely firmly aware of their hopeless condition and of their impending demise. It is a period of loneliness. People can do nothing any more to stop death; they can only delay it by artificial means. It is like throwing pebbles in the way of the gods of death: Nothing will deter them. Any meaningful and satisfying interpersonal relations (except alleviation of pain) cease gradually. One question remains unanswered: Were those typical terminal dreams produced in sleep (that is, under mental conditions that precluded relevant and critical analysis of the dream by the dreamer), or were they hypnagogic images (that is, images resembling dreams and produced during the drowsy period preceding sleep, when consciousness and voluntary critical thinking are not completely suspended)?

Human movement responses elicited by the Rorschach inkblots (Piotrowski, 1977) and verbs contained in stories prompted by Thematic Apperception Test (TAT) pictures can be interpreted in a manner similar to that applied to dream events. Rorschach movement responses and TAT stories collected at one time from patients who carry suicidal intentions or who fear to kill themselves undergo consistent changes when the patients are retested some time later, shortly before they commit suicide and contrary to professional expectation. A 43-year-old man gave the following Rorschach responses: "two people walking home"; "dancing around the fire"; "two men holding two things together." His TAT response was "boy looking at his violin, he's a genuine genius." The patient returned to the hospital 14 months later, again suffering from depression and trying to control his suicidal thoughts. Treated successfully, he was discharged as being very much improved. Shortly thereafter, he died by his own hand. He had no physical diseases. The man's second hospital visit resulted in the following responses: "firemen holding on to a pole in order not to fall"; "mixing a bowl"; "two men holding a pot, looks like they're letting it down." The second TAT response was: "The boy became thwarted at reproducing something he hears and cannot recreate." The types of human movement responses stimulated by the Rorschach plates during the first admission were relaxed, spontaneous, whole-body movements on the ground; vigorous, pleasurable, exhibitionistic, whole-body movements on the floor; useful and cooperative social effort to prevent something from falling and breaking. The TAT response alluded to a physically inactive state of gratifying self-confidence.

Shortly before suicide, the patient did not repeat any of the foregoing responses, although only a little more than one year had passed. The new Rorschach responses were: "stationary great effort to prevent falling down and prevent injury or death (fireman whose main purpose is to save people have their hands full to save themselves)"; "two men bending and lowering a pot cautiously"; "stationary bending and moving of arms in order to combine different ingredients together into a compound that would be different in quality from any of its ingredients." The new TAT response was most striking: "The boy musician became thwarted at recreating something he heard." The change in all these responses to the same indeterminate visual stimuli was depressingly consistent. The reduction in expansiveness, extent, freedom, amount of overt movement, and associated self-confidence of each response was also significant (Piotrowski, 1968, 1970). Clinically, the patient's behavior showed less movement and purposefulness. The patient was quieter. In retrospect, these signs seem to have indicated increased resignation and acquiescence to, rather than abandonment of, the idea of suicide.

11 PERCEPTANALYTIC DREAM SYSTEM (PDS)

4 The Process of Dreaming

Dreaming is sleep thinking. However, it is not thinking in words but in visuomotor imagery. Most of this imagery can be easily and immediately understood, but the meaning of some of it is implicit. The chief aim of the PDS is to formulate and to dramatize dreamers' intrapsychic conflicts and to indicate what dreamers are doing about these conflicts (Piotrowski, 1971). Conflicts, with concurrent anxiety and decreased self-confidence, aggravate concern for the future. Lack of sensorimotor contact with the physical environment during dreaming facilitates the organization of effort to do something about disturbing conflicts, which take the form of the subjects of dreams. The central nervous system, which is active even in sleep, can pay full attention to a dreamer's intrapsychic processes only when it is not distracted by environmental stimuli. If these stimuli exceed a certain intensity, they interrupt dreams, just as acute anxiety associated with fears of a dreamed conflict stops the process of dreaming. Mild, subliminally perceived environmental distractions are usually incorporated into dream events without misrepresentation of the main dream message.

To specify conflict, dream analysts specify attitudes, affects, thoughts, intentions, actions, counteractions, and any revealed personality traits that bear on the conflict. Analysts also look for any allusions to the manner in which dreamers guide, control, or curb their overt social behavior. When dreamers' personalities change, dreams change also. *Personality* means the role an individual plays, consciously or unconsciously, in psychosocial relationships; *role* comprises the intrapsychic processes and the conscious or unconscious overt behavior of the individual. It is not possible to divide cognitive functions into perception (the senses) and reason (thinking) because action as a whole is both the point of departure for reason and a continuous source of organization and reorganization for perception (Piaget, 1969, p. 354). Desire prompts action; desire is the root of perception, thought, and action.

While sleeping people view their dream events, they are somewhat like people witnessing empirical events that occur independently of themselves. However, the similarity does not exist in people's looking at real likenesses of empirical events; it exists in their *seeming* to see empirical events when they are not really seeing them. They are not spectators of resemblances to empirical reality; the *dreamers resemble* spectators of empirical events. Contrary to frequent assertions, dreamers do not hallucinate (if by hallucination is meant a sensory perception for which no environmental sensorimotor stimulus exists). Furthermore, during sleep dreaming (excluding hypnagogic dreaming), conscious self-monitoring and self-evaluation (SMSE) of mental processes in terms of reality criteria are dormant. Having no visual sensations of the surrounding environment, sleep dreamers do not really hallucinate. "Lucid" or hypnagogic dreams can initiate sleep dreams but differ from them in etiology and psychological significance. Hypnagogic imagery means literally "imagery leading to (sleep) dreams"; it can be spontaneous or deliberately induced and is conscious or semiconscious. It can help people to fall asleep. Hypnagogic dreaming is a state between wakefulness and sleep dreaming. Hallucinations occur in hypnagogic states. A pathognomonic sign of schizophrenia seems to be the presence of intermittent non-SMSE states; rare in the beginning, these states become permanent in the most intellectually disordered and deteriorated chronic cases. The length and frequency (over unit of time) of non-SMSE episodes increase with progressive personality breakdown. These episodes may stop getting worse at any time, but then they continue. Patients with mild conditions can learn to live with the psychosis by avoiding anxiety-arousing psychosocial situations. Deterioration can be measured in the percentage of time during which patients are incapable of SMSE (Piotrowski, 1969). These recurring semiotic blackouts, which deprive patients of voluntary mind control while sensorimotor orientation is retained, may explain why mild psychotics are fearfully alert and self-controlled. Adequate SMSE depends on normal functioning of cerebral frontal lobes.

Dreams concern intrapsychic conflicts related to potential and actual interpersonal relationships that are important to the dreamers. Dreams help people to clarify conflicts and attitudes toward conflicts. This function of dreams is practical and more intimately personal than any other mentation in which both inner psychic life and intentions regarding relationships are embraced. Dreams are connected in very intimate and pertinent ways with actual, everyday living. Dream content is not theoretical or impersonal. That the language of dreams is basically visuomotor is therefore fitting, because the language is far more informative about intrapsychic processes than is public — verbal and conceptual — language, the main function of which is interpersonal communication. Dream reports are of necessity verbal, but understanding dreams requires penetrating beyond the words of the report and reconstructing visuomotor imagery of which the verbal report may be an inadequate presentation. Anything in a report that has no specific visual referent in the dream should be eliminated. Nonpictorial additions and imagery changes distort the dream. Therefore, dreams should be recorded immediately (within five minutes) after waking; studies have shown that dreamers unwittingly change their reports when the time between dreaming and reporting is longer. Individuals are almost exclusively self-centered and narcissistic in their dreams, and they can much more easily gratify themselves in pictures than in words. Visual imagery is much more closely affiliated with affects than words are, and imagery is still more closely analogous to sensorimotor impressions of external, objective reality than words are. Individuals differ among themselves more in their pictorial language than in the standardized verbal language. Humans acquire the knowledge and use of pictorial languages early in infancy, before they are able to speak. Thus, many scenes of early childhood are innermost experiences that can rarely be put into words. These experiences, however, may surface years later in visual imagery, especially in dreams. Many seemingly irrational dreams, if interpreted as observable, lifelike events, are found to be consistent and intelligible when the main conflict, revealed intentions, and affects are extracted. Bateson (1972) noted that whereas gestures without words are common enough and are expressive, words do not exist by themselves in direct, human intercommunication; words are accompanied by gestures, by tones of voice, or by something of the sort. When interpreting a dream, we must be aware of the full meaning of all dream events — intentions, affects, moods, and specific senses that are reflected in the imagery.

To quote from Paivio's (1979) searching and exhaustive *Imagery and Verbal Responses*:

> Osgood (1953, 1961) has consistently argued in favor of nonverbal processes in his theory of meaning, where meaning is identified with the conditioned capacity of a sign (word) to arouse a fractional component of the reaction pattern originally evoked by a stimulus object (p. 7) . . . Except in the adoption of conditioning as the explanatory mechanism, such a view appears to differ little from the ancient view that "Words are the images of things." . . . The wax tablet model (Aristotle) is at once the oldest theory of origin of images and the oldest form of stimulus-trace theory of memory (Gomulicki, 1953).

According to this interpretation, sensory experiences are impressed on the mind, and the record endures more or less permanently, depending on such characteristics as the physical intensity and vividness of the stimulus input.

The theory was rejected early in the 20th century, but it persists tenaciously in contemporary thinking. Penfield (1954) presented some of the most dramatic evidence for such a view: "Electrical stimulation of the exposed temporal cortex of epileptic patients evoked memories that were described as rivaling perceptions in their vividness." On the basis of these results, Penfield concluded that the temporal cortex of humans contains an experiential recording mechanism wherein is formed a permanent record of the stream of consciousness—all the events of which a [person] was once aware" (p. 13). The existence of such an "experiential recording machine" explains dreamers' habitual illusion that they are witnessing objective life scenes and not their own subjective images. No conscious effort is needed to create dream events. Although dream events are usually lifelike, they are also changed; this change requires an explanation. Bartlett (1932) offered one:

> In general, images are a device for picking bits out of schemes, for increasing the chance of variability in the reconstruction of past stimuli and situations, for surmounting the chronology of presentations. By the aid of the image a [person] can take out of its setting something that happened a year ago, reinstate it with much if not all of its individuality unimpaired, combine it with something that happened yesterday, and use them both to help . . . solve a problem with which [the person] is confronted today. . . . The image facilitates the operation of the past in relation to the somewhat changed conditions of the present. Obviously then, since conditions are always changing, the images and particularly the visual images must be regarded as biologically useful. (p. 304)

Besides, the eye is embryologically derived from the brain, the only part of the nervous system exposed to the outer world. Reality is more comprehensibly perceived through the eye than through any other sense organ. This condition makes visual imagery and visual memories so important. What Murphy (1947) said of memory in general fits well dream events that are felt to be real by the sleeping dreamer: Dream events "are remembered in terms of a place, an act, and a feeling that they belong to the self. . . . We cannot talk about the real without talking about the self. This becomes especially clear when we encounter not loss of reality or loss of selfhood, but a tremendous intensification of both." In the depressed phase of the manic-depressive psychosis, patients are strikingly inhibited both in affects and motility; they cannot interest themselves in anything, they are incapable of joy, and they are extremely sad; they abstain from action, mental or physical, except perhaps bemoaning their fate. In this state they fail to produce images or ideas, they have only negative intentions, and they do not plan action. During the manic phase, they behave in a conspicuously different manner—exhibiting excessive merriment and feelings of extraordinary well-being. They become expansive, ceaselessly active, on the move. In this mood of unlimited self-confidence, patients have imagery and idea flights that are so rapid and that change so frequently that the patients are unable to cooperate, despite grandiose plans that include others. Patients who are great achievers in the world are significantly less exuberant but are well organized. The main point of these observations is that the degree of dynamic energy of visuomotor imagination in dreams is concurrent with the degree of stimulation of the motor system and with the readiness to act. We can say that our visuomotor images are trial actions on a low level of intensity; they foreshadow the future (Piotrowski, 1966). Assessing the strength of counterforces among dream events is essential, of course, because these counterforces exercise an inhibitory influence.

We live in a period of television. Each day, people spend long hours looking at TV pictures and being bombarded by pseudosolemn and overzealous exhortations to buy this or that item. Such vapid talk irritates many people. Favorable (or adverse) criticism of verbal advertising does not correlate with sales. By contrast, visual, kinetic advertising consisting of simple, prominent images increases sales. These findings have influenced even political propaganda. Election results and grave political decisions depend on pictures. No doubt, visuomotor stimuli prompt action more effectively than words do.

Safely, sleeping dreamers do not need to adapt to external, physical reality (adaption is contrasted with interaction). Therefore, dreamers do not experience fear or anxiety that might be aroused by thoughts of possible threatening consequences or by inadequate mastery of a conscious, real-life situation. This freedom from threat encourages imagination. How safe dreamers feel under ordinary circumstances is demonstrated by the relief they experience when they wake from the terror of nightmares. Penfield's (1954) "experiential recording mechanism" provides the necessary memory data to present a conflict on the dream stage. In actual, waking life, intrapsychic conflicts occur within the body of one person; in dreams, however, motivating forces and counterforces are, as a rule, attributed to several figures, with each figure embodying one force or counterforce and being free of irrelevant attributes. The result is an easy and reliable identification of dreamers' intrapsychic conflicts that are currently disquieting. Dreams perform a function similar to that of the Rorschach inkblot test (Piotrowski, 1977, 1979, 1980). Both dream reports and Rorschach response records can be regarded as psychological microscopes. As with the physical microscopes, users have to learn to see what is there and how to interpret the findings. Rorschach responses and dreams differ in the kinds of information they produce. Rorschach responses reveal both the assets and the weaknesses of personalities and the more lasting traits and give a much more comprehensive analysis of personality. Single dreams deal with the rather specific intrapsychic conflicts that disturb dreamers at the moment and that they try to alleviate, seeking to resolve or at least reduce enervating inner contradictions. Dreams can be simple or very complex and complicated. Inevitably some lasting traits are also disclosed in single dreams. A series of successive dreams pertaining to the same conflict literally lays open to view the dreamer's progress in fighting the problem.

Asleep, dreamers are secure; their reality criteria are not aroused. Consequently they do not react with strong, overt affects to their dream events, except in nightmares. Because the sense of physical reality is at best dim, no opportunity exists for strong, physical reactions, even when the events of some dreams are such that, had they occurred in conscious, waking life, they would arouse intense affects.

That an individual can act consistently and persistently as if driven by a desire to achieve a definite purpose — and yet be unaware of this purpose and of pursuing it over extended periods of time — is a descriptive definition of *unconscious motivation* (Piotrowski, 1979). Two-hundred years in development, this definition is generally accepted now. It has revolutionized and advanced personology strikingly (Ellenberger, 1970). The origin of unconscious intentions and behavior patterns is the subject of many diverse opinions. General agreement on etiology does not exist. That unconscious motivation exists is undeniable; frequently, however, it cannot be easily or accurately described in individual instances, and the circumstances in which it is manifested frequently cannot be specified. During psychotherapy, individuals may make, in all earnestness, observations that, according to what has transpired in treatment, illuminate the origin of their disturbing neurotic symptoms and yet not take the next logical steps of meaningfully relating the observations to the development of their symptoms and of insightfully abreacting released guilt or anxiety. How conscious or unconscious are the patients' observations, the implications of which are plain to therapists? What interpersonal relations and intrapsychic states determine whether specific mental content (motivational and affective) is conscious or unconscious, or partially conscious and partially unconscious? How do the varying ratio and quality of the mixed, conscious–unconscious states alter individuals' psychodynamics? These questions are time-consuming; they are difficult to answer reliably in specific cases. How do changing proportions of consciousness–unconsciousness depend on intraindividual and interpersonal mental states, and which states are involved? How is the significance of the degree of consciousness–unconsciousness measured with regard to different intentions and actions?

Consciousness is a great psychobiological asset. It is necessary in the acquisition and use of well-spoken and well-written language. In turn, language broadens our understanding and improves our relations with others both through cooperation and through increasing and intensifying satisfaction with social living. Moreover, conscious behavior, aided by linguistic intercommunication, can be far more easily changed and made more productive and desirable than unconscious or routine behavior can. Frequently, miscomprehension, rather than ill will, prevents a peaceful and positive live-

and-let-live attitude. Consciousness is at the source of connections that depend on systems of meaning (Piaget, 1971, p. 49). Comprehension of meaning is an eminently social function. Unless we agree on meanings of concepts and on which aspects of empirical reality are denoted by which concepts, misunderstanding results, and cooperation is frustrated. Conscious mental states mirror not only the external and internal worlds but also our attitudes toward both. Yet consciousness is incompatible with perfect performance. A perfect performance is one in which, for example, a superb concert pianist plays a perfect piece and is completely absorbed in the music — all the pianist's affects and their nuances and contrasts come into play. The pianist does not consciously place fingers on keys. Fingers automatically "follow" the pianist's mood, which is created by sounds that in turn sustain the mood and sometimes elevate it to ecstasy. Something similar happens in sleep dreaming. Ecstasies are rare in dreams, which almost always concern personal problems. Unconscious creation of dream events, however, does happen, and as long as dreaming lasts, conscious mentation does not interrupt. This absence of critically conscious evaluation makes possible the logical and affective unity of sleep dreams. The positive contribution to this cohesion derives from the intent to formulate and face a specific, disquieting, intrapsychic conflict. Unless selected and unified for a specific purpose (such as formulating a problem), unconscious mental trends are much more diversified and mutually exclusive than conscious trends are. Therefore, conscious attitudes and intentions instigate overt behavior more easily than unconscious attitudes and intentions do. They are also more modifiable — they have fewer inconsistencies among them, and they are accessible to reasoned analysis in terms of realistic possibilities and individuals' personal resources. Not only can we submit mental and physical activities to conscious evaluation and consequent change, but we can consciously assess our consciousness of our consciousness; that is, we can analyze critically the functioning of our conscious processes. This double-checking enables us to evaluate and improve our orientation and actions in the psychosocial and physical worlds.

Visuomotor imagery is adaptable to dream intent. In dreams, visual memories of familiar persons, objects, or structures are easily modified to depict dream events better. Modifications make the object more suitable for performing its intended role in the dream or for blocking more effectively a particular action. Because we are uncritical during sleep dreams, we become aware of unexpected modifications of familiar objects later, on waking, when we realize that we have experienced personal dreams. These modifications of reality in night dreams show how dreamers contemplate overcoming difficulties or why they are frustrated by them. Modification is a way by which dreams can reveal something concrete and specific about individual dreamers. To be valuable, this information must be reliable and highly valid. PDS, based primarily on visuomotor aspects of dream events and focusing interpretation on actual complications and potential implications of intra-psychic conflict that is the nucleus of every dream, is surprisingly accurate, provided the impossibility of representing in pictures the meaning of abstract nouns is recognized. Conflicts can be worked out in considerable detail. This process could not be done if dream records were reduced to verbal reports that neglect the dreamers' many minute and circumstantial remarks about some visuomotor aspects of their dreams. Sometimes sudden and great changes in dream scenes occur, changes that in verbal description sound quite different (confused or unrealistic) but that in visual description are no more odd or unexpected than scenery changes from one act to another in a theater. A picture is worth a thousand words. All forces, all the intentions creating dreams, evolve forms. Visuomotor imagery shows the mutual, in-hibitory influences of individuals' intentions and strivings, which are ex-tracted from verbal statements with greater difficulty and less accuracy.

Dreams depict in pictures the complex interactions among dreamers' psy-chosocial intentions and overt actions. PDS helps us to identify the drives contending for control over the psychomotor system. Positive correlations exist between assent (as defined in PDS) and consciousness and between dis-sent and unconscious. Preference for the terms *assent* and *dissent* is primarily methodological. Establishing with certainty that individuals assent particu-lar personality traits revealed in their dreams or dissent other traits equally re-vealed is far easier than assessing the degree of consciousness and uncon-sciousness of the traits. Thinking in terms of the degree of assent or dissent for which reliable assessment criteria are provided seems more sound. Be-sides, traits displayed in dreams are usually psychomotor and are thus closely related to intents and actions, not only to mentation but also to overt psycho-motor behavior. In human development, understanding and use of visuo-motor imagery precede the growth of verbal communication and abstract reasoning. During the first year of life, visuomotor perceptions and imagery play an almost exclusive role in the process of acquiring knowledge of and ex-ploring the world; this role remains important throughout life.

When problems become too difficult because of inner inconsistencies and persistent conflicts, some individuals "split" into multiple personalities. Be-sides the main or major personality, one or more minor or subpersonalities, dissociated from the major or from one another, is functionally quasi-autonomous. As a rule, intrapsychic processes and overt behavior are under the influence of one of the subpersonalities, but sometimes two subpersonalities can interact. Whether the split results in two or several mi-nor personalities, among them is a pair of two diametrically opposed types resembling, perhaps, Dr. Jekyll and Mr. Hyde, the good and the bad, the purposefully active and the inhibited passive. This is essentially the differ-ence between assented and dissented traits in sleep dreams of normal people. Another common characteristic of dreams and of multiple personalities is that the most active and outgoing of the minor, split personalities knows one or several other subpersonalities and their actions, but each of these other subpersonalities has only fragmentary knowledge or none at all of the others. A minor personality may appear, control the individual's behavior, and interfere with current normal functioning. In like manner, peculiar or aggressively hostile behavior may suddenly stop, and a more companionable subpersonality may begin directing the individual's attitudes and actions.

As long as individuals' criteria of reality and unreality and their application are normal and the same in major and minor personalities, these individuals will not be mentally distressed. Almost all people have functionally split personalities (for example, private subpersonalities and official or public subpersonalities). Intense and prolonged concentration on demanding problems frequently produces subpersonalities in creative artists and scientists. These subpersonalities are hardly adequate for customary social living. These preoccupied people need other personalities for the family and for other social relationships. Similar observations can be made about people working independently and in relative isolation for lifelong purposes. Only when individuals become severely mentally ill and cannot reason logically does the compartmentalization of their personality functions (or multiple personalities) interfere with normal living and turn destructive. The same is true of sleep dreamers who have illogical, bizarre, and acute psychotic disorders; under incipient and mild conditions, psychotics' dreams appear to be mostly socially unconventional and logically inconsistent, with little distortion of perceptual reality. Prince (1957/1906) wrote of his famous Miss Beauchamp:

In addition to the real, original, or normal self, the self that was born and which she was intended by nature to be, she may be any of three different persons. I say three different, because, although making use of the same body, each, nevertheless, has a distinctly different character; a difference manifested by different trains of thought, by different views, beliefs, ideals, and temperament, and by different acquisitions, tastes, habits, experiences, and memories. . . . The splitting of personality is along intellectual and temperamental, not ethical lines of cleavage. . . . Each personality is capable of doing evil to others. . . . Each secondary personality is a part only of a normal whole self. (p. 474–5)

When they were awake, secondary personalities "BI" and "BIV" were conspicuously different. Prince listed 56 physiological, psychological, and social traits in which they differed diametrically. For example, BI disliked the smell of cigarettes and never smoked one in her life; BIV was extravagantly fond of smoking and was a heavy smoker who did not feel any ill effects. BI liked black, white, and soft shades of color in dress; BIV hated black and never wore it, was most impatient, and considered only herself and her personal convenience. BI was very dependent, free from conceit, disliked writing, loved to be with ill or suffering people, and had no fear of the dark; BIV was strikingly self-reliant, extremely conceited, wrote a great deal and liked it, hated illness and had a morbid horror of everything connected with disease, and had great fear of the dark (Prince, 1957/1906, p. 288–294). Considering all the trait incompatibilities between BI and BIV, the two personalities appear irreconcilable. Two people — one possessing the traits of BI and the other the traits of BIV — would not be expected to live together long; their differences would become unbearable under conditions of close intimacy. The stress is even more painful and enervating when those two sets of opposite traits clash within one personality, one body, as in the case of Miss Beauchamp. Splitting into several semi-autonomous subpersonalities saved Miss Beauchamp from total disintegration, concomitant, acute anxieties, and intermittent total failures of self-control. Of singular interest to us are the findings: "that however distinct and separate was the ideation of BI and BIV during the waking state, during sleep these personalities reverted to a common consciousness and became one and the same; that is, the dreams were common to both" (Prince, 1957/1906, p. 342). The dreams expressed the same thoughts, affects, and intents. A fundamental postulate of PDS is that dreams display intrapsychic conflicts between traits (intentions, attitudes, driver goals), conflicts fully or partially conscious or unconscious. Dreams of multiple personality cases do the same. Multiple personality dissociation prevents simultaneous overt manifestation of irreconcilable intentions, which would otherwise meet head-on in actuation. This safety mechanism, however, brings about considerable narrowness of consciousness with resultant inefficiency. Compared with the power of intentions unopposed by other, mitigating intentions, consciousness appears weak. If Miss Beauchamp is not typical of all multiple personality cases, she is still significant in that when she dreams, she is not split.

The task of the central nervous system is to keep an individual healthy and alive. This involves alerting the individual to threatening dangers and warning of excessive stresses that reduce the capacity for serene and effective living. The sustained pursuit of security, prompted by fears, frequently causes tension, inconsistency, intrapsychic conflicts, and thus dreams. Because we observe our sleep dreams consciously, we can initiate remedial procedures after waking. This may be the chief advantage and purpose of consciously perceiving unconsciously produced dreams while asleep. It might even explain why persistent lack of dreaming throws people off balance; denying people of sleep has been one of the subtler ancient tortures.

With the exception of some dreams of the distressingly mentally disordered, nearly all other dreams are logical units; their main theme is frustration. This is true of Freud's "specimen" dream about Irma (Freud, 1900). Freud had been convinced in his waking and dream states that he had cured

Irma of her neurosis, but on the day before his dream, his assistant brought news that Irma was still sick; then, in his specimen dream, Freud himself verified her potentially serious condition. At the end of the dream, Freud denied the failure of his cure by blaming Irma's recent illness on a noxious injection given to her without his knowledge. During his free associations following his dream, Freud listed a number of rather petty frustrations and irritations, the main theme of his postdream associations. If one human problem — the conflict between drive and counterdrive, effort and frustration — conspicuously dominates dreams, then intrapsychic conflicts are an essential part of dreaming; moreover, these conflicts are understandably part of dreams because, as a product of the brain, they are of concern to the central nervous system, the guardian of well-being and survival. Empirical proof of this view of the meaning of dreams is the effect of beneficial psychotherapy on dreams (Piotrowski & Biele, 1983). In such therapy, successive dreams dealing with the same conflict present the conflict in increasingly clearer and greater detail, despite the fact that dreamers may not have mentioned the conflict; at a certain moment, they start speaking freely about the conflict. The content of successive dreams indicates progress made in facing the conflict with less anxiety and in controlling the conflict more successfully. That sleep dreams are references to intrapsychic conflicts is not a theoretical concept but a simple affirmation of fact. The history of dream interpretation supports this affirmation. By clarifying conflict, we can possibly resolve or at least alleviate it.

The PDS conception of dreams is not based on etiological and teleological suppositions; moreover, its interpretive rules apply with minor modifications to valid interpretations of other mental products: TAT stories, free drawings of human figures (including both sexes), Rorschach movement responses (Piotrowski, 1972) and the Hand Test (Bricklin, Piotrowski, & Wagner, 1981). The common element in these five types of visuomotor response is spontaneous, free association. When a dream interpretation system is based on a preconceived notion about the meaning or purpose of dreaming, conclusions drawn from the system are conspicuously affected by the notion. Freud's major premise, that the origin of dreams is essentially the same as that of hysterical symptoms, made him reject the manifest dream as an allegedly deceptive expression of personality. Any assumption that dreams are not genuine samples of dreamers' intrapsychic processes leads to interpretation, that is misrepresentative.

In Bowler's (1973) witty conception of Freud's Irma dream as a farce, dreams are functional units; all actions and actors are meaningfully interrelated. Bowler was a drama critic for radio and television stations for more than two decades. His discussion of the dream follows; except that historical references to farces that have been popular in Europe since the mid-18th century have been omitted:

Recently I read Freud's Irma Injection Dream and reacted to it as a drama critic could perhaps not avoid reacting. If a marine biologist or a theoretical physicist were exposed to it, he might react in terms of his specialty and shed some light on its obscurities in a way unlikely to occur to those outside his field. I hope my theatrical criticism of Irma Injection will do that. Dreams are plays. Dreamers are playwrights. Dreams contain all the elements of dramaturgy: plot, a cast of characters, dialogue, pantomime, choreography, props, sets, lighting, and sound effects. They obey to their credit, and violate to their loss, the rules of dramaturgy. . . . Since all factors in a dream come from the mind of the dreamer, conventional theatrical criticism is not possible. The lone aspect of a dream which can be analyzed is its dramaturgy. . . . Farces tend to be intense and are hard for the audience to take and for the playwright to sustain. Therefore they are usually not constructed in two long acts but in three short ones. So is *Irma Injection*. Act I: The discovery of the Injection; Act II: The Dysentery Diagnosis; Act III: The discovery of the Prior Injection.

Irma Injection utilizes the standard farce technique of making events appear ridiculous by staging them at a time and in a location where it is not customary that such events take place, and indeed they are thoroughly out of place here. Act I takes place in a great hall or grand salon in the midst of an elegant and formal social reception. The occasion seems to smack of high society. It is not established that Irma does not belong there; it must be accepted that she does. Yet despite her protests, she is subjected to a thorough physical examination, is forced to open her mouth wide so her throat can be peered into, and is casually frisked all over. This is the standard farce trick of imposing indignities on a dignified lady. So Groucho was always making life difficult for Margaret Dumont, who always played the dowager. Farce demands that minor characters be kept in their place and never be allowed to emerge into more prominence than necessary. They are no more than devices to further the plot or embody aspects of the hero's dilemma. In *Irma Injection* all the characters are minor except Freud, the dreamer. Irma herself becomes a mute manikin after her protests are ignored at the opening of Act II. Dr. M. merely voices his dysentery prediction, and friends Otto and Leopold are little more than walk-ons. Only hungry actors would accept such parts.

Ancient Greek tragedies ended with Deus ex Machina, a god on a machine. The plot would become so tangled no mortal could untangle it, so a god would descend on a piece of stage machinery. The Deus ex Machina is also a basic ingredient of the farce formula where it takes the form of the introduction of an entirely new element which changes the meaning of everything which has previously transpired. In farces of mistaken identity, what was thought to be a boy is revealed as having been a girl all along, so the romance between the hero and heroine is quite heterosexual after all and the fuss by their relatives and friends unfounded. In *Irma Injection* the Deus ex Machina is the injection explanation in Act III. It explains the injection and even the pains in a totally different manner than had prevailed in Act I or Act II, or indeed before the play began. The conclusion is also typically farcical. It resolves all problems. The implication is unavoidable that once the effects of the injection wear off, the infection will go away and the pains with it, and Irma will live happily ever afterwards, so long as she stays away from parties attended by doctors. (p. 605–607)

Bowler (1973) performed an interesting intellectual experiment. He analyzed the Irma Injection dream to see how closely it conformed to the nature and structural requirements of a farcical play. The parallels were astounding, despite Freud's serious concern on hearing that a patient he had discharged as cured slipped into an apparently grave illness. Freud created his dream unconsciously while asleep, and yet his dream report can be taken for a play, consciously, deliberately written according to the impersonal and formal rules of writing farces. Perhaps Freud was in a sardonic mood when his theory and treatment were being scrutinized by colleagues less qualified than himself. A more relevant explanation is that mere verbal propositions, taken out of context, are ambiguous. A sentence spoken with irony is used to express the opposite of the literal meaning of the sentence (the literal meaning is retained when the sentence is spoken earnestly). To unravel exact, intended meanings of purely verbal statements, we must know the intentions, affects, and specific purposes that prompted the verbal utterances. Certainly an author of a farce and a physician dreaming of an important medical consultation would be motivated by disparate intentions, moods, affects, and specific aims. Therefore, we need a theory that we can use to identify the psychobiological function of dreaming in sleep and that offers reliable, pertinent rules for interpretations of single dreams. A basic premise of PDS is that sleep dreams convey truthful messages about dreamers' inadequately known intrapsychic conflicts. Messages are displayed in visuomotor images that exhibit disturbing psychodynamic incompatibilities. Conscious self-criticism is dormant during sleep dreams. In addition, visuomotor manifestations of intrapsychic states differ much less from person to person than do verbal and abstract self-expressions of these states. This allows PDS to be simple as well as valid. Dreams provide psychotherapists and the dreamers themselves with incentives to the latters' self-improvement.

5 Two Dream Interpretation Axioms

Axioms are general propositions on which people usually agree without proof of validity. Axioms usually serve as primary or basic premises for deductive conclusions. Some axioms are purely hypothetical; their truth value or validity is neither affirmed nor denied (these are the axioms of logic and mathematics). In sciences dealing with empirical reality, consensus on propositions is reached on the grounds that postulated axioms are self-evident. Axioms are indispensable in systems of deductive inference. In empirical sciences, general propositions are selected as axioms when their consistent and repeated application yields information that is both valid and significant. In dream interpretation, two axioms have been used for thousands of years.

Axiom A (so called for brevity) states that sleep dreams are visuomotor dramatizations of dreamers' intrapsychic conflicts and that sleep dreams show how dreamers' divergent intentions and incompatible behavior patterns interfere with one another; sleep dreams draw conscious attention to the nature and strength of the contending inner forces. Axiom A relates to intra-individual psychic processes. Dream figures embody different, quasi-autonomous function units of dreamers' personalities. The degree of difference between personality traits of a dreamer and those of another dream figure parallels the strength of the dreamer's belief that the traits of the other figure are also those of the dreamer. *Axiom B* postulates that each dream figure's attributes reflect the dreamer's feelings, thoughts, and intentions regarding the type of person that the dream figure represents (male, female, old, young, and so forth). Thus, Axiom B relates to dreamers' interpersonal relationships.

For example, we generally like friendly and helpful people and dislike unfriendly and uncooperative ones. If people are unfriendly and uncooperative but feel no consequent fear, anxiety, or guilt, they are very unlikely to ascribe those negative attributes to dream figures other than themselves. In such cases, we conclude that dreamers fully assent their negative social attitudes (Axiom A) and do not as a matter of course attribute them to others (Axiom B). In general, dishonest and/or violent people who are not bothered by their behavior do not habitually resent or condemn others with similar behavior. However, negative-trait possessors who feel fear, anxiety, or guilt over their negative traits are likely to express their dissent in their dreams by assigning those traits to dream figures unlike themselves (Axiom A); they simultaneously indicate that people represented by dream figures with these negative emotional attitudes are antisocial (Axiom B).

Axiom B is used far more frequently than Axiom A, at least in published dream analyses. In the literature, references to Axiom A are brief. Several reasons account for this great difference in application. First, we have much more experience in the use of Axiom B, which pertains to our evaluations of others. In waking life, we do not need special analysis of evidence to form opinions of others. We have been trained since birth to use personal experience with others to form spontaneous opinions. We often do not analyze and formulate these assessments, however, into conscious, verbal terms. Moreover, in most waking situations, we are not aware how these spontaneous and intuitive attitudes influence our social behavior. This unawareness of our motives and behavior may expose us to pain or harm. If these spontaneous assessments are common in waking life — despite this danger — then they must manifest themselves even more frequently and plainly in dreaming. The reason for this seems to be that it is impossible during dreaming to be put on guard by others' negative reactions to our attitudes and behavior concerning them.

No single dream is a manifestation of a dreamer's "total" personality, but a single dream *is* a manifestation of one or several of the quasi-autonomously functioning personality units. In a single dream, therefore, the appearance of the dreamer's own traits and opinions regarding others is possible, thus making the Axiom A and Axiom B interpretations almost equally valid.

Dreams of a small group of conspicuously delusional psychotics, however, may invalidate the principle that dream figures represent traits of dreamers and also of some other people; the psychotic's defective sense of reality in both waking and dreaming states is the monkey wrench. Yet psychotics are not delusional all the time. Milder conditions correlate with less frequent manifestations of psychotic symptoms in overt behavior. This is why many dreams of mild psychotics display no psychotic features; also, dreams are products of the relatively healthiest functions of the dreamer's psychobiological organism.

The psychological primacy of Axiom A is disclosed by the frequently striking continuity of themes in a series of successive dreams. Such a series provides an excellent opportunity to observe intrapsychic development — for better in some cases, for worse in others — in the handling of personal conflicts indicated in earlier dreams.

The same tendency that makes us notice and often criticize others' undesirable traits, traits that we would like to deny in ourselves, predisposes us to disparage others' assets, assets that we lack. Disguising the carrier of a dissented or undesirable action tendency through displacement of the dreamer by a dissimilar dream figure — while leaving the action tendency itself undisguised — amounts to deflecting the responsibility for the action tendency on someone else. Deflecting an action is easier than suppressing it; hence, even inertia contributes to the validity and special importance of Axiom A.

Examples

1. Jung (1974) published a young man's dream that had "no foundation in fact":

> My father is driving away from the house in his new car. He drives very clumsily, and I get very annoyed over his apparent stupidity. He goes this way and that, forwards and backwards, and maneuvers the car into a dangerous position. Finally, he runs into a wall and damages the car badly. I shout at him in perfect fury that he ought to behave himself. My father only laughs, and then I see that he is dead drunk. (p. 102)

The dreamer was convinced that neither he nor his father had ever behaved in this manner and that there was no chance that they ever would. His relationship with his father was positive. In fact, the son admired the father for being an unusually successful man. Why, then, did the son disavow in the dream his conscious, laudatory evaluation of his father?

Jung (1974) answered this question by explaining that the son's

> unconscious is obviously trying to take the father down a peg . . . His father is still too much the guarantor of his existence, and the dreamer is still living a provisional life. His particular danger is that he cannot see his own reality on account of his father. Therefore the unconscious resorts to a kind of artificial blasphemy so as to lower the father and elevate the son . . . The interpretation just outlined was apparently the correct one, for it struck home. It won the spontaneous assent of the dreamer. (p. 103)

Jung reported the dream as an example of the caution that must be exercised in interpreting dreams for dreamers. He explained that neurotic ambivalence had not been found in the dreamer's relationship with his father. Therefore, Jung felt that he "had no warrant for upsetting the young man's feelings" (p. 103) with a destructive interpretation of the dream.

Using PDS for a blind analysis of the dream would have been quite different. Using Axiom A, we conclude that the dreamer fully assented his condemnation of intoxicated behavior (impulsive, unreasonable, destructive, and characterized by a defiant, irresponsible merriment). The son attributed these undesirable traits to the father figure, which represented his own dissented tendency to freedom, spontaneity and socially irresponsible behavior.

The young, unmarried man lived by a strict code of emotional restraint, subdued overt behavior, and earnest devotion to hard, consistent work. Jung may have sensed this and therefore was careful not to upset the dreamer by "a destructive pronouncement" (p. 103). The conflict was between a rebellious but suppressed drive for relief from the demanding consciously assented code of conduct and his great effort to retain the security and advantages that his obedience guaranteed.

Using Axiom B, we attribute to the dreamer the same traits we ascribe to him within the framework of Axiom A. We assume that the behavior of the dream father reflects the dreamer's opinion of the behavior of the real, living father. According to the information provided by Jung, this assumption is wrong. In other words, the PDS interpretation based on Axiom A is valid (the young man was proper and well behaved), but the interpretation based on Axiom B is not. If this were indeed the case, we can turn to Hippocrates for an explanation: When real past events are grossly misrepresented in a dream, the dreamer is probably illogical or dereistic; as a rule, then, when a difference in degree of validity between the conclusions of Axiom A and Axiom B exists, the conclusions of Axiom A are more valid.

Axiom A is more significant for another reason, namely for the detection and understanding of a specific, genuine problem and the concomitant, intrapsychic inconsistencies that motivated the dreamer to seek psychotherapy.

2. Another dream in which Axiom A and Axiom B conclusions differ noticeably in content concerns an unmarried, middle-age man. In the dream, the man's girlfriend passively surrendered to the embraces of an old man. The dreamer became furious and physically attacked the old man, who suddenly disappeared. This short dream is easily interpreted in terms of the interpersonal Axiom B; it is a common scene of jealousy and of defending a person's claim to "exclusive rights" to another individual. The intra-individual Axiom A reveals the intrapsychic complications of the dreamer. In the woman figure, the dreamer submitted passively to the amorous approaches of a person of the opposite sex. This trait was dissented at level 6 of the Scale of Dissent. As the old man at the much less dissented level 2, the man actively approached an opposite-sex love object. He fully assented his active defense of his exclusive rights to his girlfriend. Although he dissented and partially suppressed his availability as a passive love object, on a fully assented level he

easily stopped active lovemaking. An interesting detail is that the old man suddenly disappeared after a short while; that is, he quickly gave up his lovemaking. Under normal conditions, the dreamer and the woman would have rejoined each other. In the dream they remained apart. This suggests that the man's pride was a stronger motive than his amorous interest in the woman. (Rule of Implicit Evidence). The conflict revealed in the dream was between an affective, physical interest in the opposite sex and abstention from overt manifestation of this interest.

3.   Hervey (1964) attempted to dream about his own suicide as part of his research on the degree to which dreamers control dream content deliberately. In a dream, he saw himself walking on a boulevard in Paris and noticed an open window on the top floor of a new, tall apartment building. Suddenly the dream scene changed. He saw himself standing on the sill of the open window. He looked at the street and jumped. Before he hit the ground, the dream scene changed abruptly. This time he saw himself in front of a church on a square. A crowd of people looked at the body of a dead man (not Hervey) who had jumped from the church tower and killed himself. Seeing a corpse is not an expression of genuine suicidal tendencies or a genuine desire for death. Rather, it indicates that dreamers long for support and love from others to alleviate depression. We do not know if Hervey ever had a genuine suicidal wish. He had a stimulating, rewarding, full life. He was recognized as a scientist (sinologist) and as a member of important scientific societies; he was financially comfortable, had many friends and a rich social life, and intermingled with other outstanding individuals. He wrote several books, one of which is his large, original treatise on *Dreams and Means to Control Them* (Hervey, 1964).

Despite his persistent and numerous trials, Hervey never succeeded in committing a suicide in a dream. Even when he did something in a dream that in reality would have caused his death, he was saved in the dream one way or another. In one dream, he jumped off a high cliff into the English channel. Before he reached the ground below, however, a balloon appeared; the gondola picked him up and safely carried him away. In another dream, he tried to shoot himself with his pistol. He looked diligently for the pistol he knew was in his house, but, hard as he tried, he failed to find the weapon. Dreamers' dying in their own dreams does not mean that they wish to die in real life for the obvious reason that dreams are not physical reality. But, had Hervey's dreams shown his process of dying, they would have violated the PDS principle that every dream trait that is fully assented is a true and real characteristic of the dreamer, simply because Hervey survived his suicidal dreams. Thus, Hervey's experiments in trying to dream traits or events incompatible with the dreamers' genuine personality indirectly confirm a basic PDS principle.

4. The 37-year-old Jung (1961) had the following dream, "which pre-saged the forthcoming break with Freud":

> I was in an Italian city, and it was around noon, between twelve and one o'clock. A fierce sun was beating down upon the narrow streets. The city was built on hills and reminded me of a particular part of Basel, the Kohlenberg. The little streets which lead down into the valley, the Birsigtal, that runs through the city, are partly flights of steps. In the dream, one such stairway descended to Barfusserplatz. The city was Basel, and yet it was also an Italian city, something like Bergamo. It was summertime; the blazing sun stood at the zenith, and everything was bathed in an intense light. A crowd came streaming toward me, and I knew that the shops were closing and people were on their way home to dinner. In the midst of this stream of people walked a knight in full armor. He mounted the steps toward me. He wore a helmet of the kind that is called a basinet, with eye slits, and chain armor. Over this was a white tunic into which was woven, front and back, a large red cross. One can easily imagine how I felt: suddenly to see in a modern city, during the noonday rush hour, a crusader coming toward me. What struck me as particularly odd was that none of the many persons walking about seemed to notice him. No one turned his head or gazed after him. It was as though he were completely invisible to everyone but me. I asked myself what this apparition meant, and then it was as if someone answered me — but there was no one there to speak: "Yes, this is a regular apparition. The knight always passes by here between twelve and one o'clock, and has been doing so for a very long time (for centuries, I gathered) and everyone knows about it." (p. 164-5)

A dream interpretation based on Axiom B emphasizes Jung's amazement that a foreign city (Bergamo) and his native town (Basel, at the outskirts of which he was born and where he went to school) have striking similarities. In this Italian city, he discovered the persistence of a way of living (represented by the knight) that went back to the crusades in the 12th century. Jung was surprised that none of the numerous passersby had noticed the knight. He was immediately corrected by someone (heard but not seen), who informed him that the knight was "a regular apparition. . . . and everyone knows about it." This implies that some of the distant past survives and mixes with the present and that this survival is a regular feature of ordinary life (the people were going home to take their siestas). This dream preceded the first publication of Jung's (1961) *The Archetypes and the Collective Unconscious* (p. 392-3). Jung's personal concepts of the archetypes and of the unconscious were unacceptable to Freud; Jung was adamant. This caused the rift between them. Dream events interpreted according to Axiom B appear unrealistic; the dream appears to be a fairy tale.

Axiom A assumes that sleep dreams pertain to intrapsychic processes. Jung (1961) described the dream as "numinous in the extreme" (p. 165), that is, mysterious, supernatural, or spiritual. He added: "My whole being was seeking for something still unknown which might confer meaning upon the banality of life" (p. 165). He was to be preoccupied for the rest of his life with numinous experiences and psychic forces that he considered universal human traits; although universal, they exist in different degrees and varieties in different individuals. In the dream, feeling surprised that no one but himself "saw" the knight, Jung received a message—although there was no messenger—that he was wrong, that the knight had always passed where Jung stood and that everyone was aware of the knight. In terms of Axiom A and even during the dream itself, the message was a sudden, unexpected inner (imaginative) insight, an intuitive, cognitive act. It points to intuition as a source of knowledge about psychosocial events of interest to more than one individual. The two axioms bring out dissimilar parts of personality. The Axiom A interpretation is more meaningful; it reveals more of Jung's specific personality traits.

5.   In the dream report of a disturbed patient appeared the following sentences: "I was an observer at times, and at other times I blended with them [the male dream figures]. They were enemies who were out to kill each other." This man shifted from an Axiom A to an Axiom B attitude, back and forth, during the dream itself. The patient experienced difficulties in differentiating between himself and others in waking life. He was not sure of his identity; this depersonalization was reflected in the dream.

6 PDS Rules of Interpretation

RULE 1: ASSENT AND DISSENT

Meanings of Assent and Dissent

The terms *assent* and *dissent* connote, respectively, agreement and disagreement with a statement or proposal. In PDS, they acquire special meanings. They are used to indicate whether dreamers assert or deny that traits they attributed to dream figures are their own personal characteristics. Axiom A postulates that all traits of all dream figures are the dreamers' own characteristics — characteristics they unconsciously project on the different dream figures. Rule 1 adds an important specification to the basic postulate by stating how all traits discernible in a dream are classified in separate trait sets and how each trait set is assigned to a different figure in the dream. Traits are put in the same set (or category) when they share a significant quality, namely that of collectively advancing either the realization or the frustration of an intention or action tendency. For example, all traits that positively contribute to the accomplishment of an end constitute one set, whereas those that hamper or hinder the effort to produce a desired result form another trait set. Obviously, these two sets of traits are incompatible because they cannot be simultaneously activated without causing intrapsychic tension and lowering the efficiency of action.

The very great majority of dreams reveals the mutual interference of drives and counterdrives, of striving and frustration, of impulse and inhibition. In dreams, people face the eternal human question: To do or not to do? The answer to this question may at times be difficult. Strong irreconcilable and persistent traits (motives) unnerve and intensify anxiety.

Dreamers unconsciously ascribe each trait set to a different dream figure. Figures and trait sets are matched when they are about equally congenial or familiar to the dreamers. This matching is done unconsciously, without significant contact with physical reality; it is not submitted to a conscious, rational, critical evaluation in which it would be assessed in terms of its correspondence with personally known empirical reality. The result of matching performed during dreaming is that, as the difference between dreamers and dream figures grows, the dreamers' dissent of traits manifested by the figures also grows. This is another form of our universal human tendency to ascribe undesirable characteristics to strangers and desirable characteristics to ourselves and our friends.

To assent traits manifested in dreams is to affirm traits as genuine personal characteristics regardless of whether they are assets or liabilities in life, of whether they signify health or sickness, of whether they are good or evil. People assent traits both before and after becoming conscious of the nature of the traits. To dissent traits is to genuinely deny or doubt traits as genuine personal characteristics. Although only one degree of assent exists, many degrees of dissent are possible.

This is reflected in the Scale of Dissent, which uses a zero location for assent and 12 locations for degrees of dissent (mildest to strongest).

All traits appearing in dreams and attributed by dreamers to themselves are considered fully assented. The zero location, on top of the Scale of Dissent, is reserved for fully assented traits. Traits are classified dissented when they are ascribed to dream figures other than dreamers. The degree of dissent increases with the difference between the dreamer and the figure exhibiting the dissented trait; this difference is measured in terms of sex, age, species of organism, natural forces, and animate inanimate objects. The scale includes humans, animals, natural forces acting on their own, and animate inanimate objects. The last category includes things such as moving, driverless automobiles not controlled by any external power and uncontrolled construction cranes behaving as if they had wills.

Other Dream Figures

Ascribing dissented traits to dream figures other than the dreamers involves two separate but seemingly simultaneous and unconscious mental processes. In one process, some personality elements that are not incompatible with one another and that could constitute one of the dreamer's minor personalities are gathered into a set. In the other process, selection of a dream figure indicates the degree to which the dreamer uses the figure to dissent the traits. If the dream figure is a real, living person, its behavior and experiences may be quite different from those of the actual person. Of secondary importance to physically inert dreamers is whether dream figures act in real, waking life as they do in dreams. Considering that the pictorial language in dreams has its limitations and that it is incapable of expressing certain ideas directly, clearly, and unambiguously, dreamers are fortunate in that they can indicate dissent and its degree through unconscious use of dream figures other than themselves.

People's dissented traits make harmonious living with others more difficult. These traits are related to negative emotional impulses. Because most people do not harbor powerful negative emotions, their dissented dream traits rarely reach ordinal locations higher than 6 on the Scale of Dissent.

That dreamers unconsciously choose other figures to be carriers of their dissented traits makes it unlikely that the dreamers genuinely wish to be like those figures. Dreamers do not genuinely wish to act as those figures do or to have the same experiences that those figures have. Their desire is to shed dissented traits associated with feelings of alienation. Alienation is usually clinically noticeable when dissent reaches the highest location on the scale (see the first example in this chapter).

Personology concerns interpersonal relationships and intrapsychic processes. In PDS, sex differences play a greater role than age differences. Therefore, when dreamers distance themselves from personal traits by attributing them to figures of the opposite sex, their dissent of the traits is stronger than it would be if they were to ascribe the traits to different-age but same-sex figures. This is reflected in the Scale of Dissent. All human and human-like figures are classified as "humans." Even ghosts are included; if dreamers specify sex and age, then the specified human-like figures can be placed into one of the first 6 ordinal locations. Dreamers' projecting traits on dream figures younger than themselves indicates some immaturity, some tendency to shrink from assuming the privileges and the responsibilities of adulthood; dreamers' projecting dissented traits on dream figures older than themselves — provided the dreamers are not senile — seems to reveal a skepticism about growing wiser, better, and more mature with age.

Dissented traits assigned to animals usually are of an animalistic quality pertaining to bodily or psychophysical sensations or events, mostly unpleasant but occasionally pleasurable (examples are: a purring, licking pet cat; a friendly tiger approaching in a zigzag manner, jumping from side to side and taking its time; a wolf stalking its prey).

Dreams with animate inanimate objects are very rare. In terms of conscious and realistic consciousness, these dreams are unnatural, bizarre. People who have them are at the time somewhat alienated, feeling anxious lest they be hopelessly controlled by their own strange, inhuman forces, usually destructive and dangerous to themselves and others. The intrapsychic forces active in nightmarish dreams of this sort — not necessarily lasting or irreversible forces — depersonalize and dehumanize when they overwhelm the dreamer's self-control and sense of reality.

It is very important to bear in mind that the traits a dreamer attributes to a dream figure must be inferred from the behavior and experiences of the dream figure during the dream and not from general knowledge of the typical traits displayed by the real-life prototype of the dream figure. Building cranes do not chase people in real life.

Examples

1.   A professional man in his 50s was traveling in his car on a six-lane turnpike in a dream. The two halves of the road were divided by a sturdy guardrail. A cautious man, he kept on the third, outer lane, and moved at an even speed below the legal limit. There was no traffic ahead or behind him. Suddenly he noticed in his small mirror that a car traveling at great speed was rapidly gaining on him. What made him fearful was that the car was wildly careening from side to side as if the driver had lost control. The man could not leave the highway and became alarmed that the other car would hit his. Because the car passed without incident, the dreamer experienced some relief. However, he also felt consternation because there was no driver in the speeding car that now raced ahead of him. After a short while, the car abruptly turned left, hit the center guardrail, and turned over several times before it came to rest. The dreamer continued driving as he watched the disintegration of the car ahead of him. The dream ended as he was approaching the wreck.

Two completely opposite sets of distinct traits are dramatized in the man's dream. According to the Scale of Dissent, the traits that the man attributed to himself are fully assented and occupy the zero ordinal location on the scale. Two features of the man's personality stood out from his dream behavior: caution to escape injury or damage and punctilious respect for laws designed to regulate conduct in the public domain. These two traits greatly assured his "safety." In the dream, he kept moving cautiously and was not struck by the erratic car. Faced with danger, he limited his activities, increased his alertness, and improved his trouble-avoiding behavior. Although he escaped the immediate danger, however, the self-destruction of the driverless car warned him that some danger was still lying ahead. The racing car had broken into parts that were strewn over the highway. The dream ended before the dreamer had come close to the wreck. He woke up in an anxious, somber mood.

With the careening car representing his most dissented traits (scale location 12), the dreamer was psychologically unable to suppress these traits and put an end to the danger. His only defense was to keep to the right edge of the road to minimize the chances of being hit. This worked for a while. His conscious, rational, major personality strongly assented evasive stratagems. But this dream warned the man that his violent, self-destructive minor personality may meet with a catastrophe in real life. The dream implies that the dreamer's whole self will suffer if the minor part of his personality goes unrestrained. The locations on the Scale of Dissent of the assented and dissented traits are 0 and 12 respectively. This difference of 12 points is the greatest possible on the scale and indicates a very severe intrapsychic conflict with acute anxiety (Rule of Complementarity). The dreamer could not tell whether the other car would hit him or not, although he took whatever action he could to avoid the danger. Anxiety is dread of the unknown and thus of the unpredictable. Because of the erratic movements of the speeding car, the dreamer was unable to estimate whether the car would crash into his.

The intrapsychic conflict revealed by the dream was very intense and perturbing. Fully assented, strictly maintained habits of great self-discipline, restraint, caution, and respect for law and order conflict with the extremely dissented, frightening tendency to indulge in conspicuous, violent, lawless, threatening, completely uncontrolled behavior. The dream reveals that the man's potentially disordered behavior could be dangerous both to himself (the car, his alter ego, destroyed itself) and to others (the violent behavior occurred on a wide, public highway).

Dream scenes or the physical environments in which dream events take place sometimes contribute relevant items to dream interpretations. We rarely see real turnpikes empty of traffic. There were only two cars on the dream turnpike in full daylight, which suggests that the dreamer's conflict absorbed him so much at the time that the conflict had become the only, or by far the most important, matter that occupied his mind. When the dream was ending, the dreamer was approaching the wreck, which was in his full view (Rule of Implicit Evidence).

There is nothing unrealistic in this dream. Careening, speeding cars on a practically empty highway are not frequent sights, but they are possible. The dreamer controlled his car and himself. He did not panic, which would have interrupted his dream and awakened him (cf. nightmare). In his manifest dream, the dreamer came out of the ordeal untouched; even his car was not scratched.

The dream added to his internal turmoil. Yet the dreamer continued functioning satisfactorily, albeit with difficulty, in his exacting profession. Shortly after the dream, he requested private psychiatric advice and treatment for the first time in his life. His behavior among strangers did not betray his internal tensions and anxieties. When asked, he reported the dream; he was not prompted, however, to elaborate. Three main clinically pertinent suggestions ensued from the dream analysis.

The short-term prognosis had been that an acute and severe psychotic breakdown was highly probable within a short time. The breakdown would be characterized by overtly hostile and physically violent behavior that would possibly endanger other people. Immediate hospitalization should have been considered. The dream elements that led to these conclusions were the patient's close watch on the careening automobile; the great speed and erratic, dangerous movements of the car; the car's "disregard" of its surroundings, its smashing into the guardrail, and its gradual disintegration. Watching and affectively experiencing the destruction of the dissented dream figure (not merely an inert wreck) were associated with actual or pending personality disintegration. Personal death, however, was not indicated for two reasons. First, the patient's dominant, conscious, assented personality escaped harm but took only limited cautionary action; it could have driven onto the shoulder of the road (Rule of Empirical Evidence). The dreamer's facing rather than retreating from the danger suggested that the dreamer's courage or self-confidence was considerable. Second, terminal cancer patients who know full well that they are dying express this awareness (assent) by seeing themselves (not other dream figures) as gradually losing vitality (cf. cancer). Our dreamer, in fact, dissented self-destruction most strongly (on the highest possible scale location, 12); he put his alter ego, the violent, irrational car, out of action for good. The assented, reasonable, mature main personality took a good look at the wreck without manifesting any commotion. The inner tension created by the assented and dissented drives and intention had enervated the dreamer. He needed to consciously use his utmost strength and care to remain rational. His conflict had to be resolved to spare him a personality breakdown. A cathartic release of the powerful, antisocial drives seemed necessary for the patient's good. He dissented (mostly unconsciously) the emotional sacrifices and excessive adaptation to social rules he had been making in his life in an attempt to feel secure, unassailable. He may have been thinking about making up for the sacrifices of his youth: In the dream, he traveled on a turnpike that lead to new and distant places; this prospect, however, had its dangers.

The long-term prognosis was that, when the acute psychotic phase ends, much improvement is very probable. The defenses against conspicuous, antisocial and irrational behavior will most likely reassert themselves. This prognosis is based on the sound self-control demonstrated by the major conscious personality during the dream; this personality thus had a rather good capacity for tolerating stress.

Within 10 days after the dream, during which he received both drugs and psychotherapy, the patient suddenly went into an acute paranoid phase; he became loud, suspicious, accusatory, verbally and physically abusive. He was admitted to a psychiatric hospital immediately, in the middle of the night. After several weeks, he was transferred to a country sanatorium for treatment and recuperation. His condition improved remarkably. Four months after the dream, the patient resumed his premorbid activities and was classified as recovered. Incidental follow-up after nearly a year disclosed that he had continued his habitual and professional activities, having experienced no relapse during the follow-up period.

2.   Another man in his 50s had a dream with the same main theme as the preceding case but with a clear difference pertaining to what was assented and dissented. In the dream, the man was walking during the middle of the night, in the center of his city with its concentration of tall, darkened business buildings. He recognized the streets but was surprised that he did not see any people or cars, traveling or parked. The city was still and empty. Another cause for surprise was the street lights. They looked familiar and were lighted, but they were spaced widely apart. In addition, the placement of the lights on one side of the street corresponded to the midpoints between neighboring lights on the other side of the street. Islets of round bright spots around the lanterns alternated with dim areas between them. The total impression was one of gloom and fear of threatening danger. At one point, he passed a building site. A building crane was parked parallel to the sidewalk, and he noticed lying on the ground the triangular, movable head of the crane. After a while he felt that someone was following him. He turned his head and to his horror saw the crane crawling after him with its head close to the sidewalk. He quickened his steps and tried to remain inconspicuous, but the crane pursued him with obvious determination. Finally, the dreamer tried to hide in a new, tall building that had just been completed but that had not yet been equipped with doors and windows. The crane found the dreamer in every hiding place and chased him onto the flat roof that was surrounded by a low parapet. With no place to hide, the man crouched in a corner of the parapet and was terrified to see the crane slowly but steadily approach him with open jaws. Only two alternatives remained — to jump off the roof and meet certain death or to stay put and be crushed by the steel jaws of the crane. Anxiety became unbearable, and the dreamer woke from his nightmare.

The scale difference between the assented and dissented traits was 12 points, or the highest possible, just as it was in the preceding dream of the careening car. In that case, however, the assented traits revealed strict self-control and consistent, predictable behavior; dissented traits were uncontrolled and violent and endangered the dreamer as well as others. In this case, the opposite was true. The dreamer himself, or the assented personality, faced mortal danger; the strong, self-assured, dissented traits, represented by the building crane, were unquestionably dominant. The dreamer was very anxious yet also determined not to be overwhelmed by his dissented drives. A definitive resolution of the conflict between the two trait sets was not yet possible. The nightmare ended in a panic, without any abatement of the dangerous drives disintegrating the dreamer's personality but also without any weakening of the dreamer's determined attempts to successfully defend himself against a personality breakdown. No direct or lasting harm was done to either figure during the dream; the worst thing was the intolerable anxiety the dreamer experienced. The danger signal for the future was the persistent, methodical, unrelenting hostility of the dissented, minor personality and the fearfulness, depression, and weakness of the dreamer's assented, conscious ego functions.

Analysis of the dream scene also contributes some information. Although the dreamer immediately recognized that he was in a very familiar section of the city and that the street on which he walked led to his home, he felt estranged and fearful; he walked warily. The city looked familiar but was not. The street lights, placed far apart (not as in reality), created round islets of brightness amid the dimness of the night. The dreamer walked alternately through light and darkness. This may indicate his alternating mental states of lucidity and uncontrolled confusion — a switching that was one of his symptoms. A possible positive sign was the two references to a new building. The dreamer passed one building site and sought refuge in a newly built apartment house that needed relatively little effort to be completed. The building activity may have signified the availability of therapy and improvement.

This dreamer was also a professional man. He lived in an area different from that of the first case. He was perceptive, highly intelligent, educated. He was also efficient at his occupation, which he practiced during the long intervals between psychotic episodes. While working, he made up for what he missed when he was too anxious, phobic, and depressed to work. He supported himself through a job that permitted him to set his own pace.

3. A 14-year-old boy described one of his dreams (Hervey, 1964):

> I see a young apprentice with dishevelled hair being horribly beaten by her employer, who is a ropemaker. The young girl held a mallet in her hand. It irritated me that she was not defending herself. I could not go to her defense, I don't know why; and I shouted to her in vain to strike back. Suddenly, I became the apprentice [the girl]. Enraged, I struck the forehead of the hateful man who had been torturing me. I looked at him closely as he was bleeding and lying on his back. After that, I was afraid I would be arrested. I combed my hair, which I tied in a knot behind my head [the dreamer then had the shape of the dishevelled woman], and fled. As I ran, I made sure that my robe would not be caught by the forked branches of the trees, which were covered with twisted hemp. (p. 349)

The interesting part of this dream is the metamorphosis of the dreamer into a young woman. Neither the boy nor the young woman was capable of hitting the sadistic man; when their bodies and minds coalesced, however, they killed him in self-defense. The pictorial language of the dream thus expressed the causal connection between actual suffering and the intent to end suffering through positive action. By emotionally identifying with the physically beaten woman, the boy developed the courage to act against the strong aggressor tormenting the weak and submissive victim. At that point, the mood changed. When he contemplated the result of his overreaction, he felt guilty and feared punishment. It was only when he felt that he was acting in defense of someone else, the woman, that he raised enough courage to fight the sadist. The implication is that he could not bring himself to fight for himself but could battle authoritarian sadists for the sake of other persons, particularly women. Indicating his high degree of identification with abused womanhood was his taking the shape of the woman whose suffering he mentally shared. The dreamer felt that sadistic men were not as mighty as they appeared; even boys can defy them successfully at times. In this dream, the boy was at first outraged, but he did nothing. He then assumed the body and role of the victim. Next, he took up the cudgel to beat the cruel, authoritarian man. The dream ended with his feeling guilty and escaping punishment. This revealed that the dreamer was ambivalent about his sadomasochistic tendencies but not about those of men and women.

Let us see how the change of the dreamer's sex during the dream affects an interpretation based on the intra-individual Axiom A. Before the sex change, the greatest difference in ordinal locations on the Scale of Dissent was between the dreamer at location 0 and the young woman at location 5. Although young, the woman was significantly older than the boy dreamer. He strongly dissented suffering physical abuse without a word of protest or a gesture of active defense. Although he was outraged as he watched the scene, however, he could not move to try to stop the suffering. The dreamer assented that he was too inhibited to fight evil openly, despite his indignation. He markedly dissented his indolent and passive submission to masochistic abuse. In other words, he was only vaguely aware of his masochistic tendency. His sadistic inclination, however, was only mildly dissented. Thus sadism was stronger than masochism and less dissented.

After the sex change, the dreamer merged with the woman and appeared as her. He was fully aware during the dream that the change had taken place. The personality of a physically female figure had acquired an important trait of the male dreamer (his combativeness) and lost a relevant, original trait of the woman (her extreme passivity and masochism). The number of figures was reduced to two: the man, scale location 2; the combined figure, appearing as a woman, scale location 5. The combined figure acted as the dreamer wanted to act (but could not) before the metamorphosis. This is a revised location 0. The trait of actively trying to block a sadist's violence nearly reached the level of full assent. A telling sign that the adolescent dreamer could not trust himself in the role of a noble defender of the weak and dependent was his excessive violence, his feeling of guilt, and his flight to escape expected punishment. The main conclusion of the dream following the sex change was the same as that before the sex change — namely that the trend of sadism was stronger than masochism and was less dissented. The conflicts in the dream pertained not to incompatible intentions or motives of behavior but to different and fluid degrees of actuating the two intentions of inflicting or suffering pain, physical or mental.

Hervey was the author of this dream. He published hundreds of his own dreams in his remarkable book, *Les Reves et les Moyens de les Diriger* (1964). Hervey had an abiding and intense interest in dreams. He transcribed them since he was 13 and published his book when he was 45. What interests us here is the idea he emphasized in the title of his book and in the concluding paragraphs of the book: shifting the dream in a desirable direction. It is unlikely that he had this idea at the age of 14. Nevertheless, the cruel, persecuting man was eliminated. The boy's shout spurred himself from paralysis into lionhearted action.

4.   To clarify further the meaning of a dreamer's simultaneous identification with two different dream figures, usually the dreamer and an "other" figure, let us examine the butterfly dream of Chuang Tzu (Woods & Greenhouse, 1974), a Chinese Taoist philosopher of the 4th century B.C. Only one figure, the butterfly, was in the dream, but the sage said that, while dreaming, he felt he was that butterfly: "Once upon a time, I, Chuang Tzu, dreamt I was a butterfly, fluttering hither and thither, to all intents and purposes a butterfly. I was conscious only of following my fancy as a butterfly and was inconscious of my individuality as a man." He also described his state after waking: "Suddenly I awakened, and there I lay, myself again. Now I do not know whether I was a man dreaming I was a butterfly, or whether now I am a butterfly dreaming I am a man. Between a man a butterfly there is necessarily a barrier" (p. 42). A non-Taoist reader believes that the dreamer was Chuang Tzu. Butterflies cannot have and record dreams in which they "see" themselves in human shape. The difference between the philosopher's location 0 on the Scale of Dissent and that of the butterfly's location 8 is very great; therefore we conclude that at the time of the dream Chuang Tzu had a serious intrapsychic conflict. He was recognized as a sage and was entrusted with important public matters. Wisdom, prudence, maturity, practical sense, sound judgment, and being able to solve difficult problems was expected of him. Chuang Tzu was not certain that he possessed these traits. He was obviously very ambivalent about whether he had the traits of a sage. In the dream, he took on the butterfly traits more intensely than his human traits: "Fluttering hither and thither, to all intents and purposes [he was] a butterfly, following [his] fancy . . . and . . . unconscious of [his] individuality as a man." Following the logic of PDS, we must infer that during the period of the dream Chuang Tzu had a very dissented but incisive and conscious tendency to withdraw from public life and social duties, from premeditated and organized work, and, instead, to live spontaneously, at random.

That the dreamer both assented and strongly dissented the same sets of traits, those of himself as man and those of the butterfly, and that, furthermore, he could not decide which he assented firmly and which he dissented firmly, reveal great indecision, ambivalence, and — because of the great importance of the difference between those two opposite trait sets for survival — anxiety (dread of the unknown).

5.   Another logical situation is created when two different dream figures do the same thing in harmonious cooperation, to the satisfaction of both. This occurs, for example, when a couple engages in sexual intercourse. A married woman recounted a dream that she perceived to be inconsistent when it was interpreted according to Axiom A. In the dream, she had sexual intercourse with a high-school classmate. As the dream started, the couple embraced in the sex act. The embrace lasted for a while, which aroused the dreamer, and ended with the couple still in the amorous position. The dreamer questions the apparent conflict between two conclusions based on Axiom A — that the dreamer assented her role in the sexual situation whereas she dissented her role as the male partner (scale location 4) in the same situation. To declare that one act was both assented and dissented is an inconsistency. What are the relevant facts? In real life, while going through high school with the man in her dream, the dreamer liked him and was friendly with him. They maintained very proper social relations, however, and neither ever said a word or acted in a way that would intimate an affectionate interest in the other. After graduation, in fact, they lost contact and moved in different directions from their hometown. The dreamer's husband never lived in her hometown. Asked whether she remembered any feelings that she had experienced during the dream, she responded with very little embarrassment that she enjoyed the event, yet felt somewhat guilty and uncomfortable about being unfaithful to her husband, even though it was only in a dream; she affirmed that it had never happened in real life and never would. Thus, it was true that while the dream event was assented and pleasant for one reason it was dissented and displeasing for another reason. Axiom A was validated.

RULE 2: PRIMACY OF VERBS AND ABSTRACT NOUNS

Rule 2 incorporates the second fundamental principle of PDS. This psycholinguistic principle makes dream interpretations easier and contributes greatly to their objectivity and validity. In dreams, verbs and abstract nouns exercise a logical authority or primacy over concrete nouns in that they usually play an essential (albeit not exclusive) role in determining specific meanings of concrete nouns. This logical primacy of verbs derives from the veracity of verbs. Nouns, particularly those in the English language, frequently have synonyms. Therefore, exact meanings of nouns frequently cannot be determined without consideration of the other elements and of the construction of the statement of which the concrete nouns are an integral part. Abstract nouns perform the semantic function that verbs perform; they connote actions, activities, processes, or states of being (active, expanding, resting, self-restrained, constricted, inhibited, stopped). Abstract nouns are verbs in disguise. A verb with the meaning that an abstract noun has can replace the noun without changing the meaning of the sentence. The abstract noun *depression* means the same as *functioning at a reduced level of activity*. *Concentration* means *thinking about one topic to the exclusion of any other matter,* and *hesitation* means *acting at a reduced and uneven pace*. Abstract nouns are convenient abbreviations of verbal phrases. Empirical objects are not connoted by abstract nouns, but concrete nouns do have concrete, perceptible correlates. Examples are *chair, table,* and *beef.* In English, these and numerous other concrete nouns are also used as verbs: *to chair, to table, to beef.* However, by becoming verbs, these words change their meanings. *To chair* means *to preside at a meeting; to table* means *to postpone the consideration of a motion; to beef* means *to grumble in discontent.* By striking contrast, the abstract noun *debate* has exactly the same meaning as the verb *to debate.*

The great psycholinguistic difference between abstract nouns–verbs and concrete nouns can be traced to basic human nature. People are striving creatures pursuing goals that would secure their lives and guarantee them a degree of individual freedom. People are appetitive and are propelled by intentions. Verbs in dreams connote people's intentions (i.e., action tendencies, motives, desires, hopes, and fears), whereas concrete nouns in dreams denote objective implements for the realization of intentions, the gratification of wishes, and the prevention of harm. Because people seem to be enthralled more by their desires (or intentions) than by the objects of their desires, they change the implements of desire satisfaction more easily than they change desires. Many individuals develop a new personal virtue rather than free themselves of a vice. As there are usually several different ways of satisfying a desire, some more gratifying than others, people have the opportunity to try and to compare them. This helps to perpetuate desires. Sustained energy is required to suppress or to render social undesirable drives that press for outward manifestation. Less energy is needed to deflect a particular desire from one object to another than is needed to suppress a particular desire. The substitute object may be suitable and more socially acceptable but perhaps less satisfying. Least resistance or inertia also influences human behavior. When people are hungry, and their favored food is not available, most will eat any food within reach rather than go hungry. The same observation can be made about most "hungers" or desires, including emotional needs and intellectual interests. That desires can usually be satisfied by several different means has resulted in the conspicuous numerical preponderance of concrete nouns over verbs in Indo-European languages.

Psychodynamically, concrete nouns belong more to the actual realization of an intention in real life than to the rise and development of that intention as a desire or motive (i.e., as an idea). This is indirectly indicated by so-called deep dreams, which rarely contain concrete nouns; they usually contain only verbs. Dreams are "deep" when the dreamers can be aroused from them only with difficulty. Sensitivity to external stimuli is reduced in deep dreams so much that dreamers become absorbed exclusively with their intrapsychic processes. Under such conditions, dreamers are least likely to think of external, physical reality in attempts to actuate intended goals. As dreamers have no desire to act overtly, they have no need for concrete nouns.

Examples

1. A bright, young, unmarried woman produced the following dream on waking: "I had an awful time giving myself an injection. I had trouble pulling the things off the needle. The needle just could not go in, and I had an awful time. I thought 'I got to get through these guards.' I had to keep pulling the metal covers off." The dream ended while she was still exerting herself to make the injection.

The dreamer was not a mere observer of her dream events; she was a very active participant. Although she experienced strong fears and anxiety, she also urgently admonished herself not to let up her strenuous efforts, lest there be a calamity. Considering the circumstances, her state of health, and the probable consequences of her getting the necessary injection on time, her fear, anxieties, and behavior were appropriate. During the dream, she formulated an urgent and relevant self-admonition ("I got to get through these guards"), and she acted in accordance with this sound warning. All this suggests that the dream was close to her consciousness. As the young woman was the sole figure in her dream, she must have fully assented all the dream events, and she must have been fully conscious of her conflict between an anxiously intent desire to improve her perilous personal condition and her frightfully futile attempts to gain access to effective curative procedures.

This dream, like all others, is a confrontation between incompatible intentions or action tendencies. Dreams, however, also contain something of which dreamers are only vaguely or not at all aware and that disturbs their feelings about themselves and others. The woman's dream is missing any clue that would lead to a solution of her conflict, her inability to release the liquid from the syringe. Thus, the dream is incomplete, a condition present in nightmares. In typical nightmares, however, the dreamers are faced with destruction at the end if they do not escape from their powerful, merciless pursuers. The horror that wakes dreamers because of its intensity is the discovery that there is no escape, that they will be destroyed despite all the seemingly available means of escape they attempt. Our young dreamer was also very anxious at the end of her dream, although an external force did not threaten her. She was threatened by a psychophysical, self-destructive force that immobilized her when she should have been active in self-defense. The psychobiological forces of life and death brought each other to a standstill.

The dreamer had been a diabetic subject to all the restrictions that this serious disease imposes on patients. Resentment of the regimen she had to follow to preserve her life and health was associated with a great fear of the future. She experienced some estrangement from others and had a tendency to feel and act impulsively in an unfriendly manner toward people, which in turn added to her feeling of being disliked and avoided. She thought that she could not afford to behave spontaneously and frankly, because her behavior would attract unfavorable attention. The obsessiveness–compulsiveness that she manifested frequently (but not consistently) significantly lowered her efficiency. Dreams and personality pertain to the dreamer's psychosocial relationships, which does not exclude the possibility that occasionally dreams will reveal the dreamer's physical condition, especially if this condition influences the individual's psychosocial behavior. The woman's psychotherapist and physician were both convinced that diabetes had a marked influence on her interpersonal relationships. If the Rule of Complementarity were applied, several Freudian hypotheses could be suggested. Very strong psychosexual inhibitions might be inferred from the persistent preoccupation with "guards" that defied strenuous attempts to do away with them. The content of the syringe would put new life into her; lack of access to the content endangered her life and made her gloomy ("The needle just could not go in. . . . I had to keep pulling the metal covers off"). This may possibly allude to vaginismus; marriage might enliven her existence and give her security and perhaps some happiness. Yet her powerful inhibitory, unconscious intentions were denying her an easier life. Her psychological problems were assessed as severe. Psychotherapy was progressing slowly. The diabetes was controlled.

2.   Nudity dreams can be found in many dream collections. Apparently they have occurred in all centuries and cultures. A conflict over modesty is hardly the main cause, because they were known in ancient Greece and Rome, neither of which is known for its bashfulness. Nudity dreams are exhibitionistic, but the meaning of exhibitionism cannot be limited to the display of personal physical characteristics. Nudity dreams, then, can be taken as manifestations of inhibited desire to display personal traits, physical or mental, that dreamers believe to be assets in the eyes of others and of them-

selves (Rule of Generalization). In the typical dream, dreamers "see" themselves completely nude or scantily dressed in a public place. They feel embarrassed in the midst of normally dressed people. They try to make themselves as inconspicuous as possible, to go home, or to hide in any suitable place. Simultaneously, they make a surprising observation. They notice that no one pays any attention, as if they were not there. This discovery usually puzzles dreamers and makes them even more uncomfortable than they were when they found themselves nude in the street. Most nudity dreams end at this stage, leaving dreamers with a sense of shame and muffled relief. The typical exhibitionistic dream has two figures: the dreamer in scale location 0 and a group of people of unidentified sex or age in scale location 8. The difference of 8 points between these ordinal locations is great, leading to the conclusion that dreamers dissent highly the behavior of the strangers in the street, whereas they assent fully their own conduct (see Scale of Dissent). According to Axiom A, passersby in the street express dreamers' greatly dissented traits. The conflict dramatized in the dream is between fully assented, conscious, exhibitionistic tendencies and the strongly dissented denial of these same tendencies. Self-display is restrained for various reasons. Application of the Rule of Implicit Evidence or the Rule of Complementarity may turn up plausible hypotheses. The most frequent and valid reasons for inhibiting desires are of a psychosexual nature. Psychosexual reasons may be rarer today that they were decades ago. What is allowed and what is not allowed change gradually over long periods of time and also from one culture to another.

Another reason for inhibition may be fear of being rejected. People's outward appearance, behavior, or achievement may make individuals proud; at the same time, they might feel that if they were to attract attention, they would be scornfully disregarded or criticized outright. A similar conflict seems to be responsible for dreams in which dreamers miss trains or do not appear where they are expected or where they want themselves to be.

Unraveling the most likely origins of conflicts is much easier and much more valid when dreamers are in psychotherapy or when their dreams are investigated with their willing cooperation. Analysts must resort to probable hypotheses in blind dream analyses.

3.   Hervey (1964) reported a woman's dream with a transparent meaning. One day a "charming actress" told Hervey the "singular" dream she had had:

> I have dreamt last night that an enormous white lion had entered my bedroom. At first I was terribly afraid of him. He jumped from one piece of furniture on another, and I did not know where to flee for safety. Meanwhile, as he was approaching me amicably I lost the fear of him and I started caressing him, and I was playing with him even when I was awakening. (p. 352)

Hervey did not interpret the dream beyond saying that it was a "fusion of two arrangements of ideas simultaneously evoked." He did not give the age of the actress but did call her charming. He knew that she was the owner of a large, white cat. After telling him her dream, the actress reported that, two days before dreaming it, she had attended a circus performance of a lion-tamer. The white cat and the jumping circus lions performing under the control of their tamer probably were the visuomotor, day residuals used in the construction of her dream. One of the "arrangements of ideas" is the dream behavior of the actress. At the beginning of the dream, the actress is frightened by the size and movements of a large beast that had burst into her bedroom. Her emotional attitude was then decidedly negative toward the intruder. Not only did she not want to have anything to do with the male lion, but she wanted to flee from him because she felt endangered. She had dropped two hints, however, that she was not as frightened or imperiled as her words had implied. First, the lion was white (her cat was also white and posed no threat to her; if anything, the cat was a source of some pleasure). Second, "white" usually connotes purity of intent and innocence. The dreamer was the sole creator of her dream. Had she unconsciously wanted to escape the lion, she would have done so; every thought of the dreamer turns immediately into a dream image. Instead, the actress did not move from her bed and discovered with obvious relief that the white lion was "amiable"; at this moment her fears died, and she felt safe. The encounter ended with her becoming friendly with the lion and, in fact, liking him; her caresses were soothing and pleasant to the lion's senses and to hers. It was a rather mild heterosexual experience, one that the dreamer would have liked to prolong, as the last words of her dream report indicate: "I was playing with him even when I was awakening." The dream dramatized the dreamer's overcoming her fear of people, mostly of men who made demands of her, particularly those demands of a personal nature. The dream reassured her that she could control such situations; the expected dangers and unpleasantnesses had been greatly exaggerated, and the end experience may have been quite desirable. The dreamer projected her dissented traits on the lion, whose location 10 on the Scale of Dissent meant that the dissent was strong. She dissented her tendency to be impetuous and insistent in intention but devious in action when aiming to be emotionally close with someone (the lion zigzagged and jumped about as he neared the dreamer). The effect of such behavior was to discourage others from close, affectionate relations with her and to give them a wrong idea of her genuine intentions. The wooed partners in affection must themselves find the affectionate nature of her personality hidden behind her rather primitive, impetuous behavior. This kind of behavior must spoil many opportunities for mutually gratifying, positive relationships.

The rare feature of this dream is that both its figures changed conspicuously during the duration of the dream and that one result of these changes was the same in both figures. Both figures ended being gently affectionate with each other, manifesting their mutual attraction in an overt manner, although one was limited to subdued, quiet caresses. At the beginning, however, the dreamer assented her terror and desire to escape, whereas later she dissented her friendly though impetuous and amorous approach to persons of the other sex. The lesson of the dream, then, appears to be that a mutually shared, moderate mode of psychophysical gratification of positive emotional needs (e.g., love) is calming, reassuring, and enjoyable and chases away fears and agitation — with one qualification: The actress preferred to escape her "feminine role" (she actively caressed the "enormous lion," which passively accepted the caresses). The dreamer appeared to be in the process of becoming able to genuinely and unhesitatingly desire friendly, amorous relationships with men (and very likely with women), provided she could dominate and control the relationships. She seemed to be undergoing a personality change away from stormy emotional involvements toward calm, friendly, positive, close emotional involvements of moderate degrees.

4. A very old man who had a mind and a will of his own had been a successful and competitive businessman. He had closely supervised and controlled his dependents and staff. This man had suffered from a neurological defect that sporadically interfered with his psychomotor coordination and his voluntary attention. These occasional and brief periods of decreased efficiency, however, did not appear to interfere with the slow tempo of his current life (he had been free from any duties or serious responsibilities for many years). Although cautious, he moved with apparent self-confidence and was able to drive his car. This was his dream:

> I was driving my car some place and, when it came time to stop, my brakes would not work and the car kept going. I was frightened half to death for fear of hurting someone else. I felt helpless. Suddenly a big man appeared out of the blue. I shouted for him to jump in and put his foot on the brake and stop the car. He did and I woke up at that point, so I don't know if the car was stopped or not.

Unexpected help appeared in the person of "a big man," but the dream ended without the dreamer's knowing "if the car was stopped or not." Thus, he thought that the help he received was of questionable reliability. This means that he could not depend on his reserve strength when he faced an emergency (Axiom A). He did fully assent his inability to control the car; that is, his capacity to perform skillful actions. He realized he started things that he could not finish. In waking life, he verbally rebelled against his infirmity. Sometimes, on his own initiative, he did things that endangered others and himself. In the dream he "was frightened half to death for fear of hurting someone else." Thus, the desire for personal independence and the fear of causing serious damage as a result of his impairment clashed. The dream can be interpreted as a warning to the man to resign himself to the inevitable limitations caused by his irreversible illness; the dream also consoled him when it made him realize that he would feel more secure and relieved when he accepted reality and needed help.

RULE 3: SYMBOLISM OF CONCRETE NOUNS

Knowledge of the visuomotor content of a dream, and not just of the verbal dream report from which some pertinent visuomotor details have been omitted, usually makes plain the meaning of actions or action tendencies and of their strength, inhibitions, and blocking. Verbs in dreams are easily and reliably comprehended; concrete nouns are not (because most concrete nouns are inadequate substitutes for abstract nouns that, by their very nature, defy unequivocal visual representation). Because dreams deal with intrapsychic conflicts between incompatible intentions and drives, the essential parts of dreams consist of verbs. Intentional drives and counterdrives, however, are usually significantly differentiated, affectively and psychomotorally, by specific goals pursued and implements employed, and these goals and implements cannot be shown visually because they are abstract. A goal is something desired, imagined, and anticipated but not presently existing. Dreamers do not always try to visualize resolutions of intrapsychic conflicts of which they are beginning to become aware. When they attempt, however, to grope for solutions, their unconsciously functioning minds find, only with difficulty, suitable visual representations of conflict resolutions. Most of these resolutions consist of changes in dreamers' mental states (affects, evaluations of psychosocial attitudes, redirection of purposes and habits). These changes cannot be unequivocally visualized in images of perceptible, concrete objects. The intellectual problem is similar to that in algebra. An x or y can stand for any unknown variable; nevertheless, once the algebraic problem is correctly solved, x and y can be assigned specific mathematical values. The analogy cannot be exactly correct because dreams contain values or elements that are not perfectly quantifiable. The best dreams are like algebra problems in which the number of independent equations is never as large as the number of unknowns. This condition makes it possible to infer several different values, of about equal plausibility, for the symbolic meaning of some concrete nouns.

Some generalizations aid in the unraveling of meaning of nouns. The appropriate meaning usually conveys a human trait relevant to the activity described by the verb, which the symbolic noun complements and intelligibly specifies. If the unraveled meaning of the dream noun makes the dream events possible in waking life, then that inferred meaning is most likely correct. Occasionally a concrete noun in a dream can be taken literally or according to the standard dictionary sense of the noun. A concrete object may have different, specific meanings in the dreams of different individuals and in different dreams of the same individual. These diversities result from the dreamers' different personalities and significant experiences. The influence exerted by the principle of irrelevant differences on concept formation contributes to the diversity of symbolic meanings of the same concrete nouns in dreams and of words in general. In other words, concepts connote one or several attributes that are shared by many animate or inanimate objects that are otherwise different. Thus, concepts facilitate thinking about and handling a large number of objects and situations, the differences among which are irrelevant, in an attempt to achieve particular mental or physical purposes. When we prepare to classify objects or data, we begin with knowledge of relevant concepts and their definitions — that is, with an awareness of traits that the things (mental or physical) must share to be put in the same category. In dream analysis, this process is reversed. We know we deal with symbols (concepts), but we do not know the meanings that make the symbols fit the dream content logically. Dreamers can be idiosyncratic in their unconscious choice of a relatively least inadequate symbol when an adequate symbol is impossible to find (which is usually the case). This deficiency of distinct and appropriate visual symbols of abstract objects seems responsible for the impression that most dreams are incomprehensible or even bizarre. When interpreted correctly, however, symbols cease to be bizarre in dreams of healthy individuals. True bizarreness is found in some of the dreams of some persons having primary (not merely psychogenic) disorders of the central nervous system. Although healthy dreamers appear to be unrealistic when they create scenes pertaining to empirical reality, they do not get confused and disoriented. Dreaming is a personal, intrapsychic process dominated by the intention to resolve inner conflicts and to come to grips with inner psychodynamic difficulties. This intention not only prompts dream events; it maintains their common purpose and the meaningful connections between diverse dream elements, including concrete nouns. Individuals dream not to enlighten others, but to benefit themselves (although few appear to be aware of this). In dreaming for themselves, people use any method to express thoughts in an indirect and personal manner (they may use concrete nouns that have only a slight logical connection with images of concrete objects); this will do for the brief duration of a sleep dream. Sometimes we act the same way in waking life. When making an accurate and complete description of an unfamiliar object presents some difficulty, we simply refer to the object as "that thing" or "you know, that thingumajig"; these incomplete expressions make for quick social communication among those who know to what these expressions refer. The visual image of a concrete object or of a social event can have many separate meanings in a dream. The dream symbol and the meaning of the symbol must have at least one property in common; in all other respects, they may disagree. A schizophrenic once said that a symbol is a word that makes you think, that tells several other things. Images of concrete nouns in dreams are even more intriguing. As symbols, they are frequently visible signs of something invisible. Symbolic, concrete nouns stand for thoughts rather than perceptions.

During play, children often ascribe unlikely meanings to concrete objects. For example, in choosing building blocks to represent people (including themselves) or animals, children pick without concern for shape, color, and size. In fact, some little boys select the biggest blocks to represent themselves and small blocks to pass for their fathers. Choices are determined by affects, not by concerns with objective size differences, of which children are well aware. The sense of reality functions well when children play and when they are in actual, realistic relations with fathers and other people. Children can change their symbolic objects readily and frequently. Real, objective differences between building blocks and whom or what they represent in play do not perplex children because children feel and know well that social relations in play do not depict actual circumstances with living people. Still, that children play and engage in make-believe that dramatizes their feelings and thoughts does not mean that the emotional impulses and attitudes expressed through play are not genuine. Not only in dreams and during play, but in many other situations, precise, objective, and relevant thinking is unnecessary for satisfactory communication with ourselves and others.

Limitations of the visuomotor language of dreams necessitate the use of symbols or indirect indicators. Because dream symbols primarily denote means of intent realization, the similarity between concrete noun symbols and what they symbolize is mainly kinetic. When we read dream symbols correctly, we find very little bizarreness, except in those dreams produced by patients with seriously disordered central nervous systems. Thinking in dreams of healthy people is realistic, practical, and occasionally even inventive. Concrete nouns that serve as symbols in dreams connote means or implements needed to carry out intended actions that are indicated by verbs, which, together with the concrete noun–symbols, constitute syntactical and logical units. For example, "looking for catnip" means "looking for a means to intensify a pleasantly exciting emotion." Manifestations of love are kinetic or psychomotor. A wish to deepen a friendship implies a desire for more frequent and intense exchanges of pleasurable experiences with a friend. Dislike of a person is a negative emotional attitude that is accompanied by attempts to reduce the number and quality of interactions with the disliked person. A national flag symbolizes not only a special group and its territory, but also and more important, each group member's attitudes and duties toward the group. Group or individual psychological symbols in dreams and in waking life connote intentions and action tendencies. Even when symbols are of death or destruction, they refer to intentions and actions, albeit in a negative way; they refer to cessation, to the ending of motion and of life.

Concrete nouns in dreams frequently symbolize something other than what is indicated by standard dictionaries. A concrete noun may mean different things to different dreamers and even in different dreams of the same individual. Few valid, universal dream symbols exist. Sexual dreams tend to be universal because heterosexual intercourse leaves little room for variation. Therefore, sex dreams are rather easily unraveled. Aggressiveness, however, can be demonstrated in a large variety of ways. Aggression can be manifested even in uncharacteristic action (exaggerated, insincere gestures of concern and politeness). Symbols of dislike, hostility, and aggression are therefore more difficult to interpret correctly. Visual symbols of sexual activity do not change much, but words alluding to them change frequently and are numerous. For example, within the last few decades, the name of an item of female lingerie (panties) has changed more than 20 times, whereas names of dresses and skirts, which are worn outside, have remained unchanged.

Adjectives describing inanimate objects in dreams may symbolize dreamer traits. For example, in a dream in which the "woodiness" of the floor was emphasized and the planks were seen separated from one another (instead of fitting tightly together), the description of the floor fitted the dreamer, then a "wooden" or rigid person, insensitive and awkward in social relations; walking on a floor of spaced boards would be awkward.

Examples

1.   Derivation of the symbolic meaning of a concrete noun from a young, married man's dream (called "A Futile Search") illustrates the unraveling of the meaning of the noun in the context of the whole dream:

> My mother and I are near our country home up North [his parental home where he was born], looking for some indigenous plants. We looked at the bank or the grass, alongside the road. A woman in a car drove up, stopped the car, got out, looked around and found the plants. The plants were catnip. They're indigenous to that state. My mother and I looked in vain, but this woman reached down into the grass and picked it just like that! [Dreamer demonstrated the motion with a quick, plucking gesture of his right hand.] I was exasperated!

The dream report makes it plain that the mother and the son had been trying to find the catnip, that they had not found any ("My mother and I looked in vain"), and that at least the son was "exasperated" (irritated, mildly depressed) by the failure of their search and the speed and ease with which the unexpected female newcomer located the plant. The dreamer wanted to share the catnip with his mother, but denied himself the wish. He created the dream and used it to dramatize his wish and his denial of the wish. However, he also indicated, albeit on the dissented scale level 5 (in the person of the newcomer, a woman somewhat older than himself) a desire for finding and being exposed to whatever effects he thought "catnip" might induce. At the same time, he was irritated and angry when someone other than his mother offered the "catnip" to him. Refusal of the offer was immediate, firm, and fully assented (on level 0 of the Scale of Dissent). The person who had no difficulty finding and plucking the plants was a woman. Catnip is a common weed that grows in many places, yet the dreamer pointed out that the catnip that had attracted his interest was "indigenous to that state." His mother, however, could not help him find the plant, although the younger woman could. What, then, does "catnip," a strongly scented weed that grows quickly, represent? Perhaps the fact that catnip is a labiate plant contributed to the dreamer's unconscious use of it as a symbol. Catnip has bilabiate flowers and opposite leaves resembling a lip or labium. A lip or a lip-like object is "kissable." Cats are fond of catnip because it stimulates them pleasantly.

At this stage of the analysis, we know about the properties of the "catnip," the dreamer's qualified desire for it (with mother but not without her), and the great affective significance that it has for the dreamer. What in personological terms is the specific goal that the dreamer seeks to attain and that is symbolized by the catnip?

The capacity to stimulate and enliven seems to be the property to which the catnip owes its inclusion in the dream. This probability is strengthened by the dreamer's strong emotional reaction at the end, when he was unexpectedly offered the plant. By sharing the "catnip," mother and son would have become more lively and responsive to each other. Therefore, we infer that the symbolic meaning of the concrete noun *catnip* is the intensification of mutual love. It does not mean just *love* because of the dreamer's feeling that some love or positive emotion had already existed between him and his mother before the dream — which is revealed by the image of him and his mother, side by side, searching for the plant. Additional evidence is provided by his firm and intense rejection of the desired catnip from someone other than his mother. The dreamer acted toward the other woman in a manner opposite to that shown by the biblical figure of Adam, who accepted and ate the apple offered to him by Eve. A 30-year-old man who craves a warm and demonstrative mutual relationship with his mother probably takes little interest in younger women who would be fit and proper candidates for marriage (Rule of Complementarity) or may be an inadequate and difficult husband.

What was in the future for this dreamer? That his immature craving for increased emotional dependency on his mother was frustrated is significant. The dream revealed inner forces that pulled the dreamer away from his preoccupation with ungratified childhood wishes; it prodded him toward mature and fully developed heterosexual relationships. Remembering that the dream was the dreamer's own construction (consisting of intentions, counterdrives, and affects of his personality), we deduce that the dream showed his growing conviction that his desired deepening of emotional intimacy with his mother was unattainable; otherwise, he would not have made the frustration so striking in the dream. Moreover, he would not have the second woman appear just after he and his mother had given up the search for the "catnip." The newcomer behaved in a lively and independent manner. She arrived alone unexpectedly, walked immediately toward the dreamer, and wasted no time reaching for the "catnip" that had escaped the dreamer's eyes. At this moment, the dreamer paradoxically told himself plainly, as a result of unconscious dream reasoning, that that on which he had set his mind (i.e., more intense love) can be had with a woman not related to him by blood (the other woman arrived by car from some distance; she was not a member of the family). The acuteness of the dreamer's negative reaction to the woman's forthright offer reveals both his great interest in a mature, heterosexual relationship and his ambivalent hesitation about it. In dreams, the temporal sequence of events in a mutually related chain of experiences reveals, as a rule, causal relations, the cause preceding the effect (Rule of Complementarity). Applying this rule, we deduce that, in the first part of the dream, the young man resolved that it was hopeless to look with his mother for "catnip" near the parental home; in other words, the dreamer revealed a marked lessening of emotional dependency on his mother. This conclusion is corroborated by the second part of the dream. The weakened dependency on mother allowed an intensification of emotional interest in other women and thereby a reduction of ambivalence concerning heterosexual tendencies.

The dreamer's attitude toward whatever "catnip" symbolized to him changed during the dream. At first, catnip was clearly desired with full assent, but the search for it was a failure. Consequently, he abandoned the desire, causing some depression (Rule of Complementarity). Then, in a defensive reaction against depression, he made the desire reappear in a stronger and potentially consumable form, but he promptly and resolutely dissented it. The desire went through several phases: It was assented, dissented, repressed, and the object of acute ambivalence. Affects and motor behavior were decidedly more intense at the end than at the beginning of the dream. A great deal happened intrapsychically. Intentions went through an important rearrangement. It is striking that, as the mother left the stage, the dreamer immediately thought of a young woman. "My mother and I looked in vain, but this woman reached down and picked it just like that!" We can hear a tone of admiration for "this woman" in that vivid exclamation. The dreamer manifested a strong inhibition of desires that are pleasing to the mind and senses. Yet, in the first part of the dream, the inhibition was much more severe than in the second, revealing an alleviation of a desire for a closer and more gratifying relationship with women (and probably also with men according to the Rule of Generalization). At first he expressed the feeling that "catnip" was beyond his reach, but in the next moment, all he needed to do was to extend his hand to take hold of easily available "catnip." The inhibition eased considerably but did not vanish. It is a sound procedural assumption that the change in the circumstances of the initial and final events provides clues that can be used to explain the difference in the dreamer's behavior. The conspicuous change consisted of the disappearance of the mother from the active dream stage and the appearance of her substitute, the younger woman. We can infer that the dreamer was relinquishing his wish for a warmer emotional attachment to mother because the wish was unrealizable. At almost the same instant, the dreamer grasped that gratifying and intimate relationships could be easily developed with a younger woman. After all, he was married. Although he dared now to desire heterosexual gratification (the young woman offered him plentiful catnip), he was still too inhibited and held back from heterosexual experiences (he still dissented them).

The dream marked a decided turn for the better for him. He began talking about his mother and continually aired his affects regarding her. Several months later, he concluded emphatically: "My mother gave me everything but love." Ample evidence supported this statement. She could always be relied on for help, she was constant in providing whatever he needed, and she made sacrifices for him, but she was not as warm and demonstrative as he had wished her to be. His wife was similar in many respects. Intense psychotherapy helped a great deal. The improvement was most visible in his scholastic achievement.

2.   Very rarely do dreams contribute immediately and directly to solutions of circumscribed, technical, physical problems. Elias Howe, the inventor of the first workable model of the sewing machine, had such a dream in 1846; he was unmarried at the time and 22 years old. Both Howe and his rivals had been frustrated for years. The invention had been ready except for one essential detail that defied solution: the needle. The needle had been known for centuries, but the aperture for the thread was always located at the back or distal end of the needle. Thus, when the needle was used, it pulled the thread behind it. No one had been able to adapt the traditional type of needle to the needs of a sewing machine. During the night preceding the day when Howe successfully completed the construction of the first workable sewing machine needle, he had a dream.

Howe saw himself pushing through a dense forest in Central Africa. Suddenly he heard a rustle. He stopped, looked around, and saw himself surrounded by natives pointing their spears at him. The spearheads astounded him; he concentrated on them. They were unique in that each had an elongated, narrow, vertical slit in the middle.

Apparently, Howe's awakening coincided with a moment of enlightment. Howe suddenly realized that the sewing machine needle should have the aperture at the front end, the piercing end, not at the back or trailing end. This creative and very useful insight was contrary to Howe's personal experience and to the age-old manner of operating a needle. According to reports, Howe rushed down to his basement workshop. The repeated to-and-fro motions of the spears in the hands of the threatening natives may have helped Howe give birth to his ingenious idea. During actual sewing, the needle makes many to-and-fro motions. Howe's creative conception could be demonstrated visually in a dream. Moreover, the visuomotor demonstration had to be brief to be grasped quickly. Moments of true, valuable inspiration are fleeting and must be immediately recorded to prevent being forgotten. Howe snatched a great prize from his plight: the secret of the needle. He achieved it with remarkable calm.

We can almost say with certainty that dream interpreters, including modern ones who were ignorant of the difficult problems encountered in constructing the first sewing machine, have not seen Howe's spearheads as models of sewing machine needles. Making the connection between spearheads and sewing needles is particularly difficult for interpreters who view dreams as meaningful units; interpreters would rather meditate on the possible meaning of the peculiar spearheads within the context of the whole dream (and would omit knowledge of Howe's waking activity). Taken as a whole, the dream showed the dreamer in immediate and potentially grave danger in an unknown territory, unable to escape from reputedly wild, hostile, armed men who threatened him. The situation was hopeless. All the prerequisites for panic were there. Yet after a moment of anxiety, Howe felt pleasantly attracted to the sight of the spearheads. He was even exhilirated. Panic never materialized. The final solution to an arduous and important problem, the cessation of a series of enervating failures, and the victory over many rivals raised Howe's confidence in himself and his feelings of security and freedom. Such feelings of personal power are incompatible with panicky powerlessness. They not only stopped Howe's panic but contributed to the ecstatic birth of his image of the sewing needle.

Howe's dream contained only two figures. One was Howe, whose dream traits were fully assented on level 0 of the Dissent Scale. The other was a collective of undifferentiated, armed men, all of whom acted in the same way; their traits are on level 8 of the Dissent Scale. We conclude, therefore, that Howe tried strongly to repress external manifestations of his defensive aggressiveness in an attempt to remove inhibitions and obstacles put in his way. Aside from stopping Howe after he had entered their overgrown, uncultivated, and hardly penetrable land, the natives threatened but did not harm him. After an initial instant of shock, Howe studied their weapons with curiosity and treated the men as if they were not there. Instead, he became absorbed in his own thoughts. In conclusion, Howe intensely dissented making strong, aggressive gestures that stopped others from making new discoveries (his rival inventors, as well as other rivals?). On a fully assented level, however, he did not mind and rather welcomed sharp competition because it stimulated his creative mind and kept him concentrated, purposeful, productive. He alleviated anxiety and depression by intensifying his ambitious strivings. Apropos, Howe hurried to complete the sewing machine because people had already been waiting for him in London, where he had a signed contract to work on something new: corsets.

Now, assuming that we knew nothing about the dreamer except his sex and age, nothing about the history of the sewing machine, and nothing about the dreamer's behavior on waking, how would we proceed? We would first scrutinize the dreamer's actions and experiences; Howe was aware or easily made aware of the traits revealed in his active and passive conduct (Axiom A). We would then turn our attention to the other dream figure, the group of men acting in unison; they stopped him. Most dreams consist of action and counteraction; the aim of counteraction is to stop, delay, or divert action. Howe was not stopped or delayed from his penetration of the jungle. He was clearly diverted and entered a state of ecstasy in which he contemplated the spearheads and became insensitive to everything else, including the threatening men who had surrounded him. He woke up fascinated. What he affirmed in himself was his quick escape of serious difficulties; thus, he boosted his feelings of self-confidence and mastery over his life. He had ventured boldly into unknown dangers as an explorer, despite his self-inhibitory tendencies (dramatized by the anonymous spearmen). His progress into the dark, unknown territory ended simultaneously with his perception of a fascinating, original version of a known object. The vision of the newly envisioned object dissipated his depression (walking in the dark) and any fears or anxiety he might have had.

In dreams of subjects with normal central nervous systems, concrete nouns that function as symbols most significantly supplement the meanings of verbs with which they form logical and grammatical units. Sometimes, however, concrete nouns considered alone, with no references to verbs, bring to mind meanings that then specify the meanings of the pertinent verbs. When, in this dream, the spears are regarded as physical weapons, they are not symbols but names of existing, physical objects. The *natives pointing spears* phrase then means literally what it says. If, however, the spears are taken as symbols of any form of aggression, physical or mental, then *pointing spears* does not necessarily mean a physical threat. Furthermore, if the spear, or particularly the head, which elicited such a strong response from our dreamer, is viewed as a phallic symbol, then *pointing spears* means sexual aggression. As the aggressors are men, male sexual aggression is indicated. Moreover, the intended object of the aggression is a man—which points to a male homosexual bid. The dreamer was not harmed by the spears and escaped them without apparent fear or effort. The spearmen consisted of undifferentiated individuals. This indicates that the dreamer liked to keep his homosexual inclination secret. He seemed to successfully prevent its outward manifestation.

The different interpretations of the meaning of the spears show that none of the dream interpretations excludes the others. Similarities are especially close between the properties of the phallus and the sewing machine needle. Both share the repeated in-and-out motion, both bring separate things together and unite them, both are elongated, and both have a narrow opening at the penetrating end. The assumption of a homosexual inclination and of strong suppression appropriately fits the context of the dream:

1. The secretiveness of the deindividualized spearmen who wielded the spears.
2. The darkness and isolation of the place where the event occurred and where the dreamer was unknown.
3. The event occurred in a land where people lived close to nature, where they were mainly occupied with satisfying elementary human needs.
4. The fascinating visual experience that enthralled the dreamer kept him detached from everything else.
5. The sight of the spearheads was associated with the strongest and most unexpected emotional reaction — which resulted in a remarkable uplifting of mood.

Thus, whatever the spearheads symbolized for the dreamer was something that meant a great deal to him.

The purely verbal dream interpretations, neglecting fine, necessary details that convey the basic meanings of the dream, make the similarities among the different verbal versions stand out. By contrast, when we become aware of and visualize the visuomotor aspects inevitably involved in the enactment of dream events, we obtain more detailed and more differentiated versions of the various interpretations. Such interpretations convey more meaning and are more easily verifiable.

As differences among the different versions become visibly greater, the complexities of the dreamer become more apparent. As the Howe dream illustrates, several different problems, not clearly related in the dreamer's conscious mind, can surface simultaneously in unconsciously produced dreams. In sleep, the mind is free from the surrounding physical world; it is therefore almost exclusively influenced by intrapsychic processes. At times, as in Howe's case, the sleeping and consciously uncontrolled mind can grasp the similarity of motions — hostile attitudes, sexual arousal, sewing machine — that the dreamer experienced or observed under very different, waking-life circumstances. Among the contributions of Howe's dream was a very rare one: the successful and creative solution of a technical, physical problem.

In conclusion, the visuomotor imagery of the dream pertains to the dreamer's intentions and actions. Therefore, dream symbols are not arbitrary or conventional but individual; they symbolize an implement intimately related to the dreamer's intention revealed in the dream. Only when the symbolic meaning of a concrete noun is disregarded do dreams appear bizarre. In unraveling dream symbols, we must consider the dynamic structure of the whole dream and the role that the symbolized implement or action plays in the whole dream. The interpreter should think not primarily in terms of verbal dictionaries but in terms of the dreamer's dynamic intentions.

Some intents are abstract (i.e., they cannot be visualized in the pictorial language of the dream). Many ideas cannot be presented visually and intelligently. For example, "desire for being given more love" cannot be represented directly by a single, concrete object. Public, verbal language serves mainly the needs of intelligible, inter-personal communication as a means toward the development of effective, mutual cooperation. Verbal language is the means in expressing the absence as well as the existence of things and relationships. Pictures are positive. They represent something existing independently of their pictorial counterparts. Pictures, including dream imagery, are substitutes for real things or experiences. Therefore, dreams must revert to visible symbols (or indirect indicators) of unfulfilled desires, as for example, for more maternal affection. A second reason for the ambiguity of concrete nouns (which frequently serve as symbols in dreams) is the dreamers' inert physical state. Dreamers will not act; if they try to carry out some of the activities of which they dream, they would wake up, and the dream would end. This typically happens in nightmares: the dream events so frighten and endanger the dreamers that their anxiety wakens them to stop the terror. Thus, whereas dreamers conjure up intentions and potential activities that rarely wake them up, they cannot feel a strong impulse to act out the content of their dreams in waking reality.

Another reason for the ambiguity of concrete nouns in dreams is the suspension of self-monitoring of mental processes and actions. Critical assessment and conscious control of these processes and actions is turned off during sleep dreaming. Furthermore, dreamers do not discuss their intrapsychic conflicts and possible resolutions with other dream figures. However, they are brought together face to face. This confrontation furthers self-knowledge; it is the most important function of sleep dreams.

RULE 4: IMPLICIT EVIDENCE

The Rule of Implicit Evidence applies mainly to the endings of dreams. The task of interpreters is to analyze the ways in which dreams terminate, and thereby to extract any implicit indication of how the dreams would most likely evolve if they were to continue. By inferring continuations of dream events, interpreters rely on the fundamental PDS postulate: that dream events be evaluated as if they were real events observed consciously in active, waking life. Endings of dreams are important because they usually reveal what dreamers are inclined and ready to do about conflicts dramatized in their dreams. Evidence derived from dream endings is implied and indirect because it is based on comparisons between reported terminations of particular dreams and possible dream event continuations formulated by interpreters on the basis of empirical knowledge of human behavior. When dream interpretations are not "blind," knowledge of dreamers' personalities, health, and important living conditions help in making predictions based on implicit evidence more specific, relevant, and valid. Predictions based on implicit evidence can be doubtful or wrong in the case of subjects who suffer from organic illnesses that conspicuously and unpredictably affect personality and behavior. In general, implicit evidence pertains not only to what dreamers are likely to do next, but also to what they will try to avoid in the immediate future.

Nightmares are dreams with special endings—dreamers panic and behave irresolutely at the end because all their options are dangerous. Nightmares are aborted dreams in the sense that they terminate before creating any model for handling the difficulties and conflicts that are the main themes of dreams. Nightmares do not offer solutions. Faced with limited, dangerous choices, the dreamers panic; their fear of destruction brings dreams to sudden ends. A measure of this panic is the great relief dreamers feel when they wake and realize that the dream events were imaginary. As a rule, personality changes following nightmares do not have bad prognoses. Favorable prognoses are probably the result of the impressive amount of energy that is quickly and effectively mobilized against potentially mortal danger. Nightmares reveal dreamers' strengths, their resolve to survive by escaping great dangers, and, implicitly, their alertness to threatening, personal, physical and/or mental destruction.

The usual choice left to dreamers in nightmares is between being killed or committing suicide. A typical example is provided by a dreamer who has been cornered by a pitiless monster on the roof of a tall building. Only two options are available. The dreamer may jump off the roof to a certain death or may remain immobile with panic and await being killed by the monster. This raises the possibility that people who experience nightmares are likely to consider suicide, but that, in their ambivalence toward it, they may also try to save their lives. When life becomes unbearable, suicide may seem to be a relief, a way to evade the horrors and suffering of existence. Whenever people struggle against giving in voluntarily and try to free themselves from danger, they do not abandon hope.

The very dissented traits of ogres and wild beasts in nightmares are modifiable. A dreamer's panic is a function not only of the dangerous nature of the threatening beasts, but also of the dreamer's reaction to the dangers implicit in overt, defensive behavior. The emotional upheaval and violent motor activity experienced during nightmares are prognostically far more favorable than emotional flatness, indifference, or passive resignation. In fact, one way dreamers can stop recurrent nightmares is by teaching themselves to stop running away in the nightmare, to turn around, face the approaching monster, and attack it with angry, bellicose shouts. This is ancient and apparently sound advice that was known even in some illiterate societies. In accordance with PDS, dreamers are more likely to cope and deal with dissented traits than with assented traits (assented traits are felt to be part of the genuine core of a dreamer's personality).

With the majority of nightmares, progress can be observed over subsequent repetition. Progress is manifested by the development of an interaction between the dreamer and the threatening dream figure, first by a decrease of terror and anxiety, then by clarification of the conflict and formulation of a possible intrapsychic solution to the conflict.

However, favorable remarks about nightmares are limited to dreamers with intact central nervous systems. In patients with serious brain disorders or grave, progressing devitalization, nightmares may be indications of patients' convictions that deterioration can be delayed (though not reversed).

Examples

1.   An unsolicited series of four personal dreams was told to me spontaneously during a pause at a large meeting. The dreams concerned the same conflict, but each dream handled the conflict differently. The dreamer was a historian, biographer, and amateur musicologist. He was well read in psychology, especially in dreams and in personality abnormality. Gregarious and affable, he asked whether his night dreams had any meaning beyond that which a straight analysis of the dream report (with no aid of any dream theory) would disclose. The four dreams were interspersed among others dreamed over a period of about three weeks. The dreamer had never been in psychotherapy. He was currently in a fearful state of mind, worrying about his approaching retirement and declining literary productivity. We asked the dreamer to present the dreams in chronological order. I used PDS to interpret each dream before the next dream was read. All information about the dreamer, save his name, had been withheld until the completion of the dream analyses. The first dream follows:

A lecture had just ended and I saw myself standing in front of the auditorium facing the exit through which the crowd was pouring out. I was one of the first to get out [of the building] but not the only one who had turned around to watch the other people. I had a vague hope of spotting someone with whom I could discuss the lecture which had impressed me although I had no idea what its topic was. I was critical of some of the lecturer's argumentation and would have enjoyed airing my views with someone. Suddenly I noticed a man rapidly descending the steps, pushing through the throng with a gun in his right hand and looking at me with intense hostility. A number of men standing near me rushed and disarmed him before I had recovered from shock and fear. I was astonished that someone wanted to kill me. I woke up, relieved that I escaped the danger.

There were four figures in this dream. The dreamer was at level 0 on the Scale of Dissent. He stood outside the lecture hall and looked for someone with whom he could critically discuss the lecture. The dreamer and the large crowd had attended the lecture, yet the dreamer made the queer remark that he "had no idea what its topic was." This remark, coupled with his previous statement that he had been impressed with the lecture, made the dreamer seem eccentric. He was critical only "of some of the lecturer's argumentation." The dreamer's criticism sounded as if it were of the manner with which the lecturer drew some conclusions, but not of the adduced premises and facts from which the conclusions were drawn. Apparently the dreamer was in a contentiously fussy mood; he was also physically inactive. He "would have enjoyed" letting people know what he felt and thought about the lecture. Just when he felt this desire, a man attempted to destroy him. The dreamer was saved by quickly acting friends, "men standing near" him, while he was immobilized by shock and fear. Relieved that he had escaped danger, he was "astonished" that anyone would want to kill him. His naivete was disclosed by his genuine surprise over people's resenting criticism. "Astonishment" is particularly unusual in a scholar and biographical historian who corrects errors in a field filled with innumerable details and inaccuracies, the validity of which is often difficult to prove. Moreover, the dreamer "had no idea what [the lecture's] topic was." How could he know what to criticize or whether there was anything to criticize at all? Taking this into account, we can see that his criticism of the "argumentation" was a false excuse for his trying to enjoy "airing [his] views with someone," that is, for finding an attentive audience that would hear him correct another person (the lecturer). The dreamer was not certain, during and after the dream, whether his assailant was the lecturer. Whoever would have discussed the lecture with the dreamer would have to have been a carrier of the dreamer's dissented traits (simply because the carrier of dissented traits would have to have been someone other than the dreamer). In this dream, the discussion would have been lacking in candor. No one, however, showed up to hear the dreamer's critical comments.

In terms of the interpersonal Axiom B, the dreamer believed that no one was interested in his opinion regarding weaknesses of other scholars' views and that he must keep his criticisms to himself. The intra-individual Axiom A leads to the conclusion that the dreamer could not elicit dissented mental processes relevant to his habit of finding fault even in things that "impressed" him. (These dissented processes would have been expressed by the hoped-for discussant.) He frequently disapproved of himself and others, albeit in a quiet and restrained manner. A mild but chronic depression (pessimism) and constant dissection of his perceived frustrations interfered with his creative work. His analytical skill and keen observations exceeded his creative capacity to draw significant and useful generalizations from amassed factual data.

Application of Axiom A brought out the complications of personal conflicts. Two tendencies were fully assented and most likely conscious: self-criticism (finding fault with the lecture) and reaction to self-criticism (self-criticism revealed to him his errors and inadequacies). Objecting to the "argumentation" amounted to accusing himself of some confused or unrealistic thinking or false evaluation of facts. This assessment, in turn, caused self-condemnation, fear, depression, and shock (the assailant and the dreamer's reaction to him). Then a curious defensive reaction set in. The dreamer's supportive and friendly forces (represented by the men near him) saved the dreamer from destruction, despite their being strongly dissented. This implies that his self-defense functions impulsively and semiconsciously (scale level 8), but with quiet efficiency. The dreamer not only dissembled his prompt and firm defensiveness, but he tried to keep it secret (as indicated by the lack of differentiation among the men who disarmed the assailant). In terms of Axiom A, the gunman "looking at [the dreamer] with intense hostility" disclosed the dreamer's self-condemnation and self-hate. The self-hate and the resulting shock and fear were not as strong as they might have been. A part of the dreamer, albeit a dissented part, was indifferent to his internal disquiet and upset—a condition that gave him a somewhat stoical mood and appearance (as if he acted on the principle that he could not avoid the inert, which impedes but does not help; the man with the gun rapidly descended the steps but had to push through the indifferent throng).

A methodologically interesting aspect of the dream was the complexity of events. The dream was busy. Toward the end occurred the stirring scene of the avenger approaching and frightening the dreamer. The fright set off two simultaneous but incompatible reactions: a fully assented and conscious shock that prevented the dreamer from acting overtly in any way (helpless passivity) and a prompt, energetic, and successful counterattack that freed the dreamer from the great danger (the very opposite of helpless passivity). The dreamer strongly dissented this personal tendency to act swiftly, firmly, and aggressively; the dreamer attempted to hide this trait from public view. Both states, incompatible with each other, were actuated simultaneously. The conjunction in time and space of incompatible activities that do not interfere with each other presupposes dissociation (split personality). This was manifested in the great external calm and resoluteness that the dreamer brought to aggressive disputes with opponents—the disputes were more frequently in writing than in spoken words—and the simultaneous feelings of considerable insecurity and internal fright. His condition recalls that of great actors and actresses who give excellent performances despite stage fright. An autobiographical remark made by the dreamer at a time when we were not talking about his four dreams seems pertinent. He reported, in passing, that he was surprised at family members or friends who had tried to calm him when he spoke about controversial matters. What really surprised him, he said, was their misperception of his inner state, which, he insisted, was unruffled on such occasions; they thought he was tense and excited. His external behavior did indeed give few if any clues to his inner reactions to fears and frustrations. When he felt secure and enterprising, however, he manifested his moods freely both in speech and in body language, and he was a lively and pleasant companion.

The Rule of Implicit Evidence pertains primarily to any psychodynamic changes resulting from dream events. Emotions and intentions displayed by different dream figures were diverse. Passive, tacit acquiescence to nearby, violent hostility (the silent crowd) existed side by side with intense, overt hostility that was soon "disarmed" (the assailant). In addition, the dream displayed the dreamer's entourage's effective, firm squelch of threatening, overt hostility at the same time it displayed the dreamer's futile attempts to elaborate and disseminate negative criticism of other lecturers. This, in turn, provoked violent opposition, which caused transient shock and fear (in the dreamer). The dream events brought about only one significant change; otherwise the dream figures and their relations were the same at the end of the dream as they had been at the beginning. The entourage promptly disarmed the assailant, deprived him of his gun. We concluded that the dreamer was well able to silence any aggression elicited by his critical comments, despite his "astonishment" that his ideas prompted the hostility of others and his temporary self-prostration.

The dreamer must have anticipated the violent defensive reaction to his criticism because he had dramatized it strongly in the unconsciously produced dream. In fact, his nemesis, the assailant, had started to move against him even before the dreamer "spotted" anyone with whom he could discuss the lecturer's poor "argumentation." This affectively intense dream scene demonstrated that the dreamer's intention to publicize the lecture's weakness was stillborn. We concluded then that many of the dreamer's plans to write about and publicize the shortcomings of his fellow specialists had never been carried out; this indeed was the case. The dream revealed self-punitive tendencies (Axiom A) and fearful expectation of retaliation for any wrong done to others (Axiom B). Also, it disclosed a very strong tendency to curb impulsive and frank displays of thought, which was ultimately responsible for some of his disappointments and failures in life.

The prognosis for a favorable personality change seemed warranted. Much energy was expended during the dream. This is always a good prognostic sign. What strengthened the favorable prognosis was that the dream had exhibited very good, firmly functioning control of undesirable social behavior. The dreamer's tendency to cause trouble or difficulties for himself through his intellectual attacks on others was fought. He was not, however, in complete conscious control of the reality-oriented forces that would have inhibited his irritating challenges to others. His indifference to interpersonal relationships (manifested by the indifferent crowd) was dissented strongly. Nevertheless, his indifference weakened the power of his antagonistic and pugnacious intentions, which had agitated him. This indifference, a sign of depression, is not a desirable trait. Although it kept him out of many troubles, it slowed him down. He could improve himself by eliminating this recurrent indifference. It impeded his drive for improvement, that is, for reduction of his antagonistic attitude. At the same time, the dreamer effectively curbed his unfriendly and critical attitudes when he became frightened by the possible and actual retaliation of others. His desirable traits were stronger than his undesirable traits, but his need to use the desirable ones to control and thus save himself from the hostility of others was enervating.

He assented "fear and shock" when he was threatened with retaliation, and he assented his censure of others from a safe distance (the criticized lecturer did not appear in the dream). Both these traits showed his growing attention to the sensibilities of others — which leads to a favorable prognosis. His most emotionally intense trait was the reaction to his criticism of others (dramatized by the assailant). This indicated great sensitivity to being rejected or hated; it also showed promptness and the strength of his desire to nullify criticism. His intention to curb his own tendency to criticize others (Axiom A) and the dream criticism of himself by others (Axiom B) were prognostically favorable. At the end of the dream, calm and peace prevailed (Implicit Evidence).

Axiom A and Axiom B interpretations differ noticeably in this dream. Axiom A brought out the intricate personality pattern.

2.   Within the next four months the dreamer had — in addition to a number of dreams with other content — three dreams with essentially the same problem as that in the first. In the second dream, two differences arose. A crowd was not mentioned, and one sentence was dropped (namely, "I had no idea what [the lecture's] topic was." Otherwise, dream events were identical to those in the first dream. In the third dream, the dreamer woke up when the assassin was raising the gun toward him. The anxiety was intense and caused the dreamer to wake in fear. The fourth dream was the shortest. Content was limited to two events: the dreamer's looking for someone with whom he could discuss the inadequacy of the lecture; the dreamer's noticing an intensely angry, armed man running toward him. The dreamer, not "men near him," disarmed the assailant. He also stated that the assailant had been the lecturer the dreamer had censured. Events in this fourth dream were fast and more deter-

mined than in the preceding dreams. The dreamer was not in psychotherapy. The main conflict remained the same throughout the four dreams, but at the end the dreamer had insight into his conflict, and he was freed from secondary complications that had been blurring an acute perception of the conflict. The dreamer did not give up his critical attitude, which, by the way, he contended was inherent in any objective and thorough historical investigation. He remarked that truth always has its enemies, especially in social and historical studies. But, objectivity requires that people be truthful even if being truthful resulted in unpleasant consequences. The series of dreams had one result: The dreamer did not hesitate from or dissent defending himself against reactions to his writings. He now affectively and intellectually accepted the inevitability of people's making arguments and counterarguments in life and particularly in historical research. He still dissented his own reaction to being criticized by others; he tried to suppress his resenting his work's being reproved by himself (Axiom A) and by others (Axiom B).

The illusion that no one would want to harm him in return for his adverse criticism had been shattered in the dream series. In the last dreams, he fully realized that self-defense was to be expected and that it was something quite acceptable and normal. He also realized that he was not so exceptional and loving a person that he could give no cause for resentment. In all four dreams, he dissented the physical aggressors. He mildly assented only self-defense: The defenders simply "disarmed" the attacker and otherwise did not hurt him.

3.   A young woman requested psychotherapy. She wanted relief from chronic, anxious tension. She was described by her therapist as being cooperative and intelligent. Sessions were attended regularly, but therapeutic progress was very slow, slight, and inconsistent. The patient brought a dream (written immediately on waking) that the therapist submitted for blind analysis and prognosis:

> I was on the beach and the waves were coming closer and started covering me. I saw a door under the water and tried to open it. I knew that if I opened the door, I would live, but I couldn't open it. I was drowning and could not breathe. I woke up in a panic and could not breathe.

The blind-analysis reported stated:

> The dream expresses a great fear and expectation of a severe and imminent mental breakdown. Ineffectual attempts are made to prevent the acute episode but confidence is lacking in the success of these attempts. Feelings of helplessness, defeat and depression are intense but there is no complete resignation. The patient is still considering possibilities of escaping a psychotic breakdown. However, a stormy breakdown seems highly probable soon.

Within a week after the nightmare, the dreamer entered a hospital. She had become openly psychotic. Her behavior alternated between violent, physical aggression and withdrawal during which she was silently hostile, unapproachable, and unresponsive. A year later, she was still clinically psychotic, and she was still hospitalized. She had quieted down noticeably and appeared less depressed; her periods of aggression had become less frequent and less intense. The time she spent withdrawn in passive inactivity had lengthened.

Her dream of impending death was the most unfavorable part of prognosis. She emphasized her inability to breathe properly as the most outstanding subjective symptom. She felt in danger of drowning. Her anxious reaction to this danger was very great, and she did not succeed in escaping the danger — "I knew that if I opened the door, I would live, but I couldn't open it . . . I woke up in a panic and could not breathe." Her resignation was plainly indicated by her search for an unrealistic escape from the waters through a door at the bottom of the ocean. Applying realistic criteria of waking life to the dream, we concluded that her desired escape was not only bizarre but fictional. Moreover, according to her own dream, she had an effective escape in simply turning around and walking away from the rising water on the beach. Instead, as the dream ended, she stood immobile and tried to open the door in the bottom of the ocean. Such lack of realism in an intelligent, educated, young, physically healthy person revealed grave psychotic thought disorders and conspicuous breakdown in the sense of reality. This dream was a notable example of the postulate that dream events should be evaluated as if they were real events observed consciously in waking life.

RULE 5: COMPLEMENTARITY

The Rule of Complementarity extends interpretations of dreams beyond conclusions obtained with the first three, most reliable, and most valid rules: Assent and Dissent, Primacy of Verbs and Abstract Nouns, and Symbolism. Rule 5 is used to tell what effect character traits revealed by PDS have on dreamers' subjective feelings and overt behavior. Age, family, occupation, social milieu, general responsibilities, and privileges modify to some extent the way in which traits revealed by dreams affect total behavior. The ultimate goal of Rule 5 is to use knowledge of dreamers' general life conditions as much as possible to interpret dream interpretation results.

For example, depression in people with few responsibilities, easy jobs, and no fears for their financial futures is quite different from depression in people with scarcely any means to meet emergencies and poor prospects for the future. More details, more *relevant* details can be used to interpret dreams of patients with severe physical illnesses when patients' environmental conditions are known. The Rule of Complementarity can be applied in two ways: Knowledge of dreamers' life situations can be logically combined with PDS interpretations of dreams; general principles regarding human personality can be applied to dream findings (doing this, we assume, of course, that the dreams have revealed valid personality traits). A young woman had a nightmare in which she had faced imminent death — whether she acted or remained immobile. A monster threatened to kill her at the entrance to a cave inside of which was a fire that would burn her alive. She developed such a state of panic that she woke from the dream. Her dream complemented the observation that, on the whole, nightmares do not have bad prognoses. Nightmares end with powerful mobilization of dreamers' defensive strength in anticipation of great dangers. In an extreme case, a patient did not avoid a danger but rather rallied to escape it and regain use of her conscious orientation and decision making.

Examples

1.   This dream report was from a man in his 60s. He was intelligent, highly educated, physically and mentally active, alternately gregarious and preoccupied with scientific problems. Imminent retirement, separation from his laboratory, and old age frightened him. He was interested in another opinion about the meaning of his dream because he was puzzled.

In the middle of the night, he saw himself returning home through dimly lit, silent, deserted streets. He entered the lobby of his building and walked up a flight of stairs to his apartment. Light came through a large window and fell on the landing. Somehow he was not surprised that the building was dark. As he walked up, he noticed a woman wearing a black dress and sitting on the bench that was halfway up the landing. The woman was silent and immobile. The man could not see her features but noticed that she watched him intently with piercing eyes. In passing, he had to squeeze by her; their knees touched. She appeared to be in her 30s. He was an adult in the dream, about 60. When he reached his apartment, he was surprised that the door was ajar and that the apartment itself was brightly illuminated. He had expected to find it dark and unoccupied. He entered and stopped in the foyer, fascinated by what he saw. He recognized the layout of his apartment, but the walls between the rooms had been removed; only foot-high partitions remained between the four rooms and the foyer. In the room straight ahead were two figures involved in a dueling match. This sight amused him, particularly because the two antagonists were identical copies of his adolescent self. The duel was not a serious fight but a rather relaxed game of skill. He "saw" himself again in the room to the right of the first, but the age of this figure matched his current age; "he" was dressed as a scientist of several centuries ago and was experimenting with chemical elements, trying new and desirable effects. Liquid was boiling in a beeker, and steam was escaping. The experimenter looked very busy and was bent over the equipment with his back toward the dreamer. In the room to the right of this one was another rendition of the dreamer, this one being a very old, gray-haired man. He wore a wide coat with a fur collar and stood erect with his back to the dreamer, seemingly lost in deep thought. He was "obviously" thinking of a difficult theoretical problem. Large, opened volumes were lying on small tables, which suggested that the theorist had been consulting the books. This was a step beyond the preceding experimenter's empirical fact finding. The first experimenter had a fire burning in an old-fashioned stove that gave the room a reddish glow; apartment lights and a very bright streetlamp illuminated the theorist's room. The dreamer had not noticed the streetlamp before. The three rooms were in a straight line and were facing the street; the theorist's chamber separated the fourth room from the street. The fourth room was also to the right of the foyer and looked like a large, windowless closet. It contained only one object, a large, open, wicker basket with two oval-shaped handles. Dirty linen collected for the laundry was in the basket. The only person in this room was, again, a version of the dreamer; here he was 8 to 10 years old. The boy used a stick to poke inside the basket. He pulled the pieces of clothing out one by one and examined each. The boy stopped when he pulled out his mother's bloodstained panties with the stick. Watching his boyish self, the dreamer became aware of the heavy pounding of his heart, although he did not wake. The thought passed through his mind that his multiple selves were not aware of one another or of him, the dreamer. Meanwhile, unbeknownst to the dreamer, the woman in the hallway had silently followed him to the apartment and now stopped behind him so close as to be able to rest her chin on his right shoulder. She had also watched the extraordinary spectacle in the apartment. As the dreamer became aware of her presence, he tried not to move so as not to disturb his deeply satisfying sensation of affectionate amiability. Thinking only of the woman, the dreamer woke after some time and felt pleasantly enamored. He was puzzled and wondered what the dream could mean.

This long and unusual dream consists of many distinct scenes. Initially the dreamer and the woman barely interacted; later they were brought into intimate bodily contact. When dreamers share traits with figures unlike themselves, they are said to have gained the insight that they possess the traits in question. This dream is extremely rare in that the dreamer appeared as six unlike figures from various periods of his life. He fully assented the traits of the same-sex, same-age figure. He somewhat dissented the others, who differed from him in age. Because these traits or intentional behavior patterns were assigned to discriminate figures, they are not likely to be actuated simultaneously. This seemed to be true in the man's waking life. In his youth, the dreamer had strong social and political interests. His ideas were usually individualistic, though relevant. He took every opportunity to expound and debate his ideas and to criticize the views of his opponents. He was also considerably obsessive. He took years to decide which career to pursue, and having done that, he then compulsively performed his job of historical–literary criticism. He then became a teacher and gave up reviewing contemporary books. Finally, he started an inquiry to ascertain whether cultural and political changes occurred with any regularity throughout history. The several different dream figures, each of which demonstrated a specific aspect of the dreamer's personality, seemed analogous to multiple personalities loosely integrated into a whole. If this were the case, we can understand why each figure (excluding the same-age experimenter) was somewhat dissented. The minor or subpersonalities had incomplete or no knowledge of one another in waking life. In other words, they dissented one another and consequently required different dream figures for representation. The dreamer did indeed say that he relied a great deal on the spontaneous (unconscious) activity of his brain.

Results of free-associative, undisciplined thinking are sometimes completely unanticipated. In this dream, the oddest association was the blood-stained garment. The dreamer called the association "odd" because he was "past sixty," and the figure was 8 to 10. Preoccupation with whatever thoughts and feelings that this dream element represented probably originated in the dreamer's preadolescence. An event from that time in the dreamer's life seemed to be the kernel of an emotional complex that was manifested in the dream; the dreamer's "heart pounded" as he lifted the panties. From this childhood scene, he shifted to the woman with the piercing eyes. He willed himself to be as immobile and silent as possible, so as not to lose the woman's caress. His excessively restrained behavior suggested that he had believed that her attraction to him might have been momentary; this, in turn, implied a feeling of inferiority, a presumption that he was incapable of eliciting strong, positive emotions from women. He was reaching out, but in a meek fashion. He was motionless, as if nothing agitated him. With such an attitude, he would have easily surrendered to the direction and control of others.

The dream had two themes: the story of the man and the woman and the man's survey of his past. They do not overlap. When the man felt the presence of the woman near him, he stopped paying attention to the scenes from his past; he was aware of them only when he was alone. His interest in the woman suppressed his analysis of his past social and scientific activities, as did the reference to the dreamer's preadolescent concerns. These concerns caused anxiety and made his heart pound, whereas the closeness of the woman calmed his heart and reinstated his self-control. The concerns suppressed action. Dream activities were never completed, their eventual outcomes were never decided: The duel was playful, not in earnest; the experimenter fussed but did not achieve; the theorist looked through the window but remained undecided. The boy and dreamer–woman couple, however, were moderately active and reached goals. The intellectual and objective preoccupations that had dominated the dreamer up to this dream began to weaken, and he began to place new emphasis on developing his emotional and subjective sides. His former preoccupations were only images (similar to dreams within dreams), whereas these new preoccupations constituted the main part of the dream. Activity in both parts was subdued, although it was accompanied by intense feelings in the main part.

The dream illustrated the soothing effect of feminine attention and affection. The dream began with darkness, gloom, and loneliness and ended with the dreamer's warm glow. Despite this improvement in mood, the man's inhibitions, rigidity, and restraint did not disappear from his close relationships with women and with others. According to the Rule of Implicit Evidence, the dreamer still had conflicts. The complement of this interpretation is that the dreamer solved some of his important contradictions. He criticized and partly rejected his previously strong conscious and spontaneous occupational goals, and he unhesitatingly affirmed that he would seek security and freedom from inner tension in emotional union with women (mother). This rearrangement of intentional structure was realistic in light of the important changes in the dreamer's life, but his psychological nature underwent a serious change. Suddenly, he felt decrepit.

Compulsory retirement precipitated the loss of the man's main workshop and denied him easy access to research aids (staff, books, meetings at which personal ideas could be tried out, and so forth). He particularly missed stimulating contact with students and colleagues. His somewhat undisciplined work habits had needed the stimulus of challenge and the exchange of frequently incompatible viewpoints. He had relied greatly on his good presence of mind. Opposition had prompted him to clarify the expression of his views. He had always been eager and ready to participate in debates. In his replies, he had been good at repartee. He remarked that he had enjoyed "friendly intellectual contests," and he described them as being a remedy for his tendency to indolence.

The man accomplished something positive during the dream; among other things he alleviated his depression. The dream started in a minor key. Streets were abnormally dim. In the house in which he lived, the lights were off. The woman on the landing was dressed in black and her head was covered. As a matter of course, the dreamer expected to find his apartment dark and locked (although he actually lived with his wife). He had a slow gait and was in a low mood. Nonetheless, he stirred as he climbed the stairs (symbol of sexual arousal?). Although the woman's head was covered with a shawl, her eyes pierced him. He began to breathe more deeply after entering his apartment. The bright illumination of the apartment revealed an interesting spectacle. He watched it carefully, and found that he did not care for this display of his indecisiveness in past activities. His emotions and energy quickened when he had started to think of his mother (in the windowless dirty-linen closet). The associations were accompanied by a heavy pounding of his heart. But nevertheless, the pounding was promptly allayed and the dreamer's mood suddenly changed to a happy one. In fact, it made him feel so good that he wished to perpetuate this happy mood by remaining completely motionless. This change was brought about by the 30-year old woman on the landing (the dreamer was 60). The young woman approached him from the back, stopped behind him and gently put her chin on his right shoulder. The man felt much better at the end of the dream than at its beginning. The working through of the dream marked a better reconciliation with objective and intrapsychic realities.

2. A young woman had the following dream before her first psychotic breakdown:

> It was dark ("a moonless night") and I didn't know where I was and what I was supposed to do there. I was in a poorly lit square, surrounded by tall buildings. I was looking for a way out. I wanted to get away. I looked for the street (but could not find one). Before I knew what was happening, I fell into a dark and deep hole. And I woke up.

The dreamer reported that she had, in acute anxiety, experienced the sensations and feelings revealed in the dream. She was particularly frightened by her helplessness and disorientation, and at the end of the dream, by her sudden loss of physical support as she dropped into the "dark and deep hole." Her failure to find a street that would lead from the square made her particularly anxious. She realized that there was no way out. The function of PDS is to directly disclose intrapsychic processes that matter to dreamers at the time of their dreams. In this case, the dreamer's perception of her surrounding environment was limited because of the darkness. Thus, the dreamer was, figuratively speaking, in the dark concerning the psychosocial relationships that mattered to her. She lost her affective and intellectual contact with people. She was at a loss to understand what was familiar to her. This severely constricted her movement and orientation (she could not find a street by which she could escape the tall buildings enclosing her in the square). The dream ended in acute but brief terror when she suddenly dropped into the hole. This confinement, the darkness, and the lack of visibility imply an agitated depression. In this endoscopic dream, the verbs alone accurately described her feelings and hopelessness. She could not help herself but was seeking help. She desired to escape the entrapment and darkness. She was afraid of what might happen in her immediate future and of what consequences were in store for the rest of her life.

She was the only dream figure. This implies that she assented all the revealed traits. In other words, she knew that the hopelessness, panic, and sense of entrapment that the dream described were hers and that she was facing an imminent depressive withdrawal from people and the world. Yet despite her plea for help, she withdrew most of the time and was unable to communicate (except regarding simple matters of living at home — i.e., sleep, meals, dressing, basic physiological needs). An acute hyperactive psychotic episode started within a week of her dream.

Complementarity prompted us to evaluate the results of PDS analysis in terms of our knowledge of mental disorders. The dreamer was very anxious and feared entrapment; these were affective experiences. In reporting the dream and in describing the physical dream environment, the dreamer was lucid and realistic. Under emotional stress, anyone can miss in the dark, a street that would normally be noticed. The patient was at an impasse. She could not help herself, and no one was there to help. She was isolated and incapable of action. Under these conditions, her outlook was terrifying: disaster. Dreamers who look for a way out of such conditions only to find themselves physically blocked from escaping death or serious physical danger are almost exclusively schizophrenics or cerebral organic patients threatened by impending personality disorganization, "the coming of the night."

It is interesting to note that the dreamer's condition calmed after six weeks of treatment and that she was able to return home. Although she did not need continuous care or attention, she dropped her sense of initiative and increased her caution in psychosocial relationships. She reduced the complexity and intensity of her life in all areas. This, we might argue, was foreshadowed by her ending all effort after she had fallen into the hole (Rule of Implicit Evidence). Thus, a PDS interpretation can appropriately complement an interpretation made by an experienced clinician or therapist in the diagnosis and treatment of patients.

RULE 6: GENERALIZATION

The term *generalization,* when used in PDS, pertains to dream interpreters' conclusions regarding the types of people to which dreamers' characterizations of their dream figures apply. When so defined, *generalization* can be used with Axiom B, but not with Axiom A because Axiom A postulates that all traits of all dream figures are, by definition, personal traits of dreamers themselves. The meaning of differences among dream figures within the logical framework of Axiom A is different from that within the framework of Axiom B. According to Axiom A, differences among dream figures serve to classify dreamers' traits into separate categories based on the degree to which the traits are assented or dissented (see Scale of Assent–Dissent). The main assumption of Axiom B is relevant to the process of generalization; it postulates that the psychological properties attributed to different dream figures reflect dreamers' opinions of types of persons resembling the dream figures in sex, age, and other indicated traits. Thus, if a dream figure were described as female, young, married, childless, and working, then, in the dreamer's opinion, whatever the dream figure experienced in the dream and however she behaved would likely be typical of young, married, childless working women. Such an opinion would involve the lowest and easiest degree of generalization. By disregarding any one of the dream figure's five properties (sex, age, marital status, motherhood, work), we can increase the variety of people who are assumed to be represented by the dream figure. The range and diversity of people included in one category by the process of generalization increase as the number of attributes in a set used as the criterion for inclusion decreases. As the criterion for classification becomes less exacting, the chance of error becomes greater. For example, if we were to generalize that all people share the behavior and experiences of the young woman above — which would be the highest degree of generalization — we would certainly find that a considerable percentage of the total population has not had the experiences and problems of that young woman. We should be particularly careful in ascribing the characteristics of a dream figure to real persons of the opposite sex. Psychological identity with a person's own sex and the person's awareness of true or imagined sex differences are so strong and influential that virtually all people believe that some distinct and lasting personological differences between men and women exist. Psychobiological and physiological differences are fundamental to the most affect-laden preoccupation of humans and all living organisms: survival. Experiences connected with conception, birth, danger avoidance, and death are determinative and pervasive. Without sex, life would not exist; sex and sex differences are vital.

Sometimes dream figures unlike dreamers represent single individuals of particular emotional significance for the dreamers. Such individuals are not always clearly identified in dreams. They may be physically recognizable acquaintances, emotionally indifferent to dreamers who express surprise at finding these figures in their dreams. Dreams, however, frequently contain figures with whom dreamers are very familiar; these figures play significant roles (e.g., marital partners, parents, siblings, close friends, etc.) in dreamers' lives. Very close relationships developed over many years preclude generalizations because they usually possess unique features. Dream interpreters cannot tell whom such unique dream figures represent in dreamers' lives unless they know the psychosocial history of the dreamers sufficiently well. Postdream inquiries help to identify the real individuals behind the dream figures in question.

The probable reason why dream figures other than dreamers can represent a number of different persons is that most people want to gratify their desires more than they want to have it done by specific objects or other people. In such instances, dreamers justifiably use one person as a symbol for a number of potential or interchangeable individuals. Occasionally dream figures are animals or animate inanimate objects (automobiles, violent sea storms, airplanes). These dream figures reveal the most dissented traits. Viewed as expressions of dreamers' opinions of themselves (Axiom A) or of others (Axiom B), traits of animals and spontaneously moving inanimate objects (e.g., building cranes) must be translated into human terms; these traits disclose gross, primitive, poorly controlled affects and intentions, mostly hostile and destructive. Generally speaking, nonhuman figures represent persons with strong, poorly controlled, disruptive affects and habits and tendencies to impulsive, inconsiderate, inappropriate, or threatening behavior. Dreams revealing these traits are produced, as a rule, by visibly disturbed individuals. Dreams in which inanimate forces or objects run amok and directly approach and try to destroy helpless dreamers (thus causing nightmares) usually presage acute personality problems.

Social customs and coercion produce greater similarity among people in what they dissent than in what they assent. Therefore, generalization of dissented traits is likely to be validated more frequently than generalization of assented traits. To attribute some of our personal characteristics to other people implies that none of us is unique. In other words, personality traits discoverable in dreams through the aid of PDS are shared by at least several persons and sometimes by nearly everyone (e.g., struggling with intrapsychic inhibitions is something we all share). The correlation between knowing our own personalities and those of others is positive, although far from perfect.

Within the framework of Axiom B, PDS generalization is a process of identifying a real individual or a group of real individuals in whom dreamers may see traits that are part of one or another of the figures in their dreams. When dreamers are in psychotherapy, the Rule of Complementarity is not needed because therapists have knowledge of patients' interpersonal relationships.

Examples

1. A single man in his 30s reported the following dream fragment: "I was attending a large party and when I put my arm around my lady friend's waist to escort her up a short embankment, an elderly woman interrupted her conversation with others and looked at me in a scornful and critical way."

The scornful woman in the dream may represent someone besides "elderly women" to the dreamer. Today, probably most elderly ladies, as well as young women and men, would consider the dreamer's gesture innocuous. Therefore, it is probable that a dream interpreter would not generalize in this case but would assume that the "elderly woman" who interrupted her conversation to scorn the dreamer at a large gathering most likely represented the dreamer's mother. This conclusion could be reinforced by some dream details: The dreamer was taking his friend away from the group, "up a short embankment." The dreamer, a single man, had a strict and "correct" upbringing. He had always behaved properly and would never have behaved toward ladies as freely as he did in this dream. He had not allowed himself any intimacy in public. The dream became more meaningful when interpreted in accordance with Axiom A: The "elderly woman" was the carrier of the dreamer's dissented traits. He did indeed struggle with an exacting decorum that is associated with emotional restraint and noticeable shyness.

2. A man in his early 40s dreamed of a woman about his age. She behaved in a conspicuously self-humiliating and masochistic manner. He felt very uncomfortable during the dream in which he himself appeared as a passive observer uninvolved in what was happening before his eyes. His personal history contained evidence that he was permitting others to take advantage of him, that he had been eager to please his superiors since childhood, and that he never took the initiative to improve his working conditions, income, position, or influence. At every job he had worked, he gained the reputation as the most qualified, but poorest paid, salaried employee. He rationalized that his behavior was realistic and prudent. He declared with apparent conviction: "One better be sensible. There is a power structure in every organization. You fight at your own peril!" He added that, if he had the choice, he would act spontaneously and assertively and that he did not like his quiet submissiveness, which at times was rather humiliating. However, he valued his steady income and the safety of his job. His complaints included mild and recurrent depressive moods and occasional fears of "losing [his] temper."

At first this man denied having had any feelings of inferiority; he denied his submissiveness, which sometimes approached masochism. He needed months of therapy before he became aware of his passive submissiveness and inability to fight for his rights. His superior intelligence, manner of being, and jobs made his masochistic character inconspicuous to most people. He was inclined to view his life as typical of a salaried employee in the modern economic world. Unmarried, closefisted, he spent his leisure time reading historical books. He had a trained ear for music and enjoyed the great masters. He justified his own traits by claiming that his personality was typical of wage earners in modern civilization. He dissociated himself—he performed the opposite of generalization—from the sadistic, elderly man who abused the submissive, suffering woman in the dream.

3. About 18 months later, during summer vacation, the preceding dreamer met me by chance and stopped to tell me his most recent dream. He saw himself walking in the alley at the end of which is the Parisian Grand Guignol, the theater of horrors. The real theater resembles a Gothic chapel; it

has a stage in place of an altar; the dream theater had something the real Guignol does not have, a mid-building pulpit in which an alert, serious, old man sat and from which he scrutinized everyone who arrived (the entrance in a side wall was opposite the pulpit). The old man could see everyone from his elevated position. The dream Guignol differed from the real Guignol in other ways. The dream theater had wide, comfortable easy chairs and needed no tickets to enter; people came and went as they pleased. The dreamer saw himself taking a chair near the pulpit and waiting. He was bored. A clown appeared on stage and began performing all sorts of tricks requiring great skill. The dreamer had to force himself to pay attention. He had come to the theater out of some vague sense of duty that he could not explain to himself. As if offended by the dreamer's indifference, the clown threw three soft dolls at the dreamer; they landed in the dreamer's lap, one after another. The dreamer placed the dolls on a neighboring chair. The man in the pulpit turned to the dreamer and in a friendly and encouraging voice urged him to throw the dolls back at the clown. The dreamer felt very uncomfortable. Not wanting to make a spectacle of himself, he remained silent and left the dolls behind as he walked out of the theater as inconspicuously as possible. Several other people also stepped outside. It was still daylight; the air was dry, but the sky was completely covered with clouds. An elderly man paced outside and repeatedly looked at the dreamer's eyes, as if he were hesitating to talk to the dreamer. The dreamer could not decide whether this man was the old man from the pulpit. With this doubt in mind, the dreamer woke up with a vague, uncomfortable feeling and with some shame.

The striking feature of this dream was the frustrated interest one man had in another. The dreamer assented his avoidance of men who showed some interest in him (Axiom B). Intrapsychically, he actively suppressed his own interest in closer contact with other men while he enforced preoccupation with them by genuinely dissenting them. When his temptation grew stronger (in the encounter with the colorfully dressed clown), it was immediately rendered ineffective, although his turning away from temptation caused some depression (boredom). He had his most ambivalent relation with "elders" or men of authority. They scrutinized critically but were or could have been "friendly and openly encouraging." Relations with men of authority caused his most intense and frequent fears and anxieties. Anxious thoughts about the "man in the pulpit" preceded interruption of the dream. The dreamer had no psychotherapy; he claimed to be his own analyst. The three brief, face-to-face experiences with three different men in the dream are different manifestations of the dreamer's ambivalent desire for close friendship with men. He struggled hard against his enervating ambivalence and his need for continuous, conscious self-control. As a result, the dreamer denied himself not only friendship but even good-natured companionship. Generalization seemed fully justified in this case. The three men with whom the dreamer had some give-and-take were quite different from one another; what the dreamer experienced with each man was also different. Yet the common element in these three face-to-face situations was the same and was emotionally significant in degree and quality: The dreamer became aware several times of the possibility that he could have social and emotional rapport with another man, but each time his attempt came to naught. As the number and diversity of psychosocial situations increase, — thus dramatizing a specific interpersonal relationship in a dream — the dreamer's affective and intellectual investment in such a relationship also increases. We seem therefore justified in generalizing that the dreamer's conflict "to do or not to do" (to respond or not to respond positively to encouraging signals from men) was likely to be aroused with any man of sufficient intelligence and an interest in art.

Nonetheless, comparison of this dream and the preceding dream, which occurred 18 months earlier, suggested an improvement. Denial of genuine tendencies had weakened, insight into some of his inner conflict had grown, and he had developed his capacity to recognize the psychosocial complexities ensuing from his intrapsychic conflict. The dreamer still did not feel at home in the world he inhabited.

RULE 7: PREDICTING OVERT BEHAVIOR

Generation of reliable and valid conclusions about overt behavior is proof of the usefulness of all psychological systems. Such conclusions are the most difficult problem in personology. In psychotherapy, however, using dreams as a source of information about patients' overt behavior is hardly ever necessary. Spontaneously or as a result of therapists' prompts, patients usually describe their difficulties themselves. Furthermore, therapists can make their own direct observations.

As a rule, failure is less difficult to predict than success. A few diverse factors are necessary for success, and lack of any one of them results in failure. Because most failures are due to personal weaknesses (i.e., significant deviations from ideal norms), predictions of failure are fairly accurate but far from perfect. These mistakes occur when the duration and etiological effect of one or more of the factors that seem to contribute to the current state of failure are misjudged; another source of mistakes is an inability to predict future appearances of presently unknown factors conducive to success. With respect to psychotherapeutic outcome, evaluating the effects of therapist on patient and of therapist–patient rapport is difficult.

As the diversity of tendencies or drives increases, individuals' indecisiveness and susceptibility to anxiety states also increase. Human energy and its organization are limited, and no person can pursue several divergent goals with steady success and genuine satisfaction. In general, then, great diversity of traits revealed in dreams corresponds to a large number of unresolved problems. In addition, passivity signifies a reduced capacity to solve personal as well as pragmatic difficulties. Any display of activity or inquisitiveness in a dream is thus a prognostically favorable sign. According to ecologists, animals that are good survivors show a highly differentiated exploratory behavior. We are not different from our fellow mammals in this respect. Consequently, diversification and passivity lower the chances of a clear, overt manifestation of traits in behavior and raise the probability that frustration, depression, and anxiety will be perpetuated. Because dreams reveal the struggle between incompatible action tendencies, assessing relative strengths of competing tendencies must be done when seeking a prognosis. Prognostic estimates must consider at least the main drives and the inhibitory counterdrives to be of value. Other factors relevant to overt behavior and prognosis include identification of: what pleases and displeases dreamers; affects related to preparing for action and affects related to relaxation or passivity; what increases ambivalence and delay, what alleviates anxiety, and what stimulates spontaneity. Healthy people enjoy uninhibited, productive activity, positive self-expression, and improved capacity to handle problems; they dislike being aware of their limitations and their inhibitions. For better understanding of dreamers and for more adequate prognoses, the extent to which dreamers share those normal likes and dislikes must be ascertained. We should not attribute much etiological power, however, to pleasure and displeasure because these are rather subjective reactions to action. Action tendencies charged with strong affects tend to be actuated regardless of mood. Manifestation of the most dissented traits (levels 8 and 12) is beyond pleasure and pain. Only physiological reflex movement occurs in an affective vacuum.

Comparisons of the beginnings and the ends of dreams are also of great prognostic significance. When dreamers move toward improvement during dreams, prognoses for spontaneous and therapeutic improvement are favorable. For example, suicide attempts in dreams ending with physically improbable rescues (e.g., jumping off a tall building and being picked up by a helicopter or landing in a net before hitting the ground) indicate that desire to live is stronger than desire to commit suicide. At the end of dreams, when relations among dream figures revert to what they were at the start, prognoses are guarded in the sense that, whereas dreamers may have clearly dramatized internal inconsistencies and difficulties, they have not yet advanced toward possible solutions of their problems. In the third scenario, dreamers' conflicts worsen as dreams progress. In such cases, prognoses are unfavorable. Escaping psychosocial relations, by whatever means, is contrary to dreamers' well-being; no one can truly live alone and remain sane.

Inconsistencies within dreams interfere with sound planning and effective action. Those who contradict themselves cannot give their full effort to any intention. They feel tense, dejected, frustrated, and consequently depressed. Their capacity for overcoming external obstacles is reduced. The manner in which they react to obstacles is a very important prognostic indicator. When people see themselves in their dreams as much younger persons than they actually are — relieved of the responsibilities and problems of adulthood — they exhibit a rare but significant sign of psychological distance from contemporary life. Meticulous description of dream details is another manifestation of the habit of delaying action by obsessive fussing with secondary matters. As manifest dreams become more involved, irrational, and delusional, predicting overt behavior becomes more difficult because of the variability of patients' sense of reality and their unpredictable reactions to environmental stimuli. The Rule of Assent and Dissent helps us to compare action tendencies on the basis of probability of overt manifestation. On the whole, tendencies dissented to great degrees require specific intrapsychic and social conditions to make the action tendencies realizable.

As a rule, nightmares do not augur a worsening of dreamers' personal conditions. Panic associated with nightmares is a function both of dreamers' being threatened in dreams and of their reacting intensely and immediately to the threats. Both the affective upheaval and dreamers' resultant mobility are much more favorable than affective flatness or passive resignation. In fact, one way in which dreamers stop recurrent, conscious nightmares is by training themselves to turn around during the nightmares, to face the approaching mortal danger, and to imagine attacking it angrily and violently. Nightmares end without any constructive suggestion of how to handle the panic that is creating the conflict.

Finally, the chances of making satisfactory inferences linking dreamers' overt behavior and outcomes of psychotherapy increase with the degree to which dream events approximate prevailing realistic modes of interpersonal relationships and with the quality of dramatization — that is, with how the actions and mutual interactions of dream figures are presented (preferably in an intelligible, clear manner without non sequiturs or irrelevant comments). Illogical, unrealistic, and obscure visual dream content makes for difficult predictions about the future and about the degree of meaningful cooperation expected from the dreamers.

The following sample dreams were produced by subjects with severe personality disorders of a schizophrenic nature, but the degree of severity of the illness varied among them. These dreams demonstrate that it is easier to correctly predict failure than to correctly predict personal improvement or success in life. Human behavior and quality of self-awareness depend on multiple factors, both internal and external. All the factors necessary for the performance of an act or the arousal of a desired intrapsychic state must be present if the act is to be performed or the mental state is to be achieved. Usually the absence of even a single, essential, causative factor prevents people from acting or from achieving a mental state. Consequently, failures are more easily predictable than successes.

Examples

1. A very sensitive college undergraduate interested in creative writing dreamed a lot. The following dream contains a detailed narrative of the psychosocial consequences of his disturbing mental disorder, intermittent "invisibility":

> A girl and I were walking on a sloping bluff of dune hills and spoke while the sea broke far below us. We were alone. I had a feeling of great tenderness for her but she showed no signs of interest in me. The waves were huge. When we looked down at the town below, I saw the walls of broken water burst around the houses which looked like islands standing out of the sea. The girl and I began to tease each other. She dared me to run down the bluff, in the wake of a receding wave, to see if I could reach the porch of one of the houses before the next wave broke. I would have none of that. Then, looking down, we saw an old woman struggling through the wash of the wave, holding a parchment over her head. My friend cried: "the cripple," and right away I ran down the slope. As I ran, I saw a growing wave rolling in behind the old woman. The wave thundered and was almost on top of the woman. I leaped down, the street was slick, the wave was about to break, the noise was great. And then, when I reached the haggard old cripple, she looked at me and the waves disappeared. And there was complete silence. She handed me the paper. I looked at it. It contained many incidents of my life. At the bottom was written: "killed by wave while attempting to rescue an old woman." I asked the woman what I should do. She pointed to a house nearby where I found several middle-aged women in an office, very businesslike. They informed me that I was in fact dead, and that, from this point on, no one in the living world could communicate with me or know of my existence. What seemed to prove this was the reappearance of the girl with whom I had been. I went to her and spoke to her. And I tried to embrace and kiss her, but her body and mine would not meet. They were only half-solid to each other. She continued to talk with the women and did not notice my presence. Then the scene changed completely. I was sitting in a comfortable living room with my mother and another person. Everything was fine. And then, suddenly, I felt myself dissolving away. I watched myself fade into invisibility. My mother and the other person did not notice my disappearance though they looked "through" me at objects in the room. Then, just as unpredictably, I felt myself fading back in, and returned to visibility. Then I talked with my two companions and they spoke as if I'd always been there.

The dream scene was a small seashore town with sandy dune hills at the water's edge. The mood was foreboding. A violent storm raged under a gray sky. Huge waves repeatedly inundated and battered the houses on the shore.

Unwary passersby were endangered. The dreamer endeavored to make normal social contacts repeatedly, with different people, but each time he became invisible after a while. His interlocuters showed no surprise but behaved as if he were not there. This main theme was presented in five different versions of his dream. The amount of fantasy displayed as the dreamer was constantly frustrated by his repeated, unsuccessful attempts to draw favorable attention to himself and to become companion and friend testify to the great amount of feeling and thought that he gave to his desire to be recognized and accepted as others are. People did not miss his absence; what was worse, they did not notice his presence. He had not established any positive emotional relation with anyone. No one cared about him. Even the "haggard old cripple" (same as the recorder of deaths, the old woman) silently handed him "a parchment" announcing his death. When he asked her what he should do, she sent him to "several middle-aged women in an office, very business-like" (unfeeling?). They confirmed his death and told him that "from this point on, no one in the living world could communicate with [him] or know of [his] existence." Proof of this statement was given to the dreamer immediately. The girl with whom he had walked and talked on the lonely hill (at the opening of the dream) reappeared. He said:

> I went to her . . . and I tried to embrace and kiss her, but her body and mine would not meet. They were only half-solid to each other. She . . . did not notice my presence. Then the scene changed completely. I was sitting in a comfortable living room with my mother and another [unidentified] person. Everything was fine.

However, this did not last: "Suddenly . . . I watched myself fade into invisibility." His mother and her companion did not notice his disappearance. In fact, "they looked 'through' [him] at objects in the room. Then, just as unpredictably, [he] felt [himself] fading back in." The dream report ended with this statement: "Then I talked with my two companions and they spoke as if I'd always been there." Only when he was home with mother, but not alone with her, did the symptom of "invisibility" subside and cease to terminate his desired human relationship; "invisibility" was reduced to a transient, tolerable nuisance. At the beginning of the dream the girl companion aroused "great tenderness" in the dreamer, and, for a time, he remained visible. But then the girl dared him to run down the hill and to see if he could escape the next "huge" wave. This amounted to prodding him to take great risks. "I would have none of that," he replied. He did take the risk, however, after the young girl had drawn his attention to the old woman about to be vanquished by the wave.

This is in essence an Axiom B interpretation of the dream. The intra-individual Axiom A interpretation reveals the desperate struggle with depersonalization.

The intra-individual Axiom A rests on the assumption that all traits discernible in dreams are genuine characteristics of the dreamers. Dreamers fully assent traits attributed to them in their dreams; they dissent traits of other dream figures (the degree traits are dissented is indicated by the degree of difference between dreamers and the figures that manifest those traits in the same dreams). Intrapsychic tension correlates with the numerical difference between the Scale of Dissent levels of the dreamer and of the other figure.

The most dissented figure in the "invisibility" dream was the huge waves (level 12). Therefore, the greatest intrapsychic conflict was between the assented, conscious desire for mutually close and harmonious relations with others and the intensely dissented tendency to commit violent, destructive assaults that endangered others and himself. "Huge," uncontrolled waves have tremendous power but no reason and no feeling. The dreamer dissented very strongly his possible, suppressed, acute, openly aggressive, uncontrolled rage. The dream indicated that the dreamer's greatest danger was his rage and that he tried to repress this rage. The danger of his rage was in his losing self-control and in his becoming a helpless victim of his own hostile violence. The dreamer tried to counteract the danger by seeking the support of others. He attempted with full assent to develop tender relations, but his effort failed (as is illustrated by the behavior of the young girl—level 4—on the hill). The statement that "she showed no signs of interest in [him]" suggested that his assented exertion of tenderness, softness, and delicacy of manner could not have suppressed or eliminated ("made invisible") his indifference to other persons' friendly and tender approaches toward him. This lack of emotional reciprocity was documented even more convincingly toward the end of the dream: "I tried to embrace and kiss her, but her body and mine would not meet. They were only half-solid to each other."

The difference between the scale levels of the dreamer and of the "haggard old cripple" was 5 points. Actually, the difference was greater because the cripple had several additional traits that did not have places provided on the scale but that separated her even further from the dreamer. She was a "cripple," she looked "haggard," and she had a document that "contained many incidents of [his] life" and that stated that the dreamer had been "killed by [a] wave while attempting to rescue an old woman." Moreover, the woman possessed magical power: When the dreamer "reached the haggard old cripple, she looked at [him] and the waves disappeared." The dreamer dissented the old woman's traits—her frailty, her magical trick, and especially her knowledge of the dreamer's personal history; he would have liked to be free of them. This was confirmed by the question he had put to the woman: He had asked about what he should do. Though dissented (apparently consciously), knowledge of his personal condition distressed him. He wanted to get rid of his intermittent "invisibility." On the advice of the old woman, who possessed "documentary" evidence of his death, the dreamer went to "middle-aged women in an office." They also "informed [him] that [he] was in fact dead" and reinforced their grim message by saying "that, from [that] point on, no one in the living world could communicate with [him] or know of [his] existence."

In conclusion, documented evidence showed that the dreamer had felt depersonalized at times in the past and that he was currently feeling "invisible." In this dream, however, he "felt himself fading back in, and returned to visibility." Because the old woman (level 5) had the evidence that the dreamer's slipping into these psychopathological states of "invisibility" had happened more than once over a long period of time, we assumed that the dreamer firmly dissented his periodic loss of meaningful rapport with others. The dreamer gave some details of these blocked states of active, mental rapport with others: "Her body and mine would not meet"; people repeatedly failed to notice his presence even when he had felt comfortable and "everything was fine"; "mother and another person . . . looked 'through' [him] at objects in the room"; his mother and her companion had not noticed his disappearance, and yet, when he faded "back in, and returned to visibility . . . they spoke as if I'd always been there." In other words, he felt comfortable at home with his mother only when someone else was there too. He had also felt depersonalized there as well, but these instances handicapped him significantly less than other instances had done. The dreamer needed, then, the attention and affection of women (others) to steady and reassure him.

The unusual and conspicuous symptom of "invisibility" deserves some analysis; it does not conform to the conventional definition of *depersonalization*. The dreamer had not noticed any change in the degree of reality of the physical and human environments. People could not see him, whereas he was able to perceive them — realistically. His subjective, pathological sensation was that he was absent or "invisible" at the same time he retained a normal capacity for evaluating perceived environmental phenomena. He felt that he did not physically exist. All the dream figures appeared realistic to him, and he responded to them as he very well might in waking life. His symptom, therefore, could not be called a *dream hallucination*. The symptom can be described as a special variety of depersonalization: He did not "see" or experience his body as strangely changed but simply as immaterial and not perceived by other dream figures that appeared in the dream as they would have in waking life. He was inconsistent in that he described himself as intermittently invisible and physically nonexistent whereas he "saw" himself in the dream as unchanged and acting as if he were the same as the other figures, who looked like normal people. Moreover, he displayed intense interest in the environment; several times he sought direct, physical contact. In other words, he was appropriately active, considering his peculiar, abnormal states, and he did not give any indication of feeling that he was under the influence of an outside force. His self-awareness was intact throughout the dream. He knew that he was changing from time to time, and yet, despite the change, he continued his realistic observations of what was happening to him and what was occurring around him. He never failed to differentiate between himself and others. Descartes said that we exist because we think. The dreamer did not exist physically, despite his continuing to perceive and to think during the time he felt depersonalized. He had "faded out" and "faded in" despite himself, and he remained the same throughout the dream.

What is the purpose of and gain from repeated "invisibility"? One obvious gain is that the symptom prevented effective rapport with others. The psychogenic nature of "fading out" periods is indicated by the conditions under which the symptom occurred. The dreamer faded out under emotionally charged circumstances such as when he had tried to embrace and kiss the girl and when he had been with his mother in her living room. He became invisible when he desired a close emotional tie with the person in whose presence he had felt depersonalized. He was disturbed on the two occasions in different ways. The feeling for the girl was patently stronger than that for the mother and her companion. He felt depressed that the girl had not even noticed his presence. He felt reassured at home with mother and could engage in normal, social intercourse with the two adults who had not even noticed that he had faded out in front of them; that is, he felt he was always welcome with them. His self-esteem and anxious depression were not as low in the presence of his mother as in the presence of the girl.

Withdrawal to his parental home, where he felt far less threatened, disclosed the dreamer's wish for less challenging living conditions. He preferred a well-known environment in which he could be sure that he would make fewer mistakes and experience fewer painful frustrations. This was a typical retreat to a predictable and familiar environment of individuals. People make such retreats to avoid novel, anxiety-producing life experiences they know they cannot handle. When difference between potential impulse strength and potential impulse control exceeds an empirically determined degree and lasts continually or intermittently, the principle of homeostasis is violated. There exists, then, a significant imbalance between afferent and efferent personality functions — which results in disordered, maladaptive, and unpredictable behavior. An appropriate change of behavior under these circumstances is retrenchment, a reduction of emotional involvements and ambition, a limiting of activities to simple tasks than can be handled effectively, an avoidance of burdensome interpersonal relationships and mental performances. This dreamer retrenched for the sake of improved internal stability; he returned to his mother and her companion — a guard of manners? — with whom he felt comfortable and accepted.

My experience indicates that people who see themselves motionless and dead in dreams or who say that they are dead do not have death wishes but rather are depressed, lonely, and desirous of nurturing support from others. The specific meaning of "being dead" in this young man's dream does not make the dream inconsistent or bizarre. A simpler and less assumptive explanation (in terms of Axiom A) is available. Perhaps the danger to his personality was not as great as it had appeared to him at first. In PDS translation, this means that the dreamer had exaggerated the danger of depersonalization and regression and, after some doubt (the second encounter with the girl) his mood improved, despite the "invisibility" episode. As the dream ended, the dreamer was feeling "fine" and was conversing freely with two companions. He had recovered from the great shock caused by his repeated fadings, and he accepted the fact that familiar nurturing and undemanding life made his symptom of feeling unreal tolerable.

The dream was positive in that it dramatized reduction of ambivalence and of associated stress and anxiety. It showed the stages of the dreamer's reconciliation with the unchangeability and endurance of his sporadic, very frightening, deeply depressing depersonalization states. The dream was also positive in that the dreamer discovered and authenticated a suitable life style that could significantly limit frustration and alleviate pain and depression — despite the persistence of the pathological symptom. The degree of severity of the pathological mental symptom can be measured by the effect it had on other mental functions. The grammar and syntax of the long and involved dream report, the consistency and logical sequence dream events, the cause-and-effect connections (noted only after the existence of the pathological symptom was assumed), and the good emotional and psychological consistency were formally faultless. The dream began with a violent sea storm and towering waves that inundated the town. It ended with calm waves and the return of the water to its natural seabed. The dreamer was under the influence of a strong emotion stimulated by a girl, an appropriate love object. It was a relatively new emotional experience for an unmarried adolescent. The dream ended with the young man's feeling "comfortable" and calm while inside the living room of the parental home. Emotions were friendly but subdued and far from passionate. The depressing, even tragically disappointing indifference to and cold nonacceptance of him by others did not unnerve him; on the contrary, they made him find a human environment in which he could function almost normally (his companions did not notice his "fading out"), albeit on a reduced level of meaningfulness and deep gratification. His proven capacity to do something to alleviate the consequences of his serious mental symptom and his willing payment of the price for reduction of stress were prognostically favorable signs. His treatment prescription was: Try less, limit psychosocial interrelationships, reduce active ambitions; trying less, he would make fewer conspicuous mistakes and he would have fewer disturbing and anxious frustrations of all kinds.

In waking life, the dreamer's social role was that of a hanger-on. He lived at the periphery of a group and was not very active. He surprised people by making unusual statements. He talked little and avoided discussions. He was more of a listener than a talker. His spontaneous statements were short, and he did not expect anyone to comment or discuss them with him. He went home before the end of the year, leaving college for good. His best subject of study at college was the most rational — mathematics. His prevailing mood was tragic, and it pervaded both his dream and his life.

2.   An unmarried, lonely man in his mid-30s suffered from chronic schizophrenia. His conspicuous, main, lasting symptom was devitalization; formal thought disorders were mild and incidental, noticeable during occasional acute periods of exacerbation of his intermittent paranoid attitudes. He recovered from these attitudes after being treated with tranquilizing drugs and brief hospitalizations, but he rarely sought help. His insight into the pathology of his symptoms gradually worsened during his 9 years of observation but was not entirely lost. He reported the following dream:

> I was standing in front of a church. There were some other people. A girl whom I had not seen for a good many years apparently had just been married and was leaving the church. When she noticed me, she ran over and grabbed my arm. Her husband was a fellow I knew. He saw that I had attracted his wife's attention. He came over and knocked me down. I'm vague; I don't know what happened then, but I remember next that I was in the girl's home, and she was introducing me to her parents as her husband. I felt trapped into something and I thought: What am I getting myself into? I woke up, feeling happy that it was just a dream and that I was not married.

Interpretation according to Axiom B was simple and easy. The dream report might have been a description of a day in the life of a very passive man who did not defend himself at all against painful abuses by others and against being dragged into relationships he abhorred. Waking brought immediate relief; he discovered that he had dreamed the events and had not experienced them in real life.

Axiom A illuminated the dreamer's intrapsychic processes; it revealed details of the dreamer's inner conflicts and of his assented psychosocial behavior. The main conflict dramatized in the dream was between a strong and persistent desire to avoid emotional involvement with others, particularly with marriageable women (Oedipus complex?), and occasional weak and frightening impulses to seek such involvement. Every feeling stimulated during dreaming was translated into visuomotor imagery. The dream began with a scene in front of a church in which a marriage had just been performed. The dreamer cautiously placed himself outside the church and away from the altar but managed to see the newlyweds. Moreover, he knew both of them, although not recently. In addition, he quickly stopped his thinking about the idea of lasting marriage as soon as the couple had moved away from the church, away from the teachings of the church, away from their religious upbringing. The dreamer could not assent the permanence of marriage (ambivalence?). His dissent was indicated by the energetic action of the bride (another man's wife, level 4 on the Scale of Dissent), who selected a new "husband" as soon as the marriage ceremony had ended. The dreamer, in the role of the bride, attempted to attach his new marital partner to himself by trying to make the partner an accepted member of his family. The bride's parents (level 8 on the Scale of Dissent) showed no reaction whatsoever. Similarly, the impassive onlookers (level 8) were noncommittal.

Through the person of the bridegroom, the dreamer introduced a minor theme that occurred but once. The bridegroom displayed the trait; he (on the very mildly dissented level 1) was the only dream figure who acted promptly and vigorously when he "saw that [the dreamer] had attracted his wife's attention; he came over and knocked [the dreamer] down." This dream element disclosed that the dreamer felt he faced a danger, among others, of attracting, albeit without actively trying, a love object who had already had a liaison with someone else. The jealous party would be provoked to hurt the dreamer. So violent had been the bridegroom's punch that the dreamer became disoriented and did not "know what happened" next. His thinking became disturbed for a while. Rivalry with a man over the man's wife or possibly over any woman or perhaps even over a man (Rule of Generalization) was thus poignantly revealed. However, this trait was less prominent in behavior than withdrawal from emotional commitment was; withdrawal from emotional commitment was strongly emphasized in the dream.

The dream demonstrated to the dreamer the power of the weaker of his two persisting and incompatible drives; his desire for an intimate, protective, and lasting relationship — a marriage — with implications of direct and socially sanctioned sex won a short-lived and painful victory. No sooner had the relationship began than it became painful (the knockout), and the dreamer tried to break it off. At no time did the dreamer assent the idea; it must have existed, though, or he would not have elaborated on it in the dream. In the end, the stronger tendency (social and emotional withdrawal) asserted itself — to the dreamer's relief and genuine satisfaction. The dream indicated no change in the relative strength of the competing tendencies. The fear of being "trapped into something" was intense and was emphasized by the dreamer's "feeling happy [on waking] . . . that [he] was not married." To conclude, the dream was just one battle won against being "trapped" in a marriage, but it contained no evidence of any weakening of the desire to marry. This result, along with the dreamer's general passivity, the depression (inferred from his feeling of being manipulated by others), and the felt need to be ready to fight for his freedom and personal sovereignty, led to the conclusion that the chance of personality improvement was minimal. This man was sufficiently strong to fight energetically any temptation to get involved emotionally or even to maintain average, normal, interpersonal relations. Some dream scenes were statistically improbable, but nothing was bizarre or empirically impossible. Thinking, verbalization, and visuomotor imagery disclosed nothing defective. His and other dream figures' feelings and actions were appropriate, considering the events. Therefore, worsening of the dreamer's condition seemed unlikely as well.

This dream may be interpreted along psychoanalytical lines. Perhaps the dream illustrated a desperate defense against the breaking through into consciousness of feelings regarding his mother. At the time of the dream, his father was still alive; the father lived 6 more years.

He had lived with his mother and two brothers, both unmarried. The patient was a veteran who, during the war at the front line, was attached to the maintenance department. He returned home because of his severe mental disorder. As a civilian, he became a mechanical assistant; most of the time, however, he was unemployed. He had four hospital admissions within 8 years and many more outpatient contacts. His symptoms varied somewhat, but the most outstanding and lasting was extreme fear of any new situation, social or occupational. Time and again he was disturbed by hallucinations that people on foot or in cars were following him to kill him. He called the police to protect him. He lived in self-imposed, psychosocial isolation even at home, where he stayed in his own room except for meals. He had psychosomatic symptoms such as headaches, extreme physical fatigue, lethargy, depression, and complete withdrawal (during which he sat at a window and looked out for hours at a time without any movement). When his father died, he went into an acute crisis and complained of heart attacks: "My heart hurts terribly." He had a catatonic period that lasted for months; he would not eat during this time. He steadfastly refused psychotherapy. He feared drugs and took them sparingly. He had one course of electroshock treatment. A neuropsychiatric screening 8 years after the dream found him cooperative, coherent, and speaking relevantly. Psychotic ideation was not found, but insight was impaired. He was considered to be suffering from a chronic, catatonic form of schizophrenia. The dream revealed his deep-seated, persistent, consistently negative emotional attitude: the strong desire to avoid emotional involvement with others, male or female. As a mechanic, he was able to work occasionally alone but not with people. His unyielding, ever-present avoidance of any meaningful, lasting, positive, psychosocial relationship with others — even when, once in a while, he was tempted to seek out others — deprived him of any chance to develop mature human qualities.

III FREUD AND PDS

7 Dissimilarity Between Perceptanalytic and Freudian Dream Systems

Dissimilarities between the Perceptanalytic Dream Interpretation System (PDS) and the Freudian Psychoanalytic Dream Interpretation System (FDS) are diverse and fundamental. They concern the purpose and the method of interpretation, the amount and nature of information obtained, and even the subject studied.

The subject of PDS is empirical, raw data, manifest dreams, visuomotor images dreamers "observe" and remember having experienced in sleep; close attention is paid to recovering the most complete and reliable records of dreams as they were actually dreamed. Subjects are encouraged to record their dreams as soon after waking as possible and to emphasize visuomotor aspects. Freud (1933) debased manifest dreams when he wrote:

> We have listened passively (as the patient told us a dream) without putting our powers of reflection into action. What do we do next? We decide to concern ourselves as little as possible with what we have heard, with the manifest dream . . . We will disregard it and follow the main road that leads to the interpretation of dreams. This is to say, we ask the dreamer, too, to free himself from the impression of the manifest dream, to divert his attention from the dream as a whole, to separate portions of its content and to report to us in succession everything that occurs to him in relation to each of these portions, what associations present themselves to him when he focuses on each of them separately. (p. 11)

Freud was unyielding in his view that the manifest dream, as a unitary whole, has no meaning. He exhorted: "Above all avoid explaining one part of the manifest dream by another" (1933, p. 12), calling for destruction of the cohesion and coherence of the dream. He further lowered the scientific value of the manifest dream by adding:

> We often find that a dreamer endeavors to prevent himself from forgetting his dreams by fixing them in writing immediately after waking up. We can tell him that that is no use. For the resistance from which he has extorted the preservation of the text of the dream will then be displaced on to its associations and will make the manifest dream inaccessible to interpretive action. (1933, p. 14)

Moreover, he wrote: "Dreams are not in themselves social utterances, not a means of information. Nor, indeed, do we understand what the dreamer was trying to say to us, and he himself is equally in the dark" (1933, p. 9). Freud (1910) innovated the concept of the latent dream:

> You must differentiate between the manifest dream content, which we clothe in words which seem arbitrary, and the latent dream thoughts, whose presence in the unconscious we must assume . . . The manifest dream content is the disguised surrogate for the unconscious dream thoughts, and this disguising is the manifest dream . . . may be described as a disguised fulfillment of repressed wishes. (p. 200)

According to Freud (1933, p. 12), two steps are usually required to get from the manifest dream to the "latent dream." The dreamer's consecutive free associations to the disjointed parts of the manifest dream "are not yet the latent dream thoughts . . . The dream is seen to be an abbreviated selection from the associations . . . The associations give us far more than we need for formulating the latent dream thoughts" (1959, p. 141). During this "abbreviated selection" by the psychoanalyst, subjectivity influencing the content of this final selection cannot be avoided. Besides, Freud (1959) wrote also that the dreamer's association often comes to a stop precisely before the genuine dream–thought . . . At that point we (the interpreters) intervene on our own. We fill in the hints, draw undeniable conclusions, and give utterance to what the patient has only touched on in his associations" (p. 14). Thus, the latent dream is twice removed from the manifest dream, which is the dream's original version (uncontaminated by an interpreter's changes); the latent dream is even inevitably influenced by the interpreter's own subjective associations. These transformations of the manifest dream can be so great that any similarity between manifest and latent dream thoughts disappears, as, for example, in the case of punishment dreams. Freud (1959) wrote: "In the latter class of dream we are met by the remarkable fact that actually nothing belonging to the latent dream thoughts is taken up into the manifest content of dreams" (p. 14). Under these circumstances, how much does a manifest dream contribute to the unraveling of personality? PDS calls for no alteration of the manifest dream but takes a lively interest in the manifest dream as a unitary whole with logically interrelated subordinate parts.

More dissimilar conceptions of the role of the manifest dream can hardly be imagined. By reducing the manifest dream's significance to that of a starting point for free, serial associations, classical psychoanalysts assign to manifest dreams a role no more significant than that of day residuals. Dreamers and interpreters contribute to latent content; interpretations are dominated by the desire to identify the wishes that were expected to have been fulfilled in dreams but that were concealed from dreamers' conscious perception by means of disguise. By contrast, perceptanalysts pay careful attention to manifest dreams because these dreams constitute their most valuable data. They do not ask for additional associations, but they preserve the emotional, logical, irrational, and dramatic unity resulting from dream figures' involvement in developing dream plots. PDS analysts record dreams to clarify dream events, intents and activities (or postures) of dream figures, and visuomotor details of first and final dream scenes. Perceptanalysts do not limit their search for the meanings of dreams under strictures of any particular theory of personality. Thus PDS and FDS do not address themselves to the same problems, and their methods of arriving at conclusions are basically different. The two systems cannot be directly and validly compared, as their chief aims are disparate. Their reliabilities and validities are unrelated.

The two systems also have different conceptions of the psychological function of dreams. In psychoanalysis, the latent dream that is "substituted for the manifest dream content is the real sense of the dream . . . and appears as the fulfilling of an unsatisfied wish" (Freud, 1953, p. 120). Latent dream content is camouflaged so as to prevent shocking and waking the dreamer. How very different is the perceptanalytic view. The function of a dream can be perceptanalytically defined: (a) as an unconsciously prompted attempt to formulate and clarify the dreamer's personal intrapsychic conflicts; (b) as an unconsciously motivated effort to find possible solutions to these conflicts; (c) as a presentation of a conflict and its intricacies: at the time, dreamers are dimly aware of their dilemma and are getting ready to attempt a solution. When dreaming, we are in a singular state of mind: Conscious and unconscious functions confront each other. By broadening awareness of what has been unconscious, dreams facilitate the process of personality integration; they reduce tensions. Therefore, their psychobiological significance is great.

This conception of the dream function is, in fact, ancient. The belief that night dreams deal with conscious, waking-life anxieties has been strong, constant, and widespread among both investigators and people in general since time immemorial. The only time a considerable group of scientists rejected this belief was in the 19th century. Materialistic philosophy prevailed, and dreams (and sublime feelings and subtle thoughts) were interpreted as meaningless epiphenomena of physiological processes. But even at that time, the traditional view of the dream function was maintained and advanced by investigators. In this century, Jung (1974) gave impetus to the ideas that dreams are purposive and forward-looking and that they concern the dreamer's psychosocial and intrapsychic tension-producing conflicts:

> This is one of the best-proven rules of dream interpretation: What conscious attitudes does it compensate? (p. 101) . . . [We] do better to inquire not why [a person] had a dream, but what its purpose is (p. 103) . . . As a rule the standpoint of the unconscious is complementary to or compensatory for consciousness and thus unexpectedly "different" (p. 118). The ego-conscious personality is only a part of the whole man (1974, p. 78). Morbidity drops away the moment the gulf between the (conscious) ego and the unconscious is closed (1961, p. 144). The psyche is transformed or developed by the relationship of the ego to the contents of the unconscious. The transformation can be read from the dreams (1961, p. 209). Dreams are our most effective aid in building up the personality (1974, p. 101).

He continued: "Serious difficulties have arisen against the [psychoanalytic] wish-fulfillment theory of dreams . . . The first of these difficulties is presented in the fact that people who have experienced a shock, a severe psychic trauma . . . are regularly taken back in their dreams into the traumatic situation." The Freudian system also fails to discover gratified wishes in nightmares and in recurrent dreams. According to Freud, if a wish were satisfied, why should there be need for repeated "gratifications," as in recurrent dreams? Is shocking repetition of a traumatic experience a fulfillment of a wish? For a while, Freud thought so; he thought that the wish for punishment is satisfied in these dream categories. However, he later abandoned this spurious explanation. To say that dreamers wish to be frightened renders the term *wish* meaningless. "Wishing" is usually conceived as a pleasant experience. If striving for undesirable pain and frustration is lumped into the category of "wish," then any striving associated with any emotion, positive or negative, should be thus classified. Use of the word "wish" in such a way would destroy the usefulness of the word. Twenty years after the *Interpretation of Dreams,* Freud, in 1920, declared: "Anxiety dreams and punishment dreams merely put in the place of the interdicted wish-fulfillment the punishment appropriate to it, and are thus the wish-fulfillment of the sense of guilt reacting on the contemned impulse" (Rickman, 1953, p. 181). With this kind of reasoning, any human affect or action, conscious and unconscious, can be said to be an expression of a wish. To complicate matters further, Freud insisted that the fulfilled wish can be unraveled only from the "latent dream"; and the free associations to portions of the manifest dreams, which constitute latent dreams, are difficult to understand. Using Freud's (1953) own words:

> Two fundamentally different kinds of psychical process are concerned in the formation of dreams. One of these produces perfectly rational dream-

thoughts, of no less validity than normal thinking, while the other treats these thoughts in a manner which is in the highest degree bewildering and irrational. We have segregated this second psychical process as being the dream-work proper. What light have we now to throw upon its origin? It would not be possible for us to answer this question if we had not made some headway in the study of the psychology of the neuroses, and particularly of hysteria. We have found from this that the same irrational psychical processes, and others that we have not specified, dominate the production of hysterical symptoms . . . Normal thoughts have been submitted to abnormal treatment: they have been transformed into the symptom by means of condensation and the formation of compromises, by way of superficial associations and in disregard of contradictions, and also, it may be, along the path of regression. (p. 597)

Freud (1953) draws the following conclusions regarding the etiology of sleep dreams:

We accordingly borrow the following thesis from the theory of hysteria: A normal train of thought is only submitted to abnormal psychical treatment of the sort we have been describing if an unconscious wish, derived from infancy, and in a state of repression, has been transferred on to it. In accordance with this thesis we have constructed our theory of dreams on the assumption that the dream-wish, which provides the motive power, invariably originates from the unconscious — an assumption which, as I myself am ready to admit, cannot be proved to hold generally, though neither can it be disproved. (p. 598)

Freud (1953) claimed that not only hysterical symptoms but also psychotic symptoms are, like dreams, fulfillments of wishes:

My own researches have taught me that in this fact [i.e., being fulfillments of wishes] lies the key to a psychological theory of both dreams and psychoses . . . The rapid sentence of ideas in dreams is paralleled by the flight of ideas in psychoses. In both there is a complete lack of sense of time. In dreams the personality may be split — when, for instance, the dreamer's own knowledge is divided between two persons and when, in the dream, the extraneous ego corrects the actual one. This is precisely on a par with the splitting of the personality that is familiar to us in hallucinatory paranoia; the dreamer too hears his own thoughts pronounced by extraneous voices. (p. 91)

This is a striking example of Freud's hasty and irrelevant theoretical thinking. Completely overlooked is the essential and great difference between being awake (the psychotic) and being asleep, and not being aware of and not mentally responding to real sensory impressions (the normal, non-psychotic sleeper). The environmental conditions and the demands for adequate adjustment are radically different. The psychotic misperceives or, more frequently, misinterprets sensory impressions, mixing them with correct impressions and valid thoughts, which results in delusions. The non-psychotic normal clearly differentiates waking thinking from dream thinking; the moment he awakens, he regains valid recognition of reality. Freud (1953) expressed the hope that "It is quite likely . . . that we shall be working towards an explanation of the psychoses while we are endeavoring to throw some light on the mystery of dreams" (p. 92).

Today, when so much has been learned experimentally about the reasoning, affects, physiology, brain pathology, and the process and quality of schizophrenic deterioration, the difference between psychotic and unimpaired normal thinking appears striking, both in waking life and in sleep dreams. PDS contains no such dubious proposition that dreams have characteristics of psychotic mental dysfunctions. Some dream features are pathognomonic of schizophrenia, but not all dreams of all schizophrenics are pathognomonic; non-schizophrenics do not ever produce pathognomonic dreams.

In PDS, the main and central object of study, the systems are essentially compatible because they investigate different mental products. During pursuit of latent dream thoughts, the classical Freudian eliminates the manifest tions to the disjointed parts of the manifest dream. The interpreter, not the dreamer, breaks the manifest dream into fragments before asking the dreamer for conscious, consecutive associations. In PDS, meanings of concrete nouns are always inferred by relating the nouns to main themes (revealed by verbs) of whole, manifest dreams, which are always viewed as logical, unitary wholes. Freud said his free association method is useless in unraveling dream symbols. Relevant explanation of dream symbols require consideration of whole dreams as presentation of a unitary action. Psychoanalysts contribute to dreamers' latent dreams when they prompt, summarize, and abstract the dreamers' associations. Finally and most important, they interpret the abstracted associations in accordance with Freud's theory of personality genetics. By contrast, PDS treats the manifest dream as an inviolable, empirical, objective fact, a mental product produced spontaneously and unconsciously; PDS views the entire manifest dream and the arrangement of its parts as the most valuable empirical data, not to be contaminated by interpreters' interference or dreamers' additional, conscious associations to words selected by the dream interpreters.

As mental disintegration increases, frequency of dreaming decreases. In most apparently bizarre and confused dreams, this impression of unreality results from an evaluation of dream logic and the sense of reality. Evaluation is based on criteria applicable to empirical, objective reality consciously perceived. But dream images are not conscious sensory perceptions of external, empirical events occurring synchronously and independently of the dreamer and outside the dreamer's inert body resting in bed. A synchronous, empirical event perceived in waking life and an imagined dream event erroneously believed to be a real empirical event are fundamentally dissimilar happenings. Indeed, a world of differences exists between them—the world of action. Overt, psychomotor dream behavior is vicarious; it is realized exclusively in imagination and in kinesthetic sensations. Waking life and dreams share potential action tendencies, not the realization of these tendencies; dreams, however, are more likely to make dreamers aware of their action tendencies than waking life is. In waking life, we can and do repress perturbing desires and drives from awareness. In dreams, these tendencies and their countertendencies are expressed much more freely; thus, we become aware of them as we watch the dream events unfold. This is why accurately interpreted dreams throw so much light on dreamers' attitudes toward others, on psychosocial reactions and intentions, and on inner feelings relating to dreamers' roles in interpersonal relationships. We understand dream messages when we understand the visual images in which the messages are conveyed. Pictorial dream language has specific assets and limitations. When we understand the psycholinguistic structure of this language and use our understanding to translate the visuomotor dream content into public, standardized, verbal language, we make practically all impressions of so-called confusion and unreality vanish. Of greatest relevance are the Rule of Assent and Dissent, The Rule of Primacy of Verbs and Abstract Nouns, and the Rule of Symbolism. The implications of Axioms A and B are also pertinent. Occasionally the universally preferred Axiom B leads to conclusions contradicting the dreamer's attitudes and experiences; however, if the same attitudes and experiences are interpreted according to Axiom A, conclusions are found to be valid and highly, dynamically, important.

FDS looks toward the past in search of the primary and fundamental cause of personality conflicts and ungratified wishes. PDS looks toward the future and conceives the dream as an attempt to clarify current intrapsychic conflicts and to look for possible solutions. Individuals who are very ambitious, who strive to achieve something outstanding but difficult, and who sporadically become frustrated in their endeavors dream often and have complex dreams.

The two dream systems differ strikingly in degrees of objectivity, reliability, and verifiability. No formal, stable, valid guidelines are provided to keep the FDS interpeter on the path of objectivity. PDS conclusions are couched in terms that are verifiable by independent, empirical evidence. Advanced formularization of PDS greatly reduces, if not eliminates, subjectivism. PDS interpretation is largely independent of particular lexicological meanings of dream content.

To demonstrate the functioning of FDS and PDS, we compare Freud's interpretation of his Irma Injection Dream with the PDS interpretation in chapter 8.

The greatest and most significant differences between PDS and other dream systems, including Freud's, are: the advanced formularization and systematization of the process of unraveling the meanings of manifest dreams; the basic PDS postulate that dream events be assessed as if they were empirical facts observed consciously in waking life. The visuomotor language of sleep dreams, however, must first be translated properly into the standardized, public, verbal language. Thus, PDS produces personality assessments that are empirically verifiable and that relate to dreamers' current psychosocial conditions.

8

The "Irma Injection" Dream: Perceptanalytic and Freudian Interpretations

This chapter illustrates the similarities and differences between the Perceptanalytic Dream System (PDS) and the Freudian Dream System (FDS) through a comparison of Freud's own interpretation of his "Irma Injection" dream with the PDS reinterpretation of it. The differences outweigh the similarities by far.

FREUD'S "IRMA INJECTION" DREAM

During the night of July 23–24, 1895, at the age of 39, Freud had the "Irma Injection" dream. It is a celebrated dream, being the first to have serial postdream interpretations applied to it by Freud and being the dream most extensively analyzed by a host of subsequent writers. The dream led to Freud's self-analysis and, in turn, to the development of psychoanalysis. "Irma Injection" is the first dream discussed in Freud's *The Interpretation of Dreams* (1953). It is also an important seminal dream.

During the early part of 1895, Freud treated Irma, "a young lady who was on very friendly terms with [him] and [his] family" (p. 106). This treatment ended with partial success; the patient was relieved of her hysterical anxiety but did not lose all her somatic symptoms. On the day preceding the dream, Otto, "a junior colleague, one of [Freud's] oldest friends, who had been staying with . . . Irma, and her family at their country resort" (p. 106), described how he had found her: "She is better but not quite well" (p. 106). Freud was "annoyed" by these words and their tone: "I detected a reproof in them . . . that I had promised the patient too much . . . The same evening I wrote out Irma's case history to give it to Dr. M. (a common friend who was the leading figure in our circle) in order to justify myself" (p. 106). On the same day, Freud had been told by his wife that she had invited Irma to her forthcoming birthday party. The Freuds lived outside Vienna, in an impressive villa called "Bellevue"; they had rented the villa for the summer. Freud had the dream there and also placed the dream events there. He wrote down the dream events immediately on waking:

> A large hall — numerous guests whom we are receiving. Among them was Irma. I at once took her on one side as though to answer her letter and to reproach her for not having accepted my solution yet. I said to her: "If you still get pains, it's really only your fault." She replied: "If you only knew what pains I've got now in my throat and stomach and abdomen — it's choking me." I was alarmed and looked at her. She looked pale and puffy. I thought to myself that after all I must be missing some organic trouble. I took her to the window and looked down her throat, and she showed signs of recalcitrance, like women with artificial dentures. I thought to myself that there was really no need for her to do that (to be fussy). The mouth opened quite wide, and on the right I found a big white patch. At another place I saw extensive whitish gray scabs upon some remarkable curly structures which were evidently modelled on the turbinal bones of the nose.
>
> I at once called in Dr. M., and he repeated the examination and confirmed it. Dr. M. looked quite different from usual: he was very pale, he walked with a limp, and his chin was clean-shaven. My friend Otto was now standing beside her as well, and my friend Leopold was percussing her through her bodice and saying: "She has a dull area low down on the left." He also indicated that a portion of the skin on the left shoulder was infiltrated. (I noticed this, just as he did, in spite of her dress.) M. said: "There is no doubt it's an infection, but no matter; dysentery will supervene and the toxin will be eliminated." We realized immediately, too, how the infection originated. Not long before, when she was feeling unwell, my friend Otto had given her an injection of a preparation of propyl, propyls . . . proponic acid . . . trimethylamin (and I saw before me the formula for this printed in heavy type) . . . injections of that sort ought not to be made so thoughtlessly . . . and probably the syringe had not been clean (p. 107).

FREUD'S INTERPRETATION OF THE "IRMA" DREAM

To extract latent thoughts that are not "confused" and that are not selected "arbitrarily" from the unconscious, Freud divided the dream into 22 sections, each containing a distinct idea. He then consciously free-associated to each section separately, from first to last. These associations covered 14 printed pages and carried Freud far afield from what he had said was the underlying and most significant thought of his dream, namely, that he was not responsible for Irma's current illness. Actually, all serial, postdream associations that exonerated Freud implicitly and that accused Otto and Irma explicitly had already appeared in the manifest dream. For example, Freud quoted his manifest dream: "Injections of that sort ought not to be made so thoughtlessly." He also wrote that he had reproached Irma "for not having accepted [his] solution; [he] said: 'If you still get pains, it's your own fault.' " Freud explained: "At that time my task was fulfilled when I had informed a patient of the hidden meaning of his symptoms. I considered that I was not responsible for whether he accepted the solution or not" (p. 108).

Influencing people, moving them by persuasion, making them "accept solutions" concerned Freud greatly at the time. In the manifest dream, Freud easily dominated his professional colleagues and flaunted Irma's examination before the assembled guests. Only Irma was neither impressed nor persuaded; she declined the "solution." Thus, whereas he felt comfortable among his peers and was certain of his prominence, he was dubious about his therapeutic method. In his latent dream, Freud associated only frustrated attempts to influence others and to make them agree with him. Irma was joined by other dissenters — Dr. M., Freud's older brother, Otto, and one of Irma's lady friends, who also would have become "recalcitrant" had she become Freud's patient. The detailed treatment of the matter of "influence" revealed Freud's absorbing desire to improve his therapeutic technique: "Solutions" or "injections" should not be administered in haste, but with particular care.

By his own testimony, Freud was keenly aware before his dream of his strong desire to be absolved of guilt for Irma's continuing ailments. This wish was plain in the manifest dream: They were directly aware "how the infection originated . . . Otto had given her an injection." The following statement of Freud, therefore, is baffling: "The dream of Irma Injection does not at first produce the impression that it represents a wish of the dreamer's as fulfilled . . . I myself was not aware of the fact until I had undertaken the analysis" (p. 136). The conscious free associations that Freud considered the key to interpreting his dream can be summarized.

The building, the hall that was the scene of the dream events, had been intended to be a place of public entertainment; it never served this purpose but retained the name of "Bellevue."

Freud said (in the dream to Irma): "If you still get pains, it's your own fault.' I might have said that to her in waking life . . . I was especially anxious not to be responsible for the pains which she still had" (p. 107).

Irma "complained more of feelings of nausea and disgust" (p. 109) and "scarcely" of throat, abdomen, or stomach. She was not pale and puffy but "had always a rosy complexion" (p. 109). "If Irma's pains had an organic basis, once again I could not be held responsible for curing them; my treatment only set out to get rid of hysterical pains" (p. 109).

"I had never had any occasion to examine Irma's oral cavity. . . . 'There was really no need for her to do that.' [to hesitate opening her mouth at his request] . . . was a compliment to Irma" (p. 109), implying that the young woman had good, healthy teeth and needed no dentures.

"The scab on the turbinal bones [reminded him] of [his] anxiety concerning [his] own health . . . (The real) Irma did not suffer from this affliction. I wondered why I decided on this choice of symptoms but could not think of an explanation" (p. 111). In later years, whitish gray scabs were found in Freud's throat; in 1928, this condition was diagnosed as cancer, from which Freud suffered until the end of his life at 83.

Was Freud's central nervous system so sensitive so as to alert him to cancer in the dream before the disease had become manifest? Hippocrates thought this was possible. Was the Irma Dream precognitive? Freud used cocaine to alleviate his pains and prescribed it for others, some of whom died, among them "a close and helpful friend" (p. 111).

> I at once called in Dr. M. . . . The "at once" was sufficiently striking to require a special explanation. It reminded me of a tragic event in my practice. I had on one occasion produced a severe toxic state in a woman patient by repeatedly prescribing what was at that time regarded as a harmless remedy (cocaine) and had hurriedly turned for assistance and support to my experienced senior colleague. (p. 111)

Dr. M. actually had an "unhealthy appearance," but the other two features attributed to Dr. M. in the dream belonged to Freud's older brother. "I had a similar reason for being in an ill-humor with each of them: they had both rejected a certain suggestion I had recently laid before them" (p. 112). Otto and Leopold were young physicians related to each other, and they were Freud's personal friends. They were his assistants in a neurological clinic. Otto was distinguished for his quickness, whereas the other was slow but sure. "If in the dream I was contrasting Otto with the prudent Leopold, I was evidently doing so to the advantage of the latter. The comparison was similar to the one between my disobedient patient Irma and the friend whom I regarded as wiser than she was" (p. 113). Concerning the "dull area low down," Freud "had a vague notion of something in the nature of a metastatic affection" (p. 113). There was nothing wrong with Irma's left shoulder. Freud wrote: "I saw at once that this was the rheumatism in my own shoulder, which I invariably notice if I sit up late into the night" (p. 113). In the dream, Freud and Leopold noticed Irma's shoulder infiltration. "This was in any case only an interpolation . . . Frankly, I had no desire to penetrate more deeply at this point" (p. 113). "Dr. M. said: 'Dysentery will supervene and the toxin will be eliminated.' At first this struck me as ridiculous . . . There seemed to be some theoretical notion that morbid matter can be eliminated through the bowels. Could it be that I was trying to make fun of Dr. M.'s fertility in producing far-fetched explanations?" (p. 114). Freud recalled next that he could not help reproaching [himself] for having put [a patient of his] in a situation in which he might have contracted some organic trouble on top of his hysterical intestinal disorder. Moreover "dysentery" sounds not unlike "diptheria," a word of ill omen. The "no matter" in the dream was intended as a consolation . . . [He] had a feeling that [he] was only trying in that way to shift the blame from [himself] . . . Nevertheless [he] had a sense of awkwardness at having invented such a severe illness for Irma simply in order to clear [himself]. It looked so cruel (p. 114).

He continued:

I could no longer feel any doubt that this part of the dream ('no matter') was expressing derision at physicians who are ignorant of hysteria . . . Dr. M. was just as little in agreement with my 'solution' as Irma herself. So I had already revenged myself in this dream on two people.(p. 115)

The group's immediate knowledge of the origin of the infection in the dream "was remarkable; only just before [the group] had had no knowledge of it, for the infection was only revealed by Leopold" (p. 115). Freud's surprise and his exclamatory reference to Leopold imply that only thorough, painstaking research is prudent and leads to the discovery of pertinent causes of human experiences. At the same time, blaming Otto for the "thoughtless" injection, Freud condemned quick and careless fact-finding. The "preparation of propyl" that Otto had injected into Irma reminded Freud of the bottle of liqueur that Otto had presented to the Freuds as a gift: "This liqueur gave off such a strong smell of fusel oil that I refused to touch it" (p. 116). On the bottle appeared "the word 'Ananas,' [the sound of which] bears a remarkable resemblance to that of [his] patient Irma's family name" (p. 115). Freud wrote of trimethylamin:

This substance led me to sexuality, the factor to which I attributed the greatest importance in the origin of the nervous disorders which it was my aim to cure . . . If I wanted to find an excuse for the failure of my treatment, what I could best appeal to would no doubt be this fact of her widowhood, which her friends would be so glad to see changed . . . Trimethylamin was an allusion not only to the immensely powerful factor of sexuality, but also to a person whose agreement I recalled with satisfaction whenever I felt isolated in my opinions. Surely this friend who played so large a part in my life must appear again somewhere in these trains of thought. Yes! For he had a special knowledge of the consequences of affections of the nose and its accessory cavities; and he had drawn scientific attention to some very remarkable connections between the turbinal bones and the female organs of sex. (pp. 116–117)

The friend was Fliess. Freud added:

I noticed that in accusing Otto of thoughtlessness in handling chemical substances I was touching upon the story of the unfortunate Mathilde, which gave grounds for the same accusation against myself. Here, I was evidently collecting instances of my conscientiousness, but also of the reverse (p. 117). [Concerning the dirty syringe, Freud wrote:] This was yet another accusation against Otto . . . I was proud of the fact that in two years I had not caused a single infiltration. I took constant pains to be sure that the syringe was clean . . . I have now completed the interpretation of the dream (p. 118) . . . The conclusion of the dream was that I was not responsible for the persistence of Irma's pains, but that Otto was (p. 118). Otto was by giving her an incautious injection of an unsuitable drug — a thing I should never have done. Irma's pains were the result of an injection with a dirty needle (p. 119) . . . I will not pretend that I have completely uncovered the meaning of the dream (pp. 120–121) . . . If anyone should be tempted to express a hasty condemnation of my reticence, I would advise him to make the experiment of being franker than I am (p. 121).

Toward the end of his book on dream interpretation Freud (1953) observed: "There are special reasons . . . why I have not given any exhaustive treatment to the part played in dreams by the world of sexual ideas and why I have avoided analyzing dreams of obviously sexual content. . . An explanation of sexual dreams would involve me deeply in the still unsolved problems of perverson and bisexuality" (pp. 606–607).

PDS INTERPRETATION OF THE "IRMA" DREAM

The main premise of PDS is that: dreams present, in their visuomotor imagery, dreamers' unresolved conflicts between mutually exclusive intentions; dreams frequently indicate possible solutions to the conflicts. PDS aims at clear formulations of the conflicts that disquiet and are at best only vaguely conscious. According to Axiom A, all dream figures represent different aspects of dreamers' personalities — which are at different levels of assent and dissent. This amounts to confrontation between dreamers' different intentional dynamic subsystems. PDS assumes the obvious, namely, that no dreamer is a perfectly consistent psychosocial unit, and that the dreamer never actuates all his diverse drives simultaneously. Some intents (action tendencies, affects, attitudes) are incompatible with others, thus causing stress (fear of failure, feeling of personal inadequacy, anticipation of disaster, anxiety). Dreams are brought about by the desire to regain peace and security. Axiom A is the more easily verifiable one; it is also more valid and psychodynamically more relevant than Axiom B. Therefore, Axiom A is used to infer the meaning of dreams from the dream reports. It is advisable to start the interpretation of a dream by contrasting the assented traits with the most dissented traits.

In the interpretation of the Irma dream, the assented traits are those in which Freud attributed to himself. The figure that is most unlike Freud (i.e. Irma), possesses Freud's (the dreamer's), most dissented traits.

Foremost is Freud's striking, tenacious purposefulness. Freud was plainly disturbed by Irma's unexpected recent signs of illness because he had discharged her only a short time ago as being cured. He needed to clear himself of responsibility for Irma's relapse, persistently directing all his activities toward that goal. This was not easy because he himself suspected that he might "overlook something organic." He re-examined Irma, then surrounded himself with a hastily organized medical concilium whose members also examined Irma to verify, confirm, and eventually to increase the number of pathological findings. They all confirmed Freud's findings. However, the right diagnosis, remedial treatment, and causation of Irma's current organic ailment, were authoritatively formulated by Freud. He even gently ridiculed his former professor and now colleague. Freud revealed his managerial interest and ability, which suited him very well, and showed that he was the dominating figure without any doubt.

It was important to Freud to prove that he was not responsible for Irma's relapse once it had been established that she was once again ill. "The conclusion of the dream was that I was not responsible for the persistence of Irma's pains, but that Otto was" (1953, p. 118). According to Axiom A, this is a self-accusation of moderate degree. Freud became aware of it during his post-dream associations. To quote Freud's (1953) own words:

> I called to mind the obscure disagreeable impression I had when Otto brought me the news of Irma condition. . . . It was as though he had said to me: 'You don't take your medical duties seriously enough. You're not conscientious; you don't carry out what you've undertaken.' Thereupon . . . I could produce evidence of how highly conscientious I was. . . It was a noteworthy fact that this material also included some disagreeable memories, which supported my friend Otto's accusation rather than my own vindication. (p. 120)

We must also conclude that the dream traits of "slow but sure Leopold" were Freud's own personal and moderately dissented traits, as were the dream traits of Otto, "distinguished for his quickness" (p. 112). Freud demonstrated these two different trait sets both in real life as well as in his Irma dream. In the dream, Freud had the clinical facts thoroughly investigated by three experts, working independently. His unwillingness to assume any organic illness yielded in face of the empirical evidence. On the other hand, the theoretical speculations regarding the cause of Irma's organic illness and desirable treatment improvements (manner of injection and cleanliness of syringe) were products of sudden intuition: "We were directly aware, too [aside from the infection] of the origin of the infection" (p. 107). "This direct knowledge in the dream was remarkable. Only just before, we had had no knowledge of it." This difference between the watchful observation of facts and the hasty formulation of hypotheses was characteristic of Freud's thinking. His original and significant factual observations differed conspicuously in degree of validity from his conceptual innovations. It took him decades to recognize that his conception of the difference between conscious and unconscous must be fundamentally revised. In 1923, at the age of 67, Freud (1953a) proclaimed in *The Ego And The Id* (orig. publ. 1923):

> The Unconscious does not coincide with what is repressed; it is still true that all that is repressed is Unconscious, but not that the whole Unconscious is repressed. A part of the Ego, too — and Heaven knows how important a part — may be Unconscious, undoubtedly is Unconscious. . . When we find ourselves thus confronted by the necessity of postulating a third Unconscious which is not repressed, we must admit that the property of being unconscious begins to lose significance for us. It becomes a quality which can have many implications. . . Nevertheless, we must beware of ignoring this property (of being unconscious), for in the last resort the quality of being conscious or not is the single ray of light that penetrates the obscurity of depth-psychology. (p. 247)

The first pages of *The Ego And The Id* are lucid and in much closer agreement with reality than Freud's early metapsychology:

> There is a coherent organization of mental processes, which we call his (the individual's) ego. . . From this ego proceed the repressions too, by means of which an attempt is made to cut off certain trends in the mind not merely from consciousness but also from other forms of manifestation and activity. . . We have come upon something in the ego itself which is also unconscious, which behaves exactly as the repressed, that is, which produces powerful effects without itself being conscious and which requires special work before it can be made conscious. From the point of view of analytic practice the consequence of this piece of observation is that we land in endless confusion and difficulty if we. . . derive neuroses from a conflict between the conscious and the unconscious. We shall have to substitute for this antithesis another, taken from our understanding of the structural conditions of the mind, namely, the antithesis between the organized ego and what is repressed and dissociated from it. (pp. 246–247)

However, Freud retained the very effective technique of serial free associations. This technique allows the therapist and self-therapist to hold the repressed and dissociated mental processes on a "loose leash" as it were. Because of this therapeutic aid, psychotherapy became possible; it contributed greatly to the development of individual and group psychotherapy.

According to Axiom A, Freud assigned his most dissented traits to Irma; she differed from Freud in sex, age, education, duties, style of living, etc. She was (in the dream) a sick, complaining, submissive person who surrendered to the control of others with only token resistance. Having come as an invited guest to Mrs. Freud's birthday party, held in an impressive suburban location, with distinguished company present, Irma did not expect to be scolded and physically examined in front of the guests. She was unexpectedly treated with little respect. Somatic symptoms were found and there was "no doubt" that she suffered from an infection. She was sick and complained of various pains: "I feel as if I'm choking." (Respiratory difficulties are associated regularly with fear and anxiety.) She looked pale and puffy. So energetic and ambitious a man as Freud would find disturbing his partly repressed and significantly dissented traits, the passive tendency and dependency on others. Freud wrote in a letter to his "dear friend" Fliess, whose opinions he valued highly, on the day following the Irma dream: "This year I am sick after all and must come to you" (Schur, 1972, p. 88). Twelve years later Freud still remembered the period of his specimen dream. Schur (1972) states:

> For instance, in a letter to Jung written in September 1907 Freud confided: 'I would like to tell you. . . of my many years of honorable but painful isolation which started after I had my first glimpse into the new world; of my closest friends' lack of interest and understanding; of the anxious periods when I myself believed I had been mistaken and wondered how I could still turn to advantage a bungled life for the sake of my family; of the gradually growing conviction that kept clinging to the interpretation of dreams as to a rock in a stormy sea, and of the calm assurance that finally took possession of me.' Obviously, in 1895, Freud had not yet achieved this calm assurance. (p. 88)

Biographical facts confirm the inner affective tension which disturbed Freud and was painful to him. They also confirm Freud's strong dissent of his pains and worries. At this same time, Freud manifested his great strength and creativeness *The Interpretation of Dreams,* which he considered the greatest intellectual achievement of his life. It seems that his worrisome thoughts and physical distress fostered his originality. "Freud repeatedly referred to the fact that he was most creative during periods of mild physical discomfort" (Schur, p. 97).

One can interpret dreams in a great variety of ways. Obviously, those systems that best meet the requirements of empirical science, should be preferred, that is, those that provide the greatest amount of significant information: valid and objective knowledge about the dreamer's personality. In line with this criterion is the use of PDS in unraveling a second intrapsychic conflict of Freud. The Irma dream is one of those rare dreams that offers original and fruitful ideas, and solves a procedural difficulty. It cleared a conflict that Freud experienced regarding the efficacy of his psychotherapeutic method. Analyzing the dream years later, Freud (1953) wrote:

> I reproached Irma for not having accepted my solution (etiological explanation of her symptoms). I said: 'If you still have pains, it's your own fault.' I might have said that to her in waking life, and I may actually have done so. It was my view at that time—though I have since recognized it as a wrong one—that my task was fulfilled when I had informed a patient of the hidden meaning of his

symptoms: I considered that I was not responsible for whether he accepted the solution or not — though this was what success depended on. I owe it to this mistake, which I have now fortunately corrected, that my life was made easier at a time when, in spite of all my inevitable ignorance, I was expected to produce therapeutic successes. I noticed, however, that the words which I spoke to Irma in the dream showed that I was specially anxious not to be responsible for the pains which she still had. If they were her fault, they could not be mine. Could it be that the purpose of the dream lay in this direction? (pp. 108–109).

Most dreams develop a theme. In the beginning of the dream Freud reproached Irma for causing her own pains, but near the end of the dream he exonerated Irma, as well as himself, from responsibility for Irma's current illness. "I [Freud] thought to myself I must be missing something organic" (1953, p. 107), that is, something incurable by his psychotherapy. Freud suddenly became aware that a "thoughtless injection" given Irma by Otto infected her and made her physically ill (Freud, 1953, p. 107). Because the affects, thoughts and action tendencies revealed in sleep dreams pertain to human relationships that matter to the dreamer, everything in dreams must be translated into terms of psychosocial relations. This rule applies to the Irma dream's "solution," "injection," "syringe" and "clean." Thus, "solution" means explanation of the hidden meaning of psychoneurotic symptoms, "injection" means words and acts designed to influence a patient in a specific manner, "syringe" means the way in which the message is communicated, and "clean" means that the motives of the communicator be above reproach, and, in the case of a psychotherapist, be guided by the patient's best psychological interest, uncontaminated by the therapist's desire for gain at the patient's expense. Today, when we translate those four key terms into concepts that are relevant and meaningful in describing the relationship between patient and psychotherapist, we understand how Irma's recent mental difficulties and Freud's earlier successful psychotherapy of her were possible. Freud (in the person of Otto) had explained to Irma the etiology of her psychoneurotic symptoms in a heedless and ineffectual manner making her condition worse rather than better; this happened despite his conviction that his analysis of her psychodynamics was correct. Freud (1953) states:

> It was my view at that time that my task was fulfilled when I had informed a patient of the hidden meaning of his symptoms: I considered that I was not responsible for whether he accepted the solution or not — though this was what success depended on. I owe it to this mistake, which I have now fortunately corrected, that my life was made easier at a time when, in spite of all my inevitable ignorance, I was expected to produce therapeutic successes. (p. 108)

This last sentence is an appealing admission that Freud's creative work progressed gradually. Practically all great ideas developed long and gradually. This is true of individual authors and of great cooperative endeavors.

The second remark which ended the dream was: "Probably the syringe had not been clean." This means, translated into psychosocial relations: The explanation of her symptoms' meaning to Irma had probably not been quite honest. It is important that neither Otto's injection nor the syringe appeared visually in the dream, therefore their psychodynamic significance is secondary. Moreover, Freud said in surprise: "We were directly aware of the origin of the infection. This direct knowledge in the dream was remarkable" (p. 115). It was remarkable in that it did not need to be conveyed by visual images; it was a case of instant knowledge. During Irma's reexamination Freud became frightened: "I thought to myself that after all I must be missing some . . trouble" (p. 107). The last two remarks did not belong to the dream proper, which deals with intrapsychic conflicts. Those remarks do not refer to Irma's specific pains and responsibility for them, but are of a general, abstract nature. They formulate rules of correct psychotherapeutic behavior in all cases treated psychoanalytically. They constitute a step forward by improving effectiveness of treatment. Furthermore, they led to the realization of the importance of the therapist's personality in treatment, and to the questions of transference and countertransference. Entailed in the clean-syringe–concept is the demand that the psychotherapist not taint treatment by a conscious or an unconscious wish for personal gain at the expense of the patient.

Normally, dreamers are about to wake up when they verbalize thoughts in grammatically and logically correct sentences about environmental reality that is not exposed to view in the dream's visuomotor imagery.

Freud (1954) confided in a letter to his friend Fliess, dated May 25, 1895:

I have had an inhuman amount to do. I have found my tyrant, and in his service I know no limits. My tyrant is psychology. . . . I am plagued by two ambitions: to see how the theory of mental functioning takes shape if quantitative considerations, a sort of economics of nerve-force, are introduced into it; and secondly, to extract from psychopathology what may be of benefit to normal psychology. (pp. 119–20)

Freud's personal physician for more than 10 years, Schur (1972) reported:

The years 1893–1900 were in many respects the most dramatic in Freud's life (p. 5). . . . Physical illness, ostracism, prejudice, the everpresent threat of want, and nearly complete isolation, all increased [Freud's] turmoil. . . And yet during this decade Freud founded a new science, The Interpretation of Dreams. (p. 221)

In addition to Irma and Freud, there were three medical colleagues of Freud in the dream who were carriers of Freud's moderately dissented traits (Axiom A). Freud's former professor and now colleague, Dr. M., was "not his usual self." He was physically weak but behaved in a self-assured manner;

he reached his conclusion quickly and announced it with dogmatic authoritarianism, making himself appear somewhat ridiculous "in producing far-fetched explanations and making unexpected pathological connections" (Freud, 1953, p. 114). "Prudent Leopold was slow but sure (while) Otto was distinguished by his quickness" (p. 112). "When Irma was feeling unwell, my friend Otto had given her an injection . . . thoughtlessly" (p. 107). During the free-associating following the dream, Freud recalled: "I had been the first to recommend the use of cocaine, in 1884, and this recommendation had brought serious reproaches down on me. The misuse of that drug had hastened the death of a dear friend of mine" (p. 111). Biographers Ernest Jones, Max Schur, and Freud himself (in his *Letters to Wilhelm Fliess*) provide ample information that shows how Freud's PDS assented and dissented traits plainly manifested themselves in Freud's behavior and mental processes.

Throughout his life Freud was a persistent and inventive author, editor, organizer, teacher and leader. The Irma dream is a representative sample of his rich and complex personality. In this dream he snatched victory from the jaws of defeat. He improved his psychotherapeutic technique considerably by his unexpected intuitive and creative ideas about the "dirty syringe" and the incautious thoughtless manner of the "injection." Incidentally, Freud's comments about the "injection" imply that making the patient conscious of "the hidden meaning of his symptoms" is not enough. The therapist must convey the causation and meaning of the patient's neurotic symptoms in such a way that the patient accepts the explanation. In other words, assenting the explanation as PDS defines "assent" is the essential and necessary condition of success of psychoanalytic treatment. Unraveling the unconscious origin and effects of neurotic habits is indispensable but not sufficient to assure authentic and lasting cure.

The Irma dream is a story rich in content, held together well by its logical coherence, describing systematically developing activities that preserve unity of space and time. Only an exceptionally gifted, affectively complex, but strong and consistent personality, capable of great personal independence and civil courage, could produce such an extraordinary dream. Freud's desire to excel as a scientific genius and to be recognized for his great contributions is disclosed throughout the dream, from beginning to end. For example, the action took place in a suburban villa, a spacious building, in the presence of refined society; Irma's social background, the social formalities at the close of the last century, and the occasion (Mrs. Freud's birthday party) were hardly the place and time to subject a respected invited lady to an exhaustive physical examination. Freud gave priority to his intellectual and professional interests over social amenities. The PDS interpretation of the Irma dream revealed Freud's creative inner struggles in that germinal period of his industrious and painstaking life. The PDS results were obtained thanks to the basic PDS postulate: That sleep dreams be interpreted as if they were events observed in empirical reality—after pertinent elements of the dream have undergone a semantic change in accordance with the PDS interpretive rules.

According to Freud, the true message of dreams is revealed in the post-manifest dream free associations that are the "latent dreams." Yet he finished his latent Irma dream analysis with this paragraph: "I will not pretend that I have completely uncovered the meaning of this dream or that its interpretation is without a gap" (Freud, 1953, pp. 120–21). Moreover, he also said: "It was a noteworthy fact that this material [post-dream associations] also included some disagreeable memories, which supported Otto's accusation rather than my own vindication. The material was, as one might say, impartial" (p. 120). This is a courageously frank and significant admission. Both the manifest dream (interpreted according to Axiom A) and the latent dream are ambivalent concerning Freud's responsibility for Irma's recent illness. However, Freud (1953) understandably attaches greater emphasis to exculpation:

> Certain other themes played a part in the dream, which were not so obviously connected with my exculpation from Irma's illness: my daughter's illness and that of my patient who bore the same name, the injurious effect of cocaine, the disorder of my patient who was traveling in Egypt, my concern about my wife's health and about that of my brother and of Dr. M., my own physical ailments, my anxiety about my absent friend who suffered from suppurative rhinitis. (p. 120)

None of these anxious solicitudes can be called pleasant wish fulfillments even when Freud tries to make a virtue out of these worrisome preoccupations. Referring to that list of solicitudes, Freud (1953) tried to console himself with these words:

> But when I came to consider all of these, they could all be collected into a single group of ideas and labelled, as it were, 'concern about my own and other people's health—professional conscientiousness' I called to mind the obscure disagreeable impression I had when Otto brought me the news of Irma's condition. (p. 120)

Great personal ambitions easily lead to disappointments and frustrations, which, in turn, lead to depressing self-criticism or spurious self-estimate. Freud would have been able to infer from his sleep dreams more diverse and more numerous conclusions about himself, conclusions of a verifiable sort, had he not presumed that sleep dreams are a kind of hysterical symptoms. After *The Ego and the Id* (Freud, 1953a/1923) and the change in the conception of the ego (now partly unconscious), psychoanalytic dream interpretation had to change. Freud determined that:

The Id is quite amoral, the Ego strives to be moral, and the Super-Ego can be hyper-moral and cruel as only the Id can be . . . The Ego was now in the lime-light of psychoanalysis, especially as the site of anxiety, reality anxiety, that is, fear caused by anxiety. . . Freud concluded with a description of the pitiful state of the Ego, suffering under the pressure of its three masters. It was clear that the main concern of psychotherapy would now be to relieve the Ego by reducing these pressures and helping it acquire some strength. (Ellenberger, p. 516).

Freud's conceptual innovations in his *The Ego and the Id* (Freud, 1953a) made his view of human psychodynamics resemble that of other thinkers, es-pecially Nietzsche's *Genealogy of Morals* (1887). However, Freud held on to his powerful practical tool of psychotherapy (the method of serial free asso-ciations to parts of the patient's statements and behavior patterns) and to the symbolic significance of apparently inconspicuous words and actions that hide a serious meaning of great personal concern to the unaware patient.

Posthumous fame held no attraction for Freud. He was a hard-working, consistent and persistent organizer, editor, and above all, creative scientific author. Without Freud's inspiration, writings, and autocratic control of the psychoanalytic movement, psychoanalysis would not have become widely known and influential. Freud desired fame during his lifetime (Waelder, 1965). He achieved great fame in the 1920s, the same period his cancer was di-agnosed, yet Freud never gave up his work and writing. His cancer caused constant pain, necessitated numerous operations, and slowly grew worse un-til Freud's death in 1939 at age 83.

IV APPLICATION OF THE PDS

9 Blind Analysis of Sample Dream With Follow-Up

Dan was a young, married, childless man who sought treatment from Albert Biele, M.D., for severe agoraphobia. His wife brought him in unannounced during an acute anxiety attack. After this initial evaluation, the first treatment session was set for the next day. The patient was encouraged to dream, to write his dreams down immediately after awaking, and to bring them to the session. He said this would be impossible, as he had his last dream when he was 12. The next day, he appeared with the following written report of a dream:

> I was in some kind of building with a wooden floor. My wife and I and another man were there. The man pointed down to the floor, to a lizard or catfish. We (man and patient) talked about it. I reached down and picked it up, and it grabbed hold of me with a hind claw. I shook my hand and it (the animal) fell off.

In the hope of obtaining additional visuomotor elements that the patient might have forgotten to write down, Dr. Biele asked some questions about the pictorial aspects of the dream.

Dr. Biele: What kind of lizard?

Patient: The lizard was a mud puppy, an amphibian-like creature. And I felt better when I shook it off.

Dr. Biele: What kind of mud puppy?

Patient: It had funny looking gills on the side of its head, not nice arches, almost like a tree- or finger-type gills.

Dr. Biele: Where was it?

Patient: On the floor that was made with wide wooden boards with cracks between them. The animal was in a crack between the boards.

The written version of the dream consisted of seven terse sentences. Dr. Biele's questions elicited vivid, graphic details that enriched the concisely written dream report.

AXIOM A INTERPRETATION

Psychotherapeutically, Axiom A is more enlightening and consequential than Axiom B. A currently active intrapsychic conflict requires the application of Axiom A.

To extract main conflicts from dreams, therapists must contrast the trait sets that dreamers assigned to themselves — or to dream figures most like themselves, when the dreamers do not appear — with the trait sets attributed to dream figures most unlike themselves. This contrast demonstrates dreamers' intrapsychic conflicts, which are the kernels of the dreams. We cannot have sleep dreams unless we confront in visuomotor imagery at least two mutually exclusive desires (active intentions) that cannot be simultaneously fulfilled. Action is desire invigorated and made visible under the influence of cognition (of means); in this way people maintain interpersonal relations. In dreams, dominant conflicts are between the most assented and the most dissented trait sets.

The assented traits are those of the dreamer in the dream. Dan was the relatively most active figure, the only one that took the initiative to walk up to the other two figures (man and mud puppy) and to make positive contact with both. Contact with the man was low-pitched and conspirational (no one could hear their conversation); it ended as Dan willingly acceding to the man's apparent wish for Dan to pick up the mud puppy. Contact with the lizard was silent and brief but very physically intense; no sooner did Dan touch the lizard than the animal "grabbed hold of [him] with a hind claw." Dan felt better when he shook the lizard off. Translated into the dreamer's intrapsychic processes, the two visuomotor dream scenes concerned the dreamer's intimate involvement with men. He kept thinking of getting involved but was cautious and restrained. He was somewhat ambivalent, as indicated by his having two different figures (the man and himself) share their fascination with the mud puppy. The degrees of dissent were different: On the Scale of Dissent, the dreamer was at level 0, and the man was at level 1. Thus, suppression of the dreamer's desire was in flux. As the dreamer's desire gradually became more intense and conscious (the man continued to draw attention to the mud puppy), the dreamer's dissent vanished. He then assented it in thought and in action. Actual bodily contact with the object of his desire, however, caused acute anxiety and forced the dreamer to beat a hasty retreat. After all, the act of recoiling from bodily contact with men — as represented by the mud puppy — was powerfully dissented (level 11).

The appearance of animals in dreams does not mean that dreamers yearn to change into animals. Dreamers are unconsciously referring to the behavior patterns of the animals manifested in their dreams. Dan knew a lot about reptiles, especially mud puppies. Mud puppies are cold-blooded, which means that the level of their activity depends on the temperature of the environment; in human terms, the level of activity would be related to the magnitude of environmental stimulation. Dan assented strong stimulation from other men but reacted violently to close physical contact and tried to sever such contact immediately. He thus seemed to assent the temptation and also his aggressive defense against gratification of the desire for homosexual experiences. The dream dramatized both the strength of his wish and his vicious, defensive attack against successful tempters. The mud puppy exhibited by far the strongest emotional reaction, and a negative one at that. There were other signs in the dream of his ambivalence toward men. First, the mud puppy was out of its element. It was in a building that had a peculiar floor; the wooden boards had cracks between them. Dan would have needed to step cautiously on such a floor so as not to lose his balance. Furthermore, the mud puppy seemed to hide between two boards. Dan did not notice it until the other man pointed it out. Another sign was the presence of Dan's wife. She was certainly interested in having her husband all to herself, but she, too, was not decisive. She watched the scene but otherwise was a passive, noninterfering observer. According to Axiom A, all these dream characters (the three humans and the animal) represent four different aspects of the dreamer's personality. In real, waking life, these trait sets could not be actuated at the same time. According to Axiom A, the behavior of Dan's wife in the dream signifies that Dan was aware of his psychosexual problem. At times he was very anxious about it, and at other times he was able to consider it with calm attentiveness.

The homoerotic inclination was intimated in the dream by a number of elements. Foremost was Dan's preoccupation with the man and the mannish, elongated salamander. Salamanders' tails break off easily on touch and usually grow back, which suggests, on a greatly dissented level, that the organ is easily injured but does recover. Lack of close contact with the female — contrasted with the intense emotions aroused between Dan and the male dream figures — suggested that Dan was cool toward his wife, which, in turn, intimated that Dan was sexually impotent. The hind claw was also significant, because the mud puppy does not have one. The dreamer realized that fact spontaneously, when he reported the dream. Thus, Dan was markedly ambivalent about his impulsive, defensive combativeness against bodily contact with men. Vicious rejection of such contact is carried out by a frail, little animal, but one exceptionally endowed with a "hind claw." Such mud puppies do not exist in reality; therefore, Dan's acutely painful reaction had not been caused by something real but by his imagination. Dan was struggling with an acute neurotic conflict: In attempting to gratify his desire for male intimacy, Dan met with pain, anxiety, and inhibition.

AXIOM B INTERPRETATION

The basic assumption underlying Axiom B is that the traits of each dream figure reflect the dreamer's affects, thoughts, and opinions concerning the type of person represented by the respective dream figure.

From the attitudes and behavior of Dan toward the other dream figures, we can infer that he would take the initiative, friendly or not, in establishing relationships with others. He was by far the most active figure, the only one that moved within the dream scene. He did not like to be a mere observer or to take a passive role in interpersonal relationships that mattered to him. This trait should have influenced his active interactions with everyone, especially men. When the rapport became intimate, however, Dan beat a quick retreat. He thought of men as being seductive. The dream activities began with the man motioning Dan to come to him and see the mud puppy. Dan did not mind such friendly male relations as long as they did not become intimate (engaging, for example, in bodily contact).

Dream figures are not created accidentally. The visuomotor components of any dream figure originate in the dreamer's genuine and current concern with them. Therefore, Dan's wife, too, played a significant part in Dan's personality problems. He expected her to be aware of his special contacts with men but not to interfere. She was conscious of what was going on and tolerated it; she was ready to assist when the need arose. Dan obviously trusted her and wanted her to see his intense struggle to curb his homoerotic inclination. He demonstrated to her in the dream that even mere talks with men can get him into undesirable and painful situations. The presence of his subdued, understanding wife was a safety device, not a result of active psychosexual desire; the desire was visible when he was engaged with the male figures. Homoerotic desire is one form of inadequate and disordered heterosexuality (Piotrowski, 1967). The wife symbolized support, and her presence in the dream was a good prognostic sign.

Parents did not appear in the dream but parents have such a strong influence on the development of their children's personalities that psychosocial roles acquired by children while living with parents affect their future adult relationships. Therefore, in Dan's dream, his wife was likely to disclose some traits shared by his mother (Rule of Complementarity). The most apparent of these traits was her standing by Dan's side — ready to help if necessary, but maintaining some emotional distance from him. Similarly, Dan's father's traits could be determined from those of the man in Dan's dream (Rule of Generalization). The conspicuous trait of the father would be his tendency to get other people (including his son) to do things they will later regret. This implies a certain disregard for Dan's welfare (Axiom B). If this were a valid deduction, Dan would be wary of men (Axiom A). He would resent men's suggestions and orders.

CONCLUSION

The dream ended as it had begun. The situation remained unchanged. Dan posed a problem but did not solve it. Each dream figure resumed the position of isolation it had had at the beginning of the dream. Dan was in great need of help to break out of his indecision caused by the strong, well-matched, incompatible drives that were mutually inhibiting one another. The desire for therapy seemed genuine; Dan needed to allay intense anxiety and enervating vacillation. The advantage of the strongly dissented, mud puppy traits was in preventing actual, homosexually colored bodily contacts and thus in saving Dan great social embarrassment and near panic; these traits, however, made Dan feel and act in a cold-blooded, hostile manner. Dan's standards of social behavior were strongly determined by prevailing norms of personal conduct. The socially inoffensive and positive attitudes revealed in the dream were assented or slightly dissented, whereas the socially more disruptive hostility that can be manifested in violent acts was very strongly dissented (level 6). In other words, Dan fought hard against his socially and personally most agitating and frightening behavior, as dramatized by the mud puppy. Prognosis for a successful psychotherapy seemed good.

DR. BIELE'S CLINICAL VALIDATION

The following text concerning Dan consists of excerpts from the typescript left by Dr. Biele. Words in quotes are Dan's. Words in parentheses are Dr. Biele's but have been condensed by ZAP. Remaining words are direct quotations from Dr. Biele.

The purpose of Dr. Biele's analysis was to ascertain to what extent blind PDS could disclose major pathology in the first two or three sessions following initial consultation. This case is not presented as a study of therapeutic technique. The dreamer contacted the author and urgently requested a consultation because of an acute anxiety attack. Dan reported that he could not leave his apartment because he dreaded a panic state. His wife had to accompany him so that he would be able to leave the apartment. She also had to escort him to classes. He was hesitant, guarded, and had extreme difficulty in presenting his problem. He was distressed that his symptoms were occurring just when he was about to start his last year in graduate school, where he wanted to finish with a doctorate. He felt that he needed to function more efficiently and that bringing "these attacks" under control was crucial to his well-being and studies. He was concerned about his academic work, even though he was consistently a grade-A student throughout his school years. "When people tell me to do things, I resent it. Sometimes I do what I'm told, but I have mental reservations. I like to find the other person wrong." Dan was openly guarded about the relationship that might develop between him and his therapist, a matter that occupied his attention from the very onset of therapy until his departure.

"The roughest period of my life until now was adolescence." He began to think at that time that he was lacking in masculinity. He took showers in a gym only when he was assured that he would be alone. Since his marriage, he tended to be socially withdrawn. He felt more safe being withdrawn. After several months in therapy, Dan reported that he had been holding back in his sessions. (He then started to discuss his psychosexual difficulties continually.) "I just don't feel like a man." He repeatedly expressed a desire to overcome his problem. After a number of weeks, during which he experienced the most intense anxiety up to that point, he disclosed with great difficulty that he was afraid he might have some homosexual tendencies. "I'm afraid of what you will think of me. Even though you haven't forced me, I feel you are making me talk about something that is very frightening." His exploration of both his homosexual fears and homosexual impulses gave rise to extreme anxiety. He was in such distress that his having two sessions a day seemed wise. (He mentioned repeatedly that bodily contact in a spirited ball game evoked his specific fear about latent homosexuality. He also talked a lot and freely about his hostile aggressiveness whenever he felt set upon, physically or mentally. He had the greatest difficulties curbing this form of irrational defense. Later, in treatment, Dan reported a frank homosexual dream that was of crucial importance.) Dan interpreted this dream himself: "It's the old story. When I try to turn my wife off or don't feel up to having sex with her, then the old homosexual fear comes back." With this one spontaneous, associative response to the dream came a dramatic and lasting reduction in Dan's anxiety and depression. Toward the end of the 10-month treatment, Dan commented spontaneously: "I can think about it [homosexual impulses], but I don't get panicky. It occurs to me when I am in the gym, just like before, but now I can look at the guys and the problem is sort of academic" (a conspicuous gain in relevant insight). Through his insight and experiences, Dan became aware of his mild, constrained anger or anxiety that was generated in a series of current interpersonal situations. Prior to therapy, these impulses were unrecognized.

(The helpful role of Dan's wife was abundantly documented). Dan described her as "a very good person," unusually efficient, held in high regard by her employers, and able to handle all domestic matters with the same degree of efficiency. She accomplished all this with such ease that he felt all the more humiliated and became intensely angry. His wife was his most reliable shield against stresses. "She is a very good, very loving, very loyal person." Dan "kept her in place" by being uncooperative, by resisting her pleas to be of some help, and by making her daily life a little more difficult. "I wanted to make her realize that I was the man!" He was "dependent on mother" as well. The persistence of this "paradoxical tie to mother" perplexed him. He became painfully aware that his way of life was similar to his mother's style, of which he had been critical. Dan's father was prone to impulsive rages during which he would "stomp around the room, red-faced," and he became chronically depressed and irritable with little or no provocation, whereas Dan's mother rarely displayed any anger. Dan became extremely disquieted when he stated that he was "very much like my father" (Rule of Generalization).

In conclusion, Dan's dream, interpreted perceptanalytically, offered his psychotherapist sound and highly relevant information even before treatment. It was also a key to increasing Dan's self-knowledge.

FOLLOW-UP

Psychotherapy was interrupted after 10 months because Dan received his doctorate at the end of the academic year and obtained a desirable position with a graduate school at a distant university. Dr. Biele gave him several names of psychotherapists near the new university. Dan maintained spontaneous letter contact for two years and reported on his progress. Within the first year, his wife gave birth to their first child; this made them happy and strengthened their marriage and made it significantly more relaxed and satisfying. Although previous attempts at raising a family had failed, the obstacles had now disappeared. All symptoms that had been incapacitating to Dan ceased to trouble him, although he still had a rare, brief, and limited desire for some form of intimacy with men.

10 Principles and Problems in Clinical Use of PDS for Manifest Dreams—————

Albert M. Biele, M.D.

This chapter demonstrates some basic fundamentals in the use of PDS. This chapter also demonstrates some problems that may arise when PDS is implemented. PDS can be an invaluable aid in all phases of psychotherapy, regardless of the school of thought to which a therapist may subscribe. PDS is a valid means of determining very early in the course of therapy the patients who are most suitable for engaging in a therapeutic process that strives for a basic change in the patient's personality. PDS provides an early and ongoing guide as to the validity of preestablished prognostic expectations. It is also a reliable instrument for assessing the progress of treatment. It can be a clinical tool that may significantly shorten the course of therapy. Lastly, PDS is a device for clinical research. Whereas it has been demonstrated that the dream in an initial session is a valuable means of assessing the patient's capacity to engage in the collaborative process of psychotherapy, PDS also gives the therapist a guideline for selecting the precise dream aspects that can most effectively be used to activate the therapeutic capability of the patient. The procedure for collecting the dream is of crucial importance in this system.

COLLECTION OF THE DREAM

Many clinicians have stated that a written report of a dream contributed very little to clinical use of the dream. PDS, however, requires accurate dream recordings, in utmost detail and in dreamers' own precise words. The dreamers are subjective observers and participants in dramas that their minds have created while free from conscious controls and filters. PDS depends very much on syntactical constructs in dreamers' dream reports. Recording dreams as early as possible, without editing or paraphrasing, is therefore essential. Dreamers should record their dreams within the first seven minutes of wakefulness; accurate dream recall drops considerably after seven minutes of wakefulness, except when dreams have been nightmares. Thus, when dreamers fail to record their dreams in writing or on a tape recorder within a brief passage of time, they are very likely to "forget" or filter out many of the crucial details, feelings, actions, surroundings, continuity, and the precise points at which dream scenes terminate or change. Some observations of scenes, films, or drama productions record what they see in a highly particularized way. Furthermore, after a span of time, dreamers may focus exclusively on one benign aspect of their dreams to the exclusion of others and may thereby lose vital aspects of manifest content. Clinicians have had patients' reporting theatrical plays, television stories, or films on two separate occasions. On second occasions, some of the most dynamic, cogent actions of the initial reports were unconsciously omitted. Because carefully collected and recorded dreams are at best fragments of dream experiences, fragments must be reported as completely as possible. Moreover, if others "saw" dreamers' dream scenes, each would report these scenes in a highly subjective way. PDS vitally depends on dreamers' "subjective" reports of their dream scenes.

At a dream workshop, participants were given typewritten copies of the dream called "A Futile Search" and were asked to work on the dream between sessions. In the following session, the participants were asked to write the dream as each remembered it. More than half had altered the syntactical structure of the dream, beginning with the opening statement. The correct initial statement of that dream was: "My mother and I are near our country home up North, looking for some indigenous plants." Half of the workshop participants recorded the dream from memory essentially as follows: "I am looking for a plant near our summer home. My mother is looking also." By placing the mother first in the original dream report ("My mother and I . . . "), the dreamer had shown an automatized deference to his mother's desires; he implicitly revealed an ongoing goal that he shared with his mother. Thus, by applying PDS to this opening statement, we derived from the dreamer's precise report that he still very much depended on his mother — to the degree of engaging with her in an attempt to fulfill a common interest (Primacy of Verbs and Abstract Nouns). The workshop paraphrase, however, was not in the dreamer's own words and therefore did not give quite so clearly this specific dynamic information about the dreamer's intense relationship with his mother; on the contrary, we would have to depend on the dreamer and on an extended associative process to expose that specific aspect of his personality.

The same assignment was given to another workshop using Freud's "Irma Injection" dream. This dream began: "A great hall — numerous guests whom we are receiving. Among them is Irma. I at once took her on one side . . ." Most members of the workshop omitted the phrase: "whom we are receiving." If Freud had omitted this phrase, analysts would have been deprived of an important activity on the part of Freud; the dream indicated that when Freud was acting as a host, probably with his wife ("we are receiving"), he readily withdrew and indulged his own self-interests when there was an appropriate distraction. Without Freud's precise words, a blind analysis of the "Irma" dream would not give rise to this important derivative. These are two minor examples indicating the need to have a dream reported in the dreamer's own, precise words.

Occasionally individuals allege that they have not dreamed for years. Sometimes a simple clinical example that demonstrates how a dream can be informative can influence patients to keep an open mind about collecting dreams. Thereafter, their positive or negative responses and the degree of responsibility they exercise in bringing dreams to early sessions may be a measure of their genuine motivation toward therapy. Most people are quite receptive to learning about the sleep–dream process — we experience a D-state with its concomitant dream creation every 90 minutes; this occurs approximately at the third depth (Stage 3) of sleep; then we recede into deeper sleep (Stage 5) until the next 90 minute cycle; then we experience renewal of dream creativity. In an average uninterrupted night's sleep, we are most likely to awake during or shortly after the last D-state of the night; hence, we have an excellent potential to capture the last dream of the night. Therefore, certain training routines for "capturing" a dream can be established. First, patients are strongly advised to keep a pad and pen at bedside. Second, patients must gradually learn, as they wake, to detect Stage 1 sleep, a state in which they are not fully awake but rather are in a phase of reduced awareness, of barely perceiving incipient wakefulness. This is equivalent to a state of drowsiness, "half awake–half asleep." Their task is to condition themselves to preserve this Stage-1 sleep. Dreamers learn, as they become "aware" of incipient wakefulness, to remain immobile, to avoid stretching, yawning, or any bodily movement, each of which rapidly facilitates full wakefulness. They are advised to keep their eyes gently closed, their fingers and facial musculature relaxed with slow rhythmic breathing. With this training, they can sufficiently "preserve" Stage-1 sleep to capture or recall dreams that are then more firmly etched in memory. No less than 10 minutes should be spent preserving Stage-1 sleep; then dreamers should start recording their dreams.

Dreamers often report having had three or four dreams a night. Unless such dreams are separated by a period of wakefulness, they are regarded as the dream collection of a single D phase, notwithstanding length, multiple dream figures, and multiple scenes. Research has established that a single D phase and its dream creativity may last as long as 45 minutes. What dreamers may regard as several dreams may be nothing more than multiple scenes of a single dream phase. The sequential order of scenes is important in that, whereas scenes may seem unrelated, they may successively indicate covert self-confrontation with contradictory goals, attempts to resolve the dilemma, setbacks, total failures, or even some progress.

PRESENTATION OF THE DREAM

Clinical use of PDS begins with presentation of the dream. Historically, analysts have cultivated a "sharp ear" by carefully listening to every word, inflection, and nuance of feeling in patients' voices. The use of PDS, however, is immeasurably enhanced when clinicians also cultivate a "sharp eye," whereby they conscientiously observe patients as they read or report their dreams. I have noted with astonishingly high frequency that, as dreamers mention behavioral action (verbs) in dream sequences, they manifest an abrupt change in posture, signified by leg, or entire-body (covert anxiety) movement; or they may change their breathing patterns, exhibiting an expiratory sigh (overt anxiety) or a fleetingly restrained inspiration with momentary breath holding (covert anger). Other changes include: transient increase in neck pulsations; slight injection or reddening of the part of the white of the eye closest to the nasal bridge. Any or all of these subtle changes are valid, reliable indicators of subliminal changes of feeling, such as incipient anxiety or covert hostility; these subtle signs appear significantly before dreamers become consciously aware of what they are feeling. By using valid observations of covert emotions, analysts are thereby alerted to specific dream actions that trigger these changes in feeling. These physiological signals of changes in feeling indicate that specific dream actions are generally associated with emotionally charged and conflictual situations, even though dream content may at first appear to be rather benign. Sometimes feelings surface and become sufficiently overt that dreamers may become uncomfortable and may halt the presentation of dreams; they may make spontaneous associations or digress by discussing irrelevant details. Thus, halting dream presentations may be in keeping with emerging feelings of anxiety or anger and is indicative of crucial conflicts in dreamers' personalities. Furthermore, the clinical value of written dreams has been demonstrated when dreamers have been asked to repeat dreams from written records in same or successive sessions; the same subliminal or even manifest feelings consistently recur at the same precise points of action (verbs) in the dreams.

In optimal use of PDS, collection of dream data must be exhausted at initial presentation. Once dreams are presented, even in written form, additional data should be obtained through inquiry. Such additional data are frequently derived from detailed exploration of some common occurrences in dreams.

Additional Data Concerning Change of Scene

Therapists should try to clarify and sharpen dream actions that precede changes of dream scenes. Therapists must determine whether original actions are completed or remain stymied when the scene changes. When scenes change abruptly before action is completed, analysts are alerted that the original goals of the actions (indicated by verbs) are abandoned by dreamers because of one or more unconscious pathodynamic factors. When goals of dream actions appear to be close to fulfillment, and the scenes then abruptly change, dreamers may be indicating pathological personality aspects such as self-obstructionism or ambivalence; or, dreamers may be revealing at the unconscious level that being self-sufficient and self-reliant is not yet acceptable. Also by aborting actions and changing scenes, dreamers may be revealing strong tendencies to preserve their propensity to falter in some anxiety-provoking undertakings. Another dynamic possibility changes of scenes may indicate that dreamers are unconsciously avoiding anxiety associated with new and potentially healthy goals. Additional dream data can enrich the dynamic derivatives of dreams as in the following example. Initially, the dreamer reported: "I had a peculiar dream. I was driving a car and then had refreshments with my wife." After inquiry, the dream fragment involving a change of scene was: "I am driving a car and have a great deal of trouble staying on the road. The next thing I know is that I am suddenly sitting in my living room while my wife serves me refreshments."

Definitive inquiry and exploration of dream data disclosed that the car was still out of control when the scene changed. With this additional data, we conclude, using Axiom A, that the dreamer became anxious when he independently strove for new goals; he tended to lose his concentration on a goal, to deviate, and then to abandon the task as soon as he found that this new undertaking was making him anxious. From Axiom A, we see that by changing the scene and by creating a new scene wherein he depended on his wife, the dreamer tended to avoid the challenge of being self-reliant and of keeping his goal in view. Further, by applying Axiom A to the traits of the dream figure of the wife, we conclude that the dreamer dissented allowing others to depend on him attending to passive and dependent needs of others; however, he dissented this role. Further, the dreamer, in accordance with Axiom B, was more comfortable in a dependent role, especially in which a woman served his needs.

The need to inquire about additional dream data, especially details leading to scene changes, is again evident in analysis of the following dream fragment of a 25-year-old woman: "I am driving a car but a tree blocks the road." When additional data were obtained, the dream fragment was enlarged: "I am driving a car on a curved road going up a hill. Suddenly a large tree falls across the road. I got out of the car and decided that there was no way that I could continue. I backed the car downhill going backwards."

The additional dream data accentuated the richness of PDS. From Axiom A, we know from this more complete dream that the dreamer perceived that her self-obstructionism in reaching her goals was unacceptable (the falling tree represented her most dissented traits). Further, she was quite complacent when her self-defeating patterns ensured that she would not achieve her goal ("there was no way that I could continue"). When the dreamer arduously pursued a satisfying goal, she tended through her self-defeating tendencies to ward off ultimate gratification ("going up a hill . . . large tree falls . . . I got out"). Thus, her assented trait yielded to her dissented trait; consequently, her acceptance of her obstructiveness bespoke a pattern of masochistic futility in her adjustment to life. She was beset with multiple depressive practices. Without this additional data, the analysis of this dream fragment would have been limited. We have found that the inquiry for additional visuomotor dream data affords additional opportunities for illumination of pathodynamic struggles that otherwise might not have surfaced or might have required considerable time to surface; obtaining additional data helps the therapist to elicit sooner the patient's presentation of relevant, associative activity.

Additional Data Concerning Physical Relationships of Dream Figures

Therapists must learn the sex and age of dream figures. They should determine which dream figure receives the dreamer's fullest attention and which is avoided. This is vital to blind analysis of the dream, especially when the dreamer is seemingly avoiding any interest in the opposite or the same sex. PDS and Axiom B also need obtain some additional dream data that will reveal whether the dreamer shows some interest in the opposite sex and then becomes more interested in a same-sex figure, or vice versa. This situation occurs in the following dream fragment of a woman: "I was riding in a car. We didn't seem to make much progress." Additional data revealed additional content: "I was sitting in the passenger seat next to the door. A man was driving and there was a woman between us. After a while I changed seats with the woman so that I was next to the driver. We didn't seem to make much progress."

By limiting analysis to verbs and to the change of the physical, interpersonal relationship of the dreamer to other figures, we derive the following traits that otherwise might not have been decoded from the initial dream fragment:

1. The dreamer at times perceived a woman blocking off her relationship with a man ("a woman [was] between us"; Axiom B).

2. The dreamer was willing to accept a same-sex relationship but only for a limited period of time (the dreamer sat next to the woman; Axiom B).

3. The dreamer preferred to share the company of both sexes ("I changed seats . . . so that I [would be] next to the driver"; Axiom B).

4. The dreamer tended to be divisive when involved with two people who are close to each other. (the dreamer changed her seat so as to come between a man and a woman; Axiom B).

5. The dreamer was unwilling to take the initiative to achieve her goals (the male driver, bearer of dissented traits, determined whether the vehicle would reach its destination; Axiom A).

6. The dreamer found it partially unacceptable to be displaced by a woman (the female dream figure displaced by the dreamer was passive, a condition not strongly dissented by the dreamer).

These derivatives were obtained through application of the Scale of Assent & Dissent (ch 2 Ax) and of the Primacy of Verbs and Abstract Nouns.

Additional Data Concerning Change of Age of Dream Figure

Occasionally, on collecting additional dream data, we find that dreamers undergo changes of age; using PDS, we must take these changes into account. The following dream fragment illustrated the value of such inquiry: "I am singing an operative aria on the stage and Maria Callas is standing off to one side listening while the audience is spellbound." After inquiry, the dreamer revealed additional content:

> I seem to be 20 years younger than I am now, at least 5 years before I was married. I am sitting in the audience at the far end of a row listening to another singer. Then I seem to be slightly older than my present age. Next I am singing an operatic aria on the stage and Maria Callas is standing off to one side listening while the audience is spellbound.

By gathering the additional data, we learned that, at an earlier age, the dreamer had been inhibited but later became less inhibited. We clearly discerned that the dreamer was ready to become less passive, more assertive, and more self-confident than she had been previously. Her newly evolving capacity to expose her attributes before others had become more acceptable than it had been in an earlier period of life. The dreamer was currently somewhat inhibited, was in conflict over displaying her personality, and was somewhat reluctant to expose her new attributes. We discerned this from the traits depicted by the dream figure of Maria Callas (Scale of Dissent). The changes in age reveal that that which had been formerly assented was somewhat dissented at present and that the dreamer was on the threshold of overcoming symptoms of a covert depression.

THERAPY

Despite decades of discussion, psychotherapists have not yet agreed on a universally acceptable definition of their discipline. Therapists "know" they accomplish something positive and help their patients, yet they are hardpressed to define their specific processes of psychotherapy.

We review briefly certain basic clinical therapeutic principles that are objective and that therefore may be universally accepted. Personality develops slowly and gradually for a long time and functions rather consistently with little awareness of the individual. Negative feelings generated from these unconsciously determined, malfunctioning traits cause some varying degrees of impediment to the functioning of the individual's personality. The goal of therapy is to bring about a degree of basic change wherein these contradictory forces or conflicts are modified, and the negative feelings are either reduced in frequency or are no longer generated. The task of the therapist is to employ a process that will effect this basic change.

Regardless of the school of thought, certain clinical elements or techniques are observable; when manifested, they constitute a basic part of the therapeutic process. They include motivation, engagement, pursuit of feeling with some degree of abreaction, associative activity, and implementation. These elements do not, however, represent the total process. Definitions of these clinical elements are essential for illustrating how the application of PDS to well-collected manifest dreams can often significantly facilitate and potentiate these vital elements of the therapeutic process.

Motivation is a patient's active, clinically demonstrable struggle to experience the elements of the therapeutic process and at a later time to spontaneously implement these elements that have been experientially learned. Patients who elect to undertake psychotherapy are willing to invest time and expense and indicate a desire to feel better and to function better; all too often, many people believe that these characteristics are synonymous with motivation. When confronted with the task of examining their motivation, some people verbalize a desire to get well but demonstrate an unconsciously determined reluctance to become involved in the therapeutic process. Those who have difficulty in actively demonstrating motivation paraphrase their resistance, perhaps in this way: "After all, I wouldn't spend all this time and money if I didn't want to get better." Deciphered, this means that patients desire to feel better but are unconsciously resisting involvement and change. When patients bring in their first dreams and are asked to comment freely, they may handle this exclusively as a cerebral exercise — they may focus intellectually on nouns and hypothesize about the symbolism of the nouns. When clinical situations so warrant, and patients can gradually be alerted that they are experiencing unclear changes of feeling while presenting dreams, then patients' sudden recognition of some emotional shift is an observable indication of motivation. In this way, dreamers demonstrate rather than verbalize motivation, which then becomes interlocked and closely meshed with the other elements of the process of therapy. This concurrent interaction propels the therapeutic process.

Engagement is the analysts' activity that fosters patients' mobilization and use of personal resources in a joint attempt to define and solve problems of personality distortion. Dreams serve as a focus for the initiation or resumption of collaborative psychotherapeutic efforts. PDS adds an extra dimension both in demonstrating motivation and in fostering engagement; the mere task of raising a subliminal feeling from a dream entails active demonstration of patients' engagement. These matters are exemplified in the following case report of an initial dream.

A man, age 34, in an early consultive session, was asked to record any intercurrent dreams. His lack of motivation was clear when he insisted that, because he had not dreamed since he was 14, he was unlikely to start dreaming at the time of the sessions. He was even reluctant to arrange materials to record a possible dream. Much later, he asked if he could use a voice-activated tape recorder. Thus, his final willingness to share a "possible" dream was a positive sign of erosion of his resistance. When he returned, he brought a tape on which he had recorded four dreams over a period of three nights. His first dream, presumably the first recalled in more than 20 years, was as follows:

> There are a line of people. I am about the 4th one in line. At the head and facing the line is a mechanical robot. He takes a person, one at a time, and stuffs him into a cylinder and leaves him neatly compressed in this receptacle. Then he does the same to the next person. When it was my turn I became terrified and awakened.

Notwithstanding that the dream constituted an indefinable threat in that he might have unknowingly revealed some hidden truths about himself, the patient demonstrated an inherent capacity to overcome this initial resistance by sharing with the therapist a small part of what he mentally experienced while asleep. As the patient listened to his own dream, his neck pulsed, his body became restless, and he breathed irregularly. These indicated an increased heart rate and were covert signs of anxiety associated with specific parts of the dream action (the robot stuffing people into cylinders). Clinical observation of these changes became a means for further assessment of the patient's potential for engagement. By focusing on the most emotionally charged verb ("stuff"), he responded with the same anxiety that he produced when he was asked about feeling coerced, controlled, made to submit helplessly to others, impelled to function precisely as others do. This evoked a mild abreaction. He stated spontaneously that this had been characteristic of most of his occupational experiences; his inability to surrender to his employer's demands had been a major factor in his frequent change of jobs. Many other associative experiences were evoked. His employers were rigid, demanding, unreceptive to his original ideas; they required total obeisance. He then noted that this characterized his intermittent academic endeavors at various universities, where he felt he had been unable to really express his own ideas and he had been required to adopt the thinking of others. Here again, as with his jobs, he had prematurely terminated his college affiliations. These associative experiences triggered intense hostility. Next, he spoke of being extremely shy, of rarely socializing, and of claiming that most of his acquaintances were "conformists" who expected him to assent blindly to their values. His last association in this sequence was that therapy would probably replicate his lifetime experiences in that he would expect his therapist to impose personal values on him, to make him conform to some prescribed standards, and to deprive him of all his potential for individuality.

Pursuit of Feeling.   Feelings in the interpersonal–intrapersonal context underlie associations, thoughts, and behavior. Therefore, clinicians have always been aware that feelings are vital elements in the process of therapy. Overt feelings of anxiety or hostility do not constitute a clinical problem inasmuch as these feelings are readily apparent to both patient and analyst. Covert feelings do not constitute a major obstacle to the process of therapy as long as these feelings remain subliminal; at best, these are only subclinically manifested by abrupt physical changes. When patients are unable or unwilling to experience such feelings and to crystallize their precise nature, they abort the therapeutic process, and resistance dominates the clinical situation.

The use of PDS may facilitate the surfacing and crystallization of these feelings into dreamers' full awareness. A commonplace therapist–patient dialogue such as the following frequently facilitates this process:

DOCTOR: I just noticed a change of feeling while you were presenting the dream. Are you aware of this feeling?

PATIENT: No, I am not feeling anything.

DOCTOR: Will you repeat the middle scene of the dream? . . . There, I noticed again the same change of feeling.

PATIENT: Yes, now that you call it to my attention, I do feel uncomfortable, . . . I am getting tense . . . I feel taut . . . It is getting worse . . . I feel quite uncomfortable.

DOCTOR: Let us find out what kind of discomfort you are feeling . . . let the feeling come up stronger and stronger . . . I can see that this feeling is now quite intense . . . what is the feeling?

PATIENT: This is damn uncomfortable . . . I can feel my heart begin to pound a little . . . I am tense . . . I feel now like I'm starting to run a race . . . I am just plain angry . . . my mother comes to mind . . .

Thus, the feeling, when surfaced and crystallized, initiates associative activity.

When dreamers relate one dream on more than one occasion in one session (as indicated in the preceding dialogue) or in subsequent sessions, they consistently show the same covert signs of negative feeling when they repeat a specific verb or phrase. The task, then, is to pursue the feeling.

People who pursue a feeling perpetuate the feeling at a level of high intensity until some degree of abreaction takes place. Abreaction, as used in this book, is the exacerbation, intensification, and discharge of a feeling that at the start was subliminal and of which the individual was not fully aware. Once pursuit has reached this discharge level, then the dreamer's psychic system triggers associative activity. The surfacing of a dream feeling associated with a specific dream conflict bestirs multiple experiential associations, each of which may seem at first unrelated but later are found to have identical feeling tones and specific, relevant, conflictual themes.

Associative Activity.   Serial, associative activity is generally agreed to be the sine qua non element of therapy, especially when it spontaneously evokes relevant experiences that particularize identical, albeit camouflaged, pathodynamic themes. Spontaneous emergence of such relevant associative experiences pertaining to past and current living brings into stark awareness the precise personality malfunctions that generate negative feelings. When patients struggle to sustain associative activity, then still more remote experiences will be forthcoming, and light is spontaneously shed on psychogenesis; this often obviates the obsessively concretized approach to explore early life patterns exclusively.

IMPLEMENTATION

Once sufficient, relevant, associative experiences are collected, both patient and therapist mutually become aware of how consistent distortions, malfunctions, and their pathodynamic goals operate in interpersonal living. The individual is then ready for the ultimate task that leads to change. This ultimate phase is instant insight, a fulminating psychofissionable reaction that embraces several stages. First, patients become aware of the precise nature of subliminal negative feelings as they transpire in an interpersonal experience. Second, patients evolve a new awareness of their tendency to express characteristic attitudes and behavior that previously were acceptable but are now seen as malfunctions. Instant insight at this level exposes or sheds new light on contradictory tendencies as they seek manifestation, thus producing an experience of startling, new self-illuminations that initially generate extreme anxiety and turbulence. This second phase frequently consumes an extended period of time primarily because patients cannot sustain the process of giving up old, characteristic parts of themselves. Such instant insights, more often than not, are attenuated or negated at times when patients revert to the old, longstanding "blindness" to the pathodynamics of their behavior. In the third stage, patients become more and more aware of the objective of the malfunctioning tendencies as they are being manifested. Patients must unravel coexisting but contradictory feelings that have been made to surface during the course of these malfunctioning experiences, and they must clarify the contradictory goals. The fourth stage of instant insight, appearing after the first three stages have been solidified, consists of intense, repetitive, active implementation of newly found approaches to unraveling heretofore unrecognized feelings, behavior, and their goals; this occurs when patients sense the impulse to manifest old, characteristic malfunctions. Anxiety that accompanies initial inroads into instant insight frequently deters patients from the struggle to sustain this newly evolved process. The struggle for multiple experiences of instant insight is implementation, without which no basic change in personality can be accomplished.

PITFALLS IN USE OF PDS

Interpretative Exhibitionism

Patients may tempt or challenge therapists to exhibit interpretive skill: "After all, you know all there is to know about me, and you could just as well tell me about the dream and the solution of my other problems, so why should I have to waste time and expense in struggling with it?" In such situations, therapists often unknowingly gain the adulation of their patients by making complete interpretations of dreams. With the availability of PDS, the problems of clinical challenge and exhibitionistic temptation are compounded. Equipped with the sensitive PDS, therapists may be tempted more than ever to present detailed analyses of dreams. Then dreamers may cerebrally confirm the analysts' interpretations and feel "good" because they have selected wise and gifted therapists. This interpretive exhibitionism and the resulting admiration of patients constitute a major pitfall: Resistance is perpetuated, and controlling dependency is promoted. Clinical use of selected elements of dreams — the therapeutic itinerary — is thwarted, and the crucial initial element of therapy, namely engagement, is delayed if not interminably deterred. In short, the therapeutic process is stymied. No valid dream work can take place, and later attempts to have the patient independently engage in meaningful dream work will likely mobilize more intense resistance. Furthermore, the crucial development and implementation of other elements of the therapeutic process — especially the elicitation, crystallization, and open expression of subliminal feeling may be seriously obstructed and unduly delayed. Therapy can transpire only when patients have developed and experienced a means of surfacing and crystallizing subliminal feelings, of pursuing these feelings to the point of activating multiple associated memories and intercurrent experiences, and finally, of sustaining this pursuit to the point of abreaction. While abreactive decompression is taking place at the height of open expression of feelings, the most explosive and relevant associations are brought forth. This crucial clinical element of therapy can transpire only when a meaningful therapist–patient relationship has been established. Resistance to change of personality is common to all people; those who elect to undertake therapy inevitably expose this cryptic trait in the therapeutic process. Often such patients initially manifest resistance in their failure to capture dream fragments that were vividly dreamed: "I was awakened by a very frightening dream; I felt scared for at least an hour and couldn't get back to sleep, but I can't remember the dream." Nightmares are firmly imprinted by the feeling of terror and are generally recalled. Finally, when dream-forgetting individuals belatedly produce dreams, they become generally resistant to engage in dream work.

Premature Application of Axiom A

The deciphering and unraveling of multiple cryptic pathodynamics of dreamers' personalities are substantially more reliable and valid when Axiom A is used. Some therapists who become newly acquainted with PDS may be unconsciously motivated to offer entire interpretations in accordance with Axiom A, thereby blocking patients from engagement and other aspects of the therapeutic process. Most important, if therapists tend to implement Axiom A beginning with the dissented traits, dreamers are extremely likely to experience excessive, intense anxiety that will block rather than facilitate analysis. PDS alerts therapists specifically to trait dissent and the invariably resulting generation of anxiety when the dissented trait presses to gain overt expression. A major pitfall occurs, therefore, when the dreamer is abruptly confronted with such anxiety-producing traits, especially in the absence of protracted indoctrination to the relatively more benign derivatives of Axiom B.

Let us assume that a female patient's dream about "a sneaky alligator" was an initial dream; the therapist may choose to point out that the alligator is a dream figure depicting sneaky, predatory, lacerating, backbiting, devouring tendencies. The appearance of this figure in an early phase of therapy can be extremely overwhelming and may precipitate a deep, potentially serious depression. More important, the potential for implementing meaningful therapy is undermined at the very start. One of the many consequences to therapeutic strategy may be that the patient will thereafter be genuinely blocked in the ultimate development of engagement. In the instance of the "sneaky alligator," the dreamer's initial spontaneous association was: "My sister comes to mind." The dreamer then spent the rest of the session and intermittent sessions thereafter giving spontaneous, valid, associative experiences and memories that revealed her perception of her sister's relationship with her and with others as being "sneaky, conniving, and backbiting"; in short, the dreamer spontaneously implemented Axiom B and thereby averted the pitfall of premature application of Axiom A. When, however, she attempted at a later time to explore her own propensity to express these unacceptable traits, she became elusive, avoidant, and intensely anxious. She tried to minimize the validity of her associations to herself, questioned briefly the use of dreams in psychotherapy, became more overtly depressed, and aborted her capacity for therapy. After a brief period, she was able to reengage effectively and to endure the inevitably painful process of exploring her extremely unacceptable traits on the Scale of Dissent. If the patient had been initially influenced to focus exclusively on Axiom A, then she would very likely have been unable to extricate herself from such a pitfall and would have delayed, if not completely forestalled, the therapeutic process. Even under ideal circumstances, therapeutic activity with traits that are strongly dissented according to Axiom A necessitates painful self-confrontation and is always anxiety-provoking.

The Dossier Syndrome

A third major pitfall that may inadvertently evolve through the casual use of PDS is designated as the Dossier Syndrome; this is characterized by the propensity of patients to collect and store experiences wherein they feel they have been victimized by so-called remissness, insensitive disregard, abuse, and oversight on the part of others, especially family, relatives, teachers, peers, superiors, and close friends. Two dynamically different clinical aspects of the Dossier Syndrome exist. First, in therapy, patients may initially tend to expound at length how others were derelict in their relationships and responsible to a great extent for the patients' disappointments and failures to achieve goals. Such patients generally welcome the opportunity to ventilate long-existing resentments arising from an endless array of memories in which others have been regarded as culpable and responsible for the patients' frustrations. This is an important and vital part of patients' histories in the initial phase of therapy. In many ways this tendency indirectly fulfills the objectives of Axiom B, which states that all dream figures evoke dreamers' thoughts, feelings, and attitudes concerning the types of persons represented by the figures. Especially early in therapy, the unraveling of a dream in accordance with Axiom B brings into sharp consciousness many long-constrained feelings and attitudes regarding others. These feelings can eventuate into major abreactions that constitute the high point of effective therapeutic processes, especially when multiple floods of relevant associations are generated. When individuals prolong their responses to Axiom B derivatives long after therapeutic processes have taken place and engage in repetitive anecdotes of already mentioned experiences, however, then they have become bogged down in the Dossier Syndrome. This syndrome is prominent in Freud's "Irma Injection" dream and particularly in Freud's conscious, free associations to the dream. To scapegoat others evokes a paradoxical satisfaction or gloating that often becomes the primary, albeit unrecognized, action tendency on the part of an individual; dossiering is often vital to patients' ongoing functioning, and the unconscious investment to preserve it can be very intense. Individuals are prone to store these presumed shortcomings of others in a kind of "psychic arsenal" to be activated at some pathologically propitious time in the future so as to victimize other persons by making them squirm over alleged shortcomings. These resentful "dossiering" tactics become unknowingly a powerful instrument by which false self-righteousness can be enhanced even as "victims" are made to writhe with discomfort, to feel guilty, and to become obligated to the patient. By merely saying "Remember when you did such-and-such?" or "Why did you do so-and-so early in our marriage?", a person is able to achieve a covert triumph by rendering the victim anxious and guilt-laden. The Dossier Syndrome is extremely common in the interpersonal, competitive strivings of many people. Sometimes patients may emerge from incomplete courses of therapy with intensified dossiering tendencies. The scapegoating of others, especially of parents and siblings, is frequently erroneously regarded as insight.

Second, the Dossier Syndrome frequently has a masochistic element. During a time of a high, intense level of mutuality and affection, patients may reach into their "psychic arsenal" to remind other people of alleged failures in the remote and even recent past. In so doing, they despoil their own genuine pleasure in their contamination of the gratification of these others.

Axiom B is an effective therapeutic instrument early in therapy, when dreamers bring into full awareness subliminal and constrained feelings and attitudes that were up until then not within conscious reach. Dreamers may prolong responses to Axiom B derivatives long after therapeutic processes have taken place, which becomes a manifestation of intense resistance. The task for therapists, therefore, is to decide at which point dreamers have essentially achieved comparatively optimal degrees of analysis from Axiom B and then to influence dreamers to implement Axiom A — that is, to move from interpersonal to intrapersonal exploration. Granted that this is not an easy task, PDS is a valuable instrument for influencing dreamers before they become helplessly mired in the "Dossier Syndrome" and reach a state of intractable resistance.

This is exemplified by the analysis and clinical use of the dream of a 42-year-old, married man, whose tendency to dossier was extreme:

Four Facets of a Dreamer: The Three Possums

There were three animals, all of the same size, enemies to each other: They appeared to be foxes or possums but were very ferocious. I was an observer at times and at other times I blended with them. These enemies were feinting and skirmishing and were out to kill each other. In a scramble one took a bite in the neck and lower skull case of another and ripped out its next meal. The third animal attacked and stole the carcass of the dead animal and succeeded in carrying it away. I watched all this happen.

Analysis of this dream revealed four facets of the dreamer, three of which are dissented; these three would therefore generate anxiety as they pressed for overt expression. According to Axiom A, the traits of the dreamer were assented:

1. Tendency to observe passively while others attack one another ("I was an observer").
2. Tendency to involve self emotionally in highly charged situations among people ("I blended with them").
3. Tendency to remain with a group engaged in interpersonal brutality and sadism ("I blended with them. These enemies were . . . out to kill each other").
4. Tendency to be cold, unsympathetic, and without compassion when others are in pain ("I watched").

The animals are dream figures with strongly dissented traits: The traits of the first animal (the victim) were:

5. Tendency to be brutal to others ("out to kill each other").
6. Tendency to attack others regardless of the consequences ("skirmishing . . . out to kill each other").

7. Tendency to surrender rather than be assertive (the victim did little to protect itself) in accordance with the Rule of Implicit Evidence.
8. Tendency to be exploited (stolen carcass).

The traits of the second animal (the thief) were:

9. Tendency to be sly, sneaky, exploitative ("feinting").
10. Tendency to seek gains without effort ("stole the carcass") in accordance with the Rule of Implicit Evidence; the thief employed mild effort to steal the carcass, whereas the aggressor animal used far greater effort to kill the first animal.
11. Tendency to be unsharing, greedy (carrying the carcass away).
12. Tendency to deprive others of the fruits of their labors ("stole . . . and [carried the carcass] away").

The traits of the third animal (the aggressive killer) were:

13. Tendency to extract from others ruthlessly ("out to kill").
14. Tendency to emotionally "devour" one's own ("took a bite in the neck").
15. Tendency to destroy relationships beyond repair and to feed on the resources of others ("ripped out its next meal").

Most of these 15 derivatives from the analysis of the dream in accordance with the principles of Axiom A had to do primarily with dissented intrapersonal tendencies. The dreamer experienced little difficulty with the comparatively simple task of decoding these traits. His immediate associations were fortuitously in accordance with Axiom B — that is, all his associative memories and current experiences concerned his parents, aunts, and uncles; his peers in childhood, adolescence, and adult life; his wife and his children; and his relationships with people in educational and occupational endeavors. He viewed each of these relationships at one time or another as being exploitative, overtly or covertly abusive, deceitful, sneaky, lacerative, victimizing, greedy, and insensitive. His abreactions and accompanying associations were therapeutically effective and helped him to remove many of his self-deceptions regarding these people who had played and continued to play a vital role in his life.

The 15 derivatives of Axiom A remained attenuated for quite some time. Only sporadically, over a period of months, could the patient be gradually influenced to activate associative memories and experiences that surfaced an awareness of his possessing these unacceptable traits. This remarkable revelatory dream, with its 11 dissented traits, remained a challenge all through his therapy and evoked the most intense resistance. Each of the animals' primary roles was part of his personality, and the fleeting awareness of a tendency to express each was unbearable:

1. His aspiration to be the strongest (the aggressive killer) resulted in frustrations and hostility.
2. His aspiration to be the victim — having to pay for his aggressiveness — evoked anxiety and depression.
3. His aspiration to be the sneaky thief (when the aggressor was distracted momentarily) helped him to avoid the extremes of vicious competitiveness and masochistic surrender.

As an only child of alienated parents, he had been treated in an inconsiderate and cavalier fashion. His mother was self-centered, exacting, cold, and unloving; his father allowed himself to be victimized and could not render any emotional support for the dreamer. It was little wonder that the dreamer could not evolve a fixed role that would be adequate enough to allow him to tolerate either parent; because he could not play the same role with each, his role with his father had to be different from that with his mother. To sustain this division was unacceptable.

This dreamer had more than ample reason to return time and again to Axiom B derivatives long after any therapeutic efficiency had been achieved. At times, he recognized and acknowledged that he was dossiering, yet he could not spontaneously desist. The Dossier Syndrome then became a major obstacle, and his resistance seemed insurmountable.

PATIENT: Yes, I recall him sneaking up on his prey, ready to rip them — but how is that relevant now?

DOCTOR: I noticed a change in your feeling.

PATIENT: I didn't.

DOCTOR: Can you picture the alligator?

PATIENT: Yes I can . . . I'm getting a headache and a pain in my leg . . . I am feeling angry . . . I AM angry at them (family) . . . I'd like to sneak up on them . . . Sometimes I feel like tearing them apart . . . I'd like to devour all of them . . . My mother made a "Cinderella" out of me . . . I did all the hard work . . . No one cared or appreciated . . . I'd like to rip them all . . . my uncle too . . . he lived with us . . . He expected me to do everything for him . . . I was proud that I could do so much for him and the others . . . but I had headaches then, like now . . . I was proud but angry . . . My headache is leaving me now . . .

In this way, dossiering was curtailed. The patient gradually came to see how his dossiering tendencies were a means of enhancing his pathologic, unconscious, ruthless impulses. By orchestrating the prudent use of Axiom B derivatives and by timely alternating them with Axiom A derivatives, the therapist was able to influence the patient to avoid concretizing his propensity for the Dossier Syndrome. Intrapersonal insights evoked the most intense resistance, but PDS may have contributed toward reducing it and toward fostering the active, therapeutic process.

Blind and nonblind analyses of patients' dreams revealed their pathology and resistances far more readily and precisely than those that were obtained from clinical data available at the beginning of treatments. The material in the clinical assessments was limited exclusively to the hard, clinically observable and observed data. Such data could have been validated by any clinician viewing and hearing the sessions.

───────────Bibliography───────────

Aserinsky, E. & Kleitman, N. (1953). Regularly occurring periods of eye motility and concomitant phenomena during sleep. *Science, 118,* 273–274.

Bartlett, F. C. (1932). *Remembering.* Cambridge: Cambridge University Press.

Bateson, G. (1972). *Steps to an ecology of mind.* New York: Ballantine Books.

Bleuler, E. (1950). *Dementia praecox or the group of schizophrenias.* New York: International Press. (Originally published, 1911).

Boss, M. (1938). Psychopathologie des Traumes bei schizophrenen und organischen Psychosen. *Zschr. f.g. Neurol. u. Psychiat., 162,* 459–494.

Bowler, J. (1973). Irma injection flops. *Psychiatric Quarterly, 47,* 604–608.

Breuer, J. & Freud, S. (1957). *Studies on hysteria.* New York: Basic Books. (Originally published, 1895).

Bricklin, B., Piotrowski, Z. & Wagner, E. (1981). *The hand test.* Springfield, IL: C. C. Thomas. (Originally published, 1962).

Brill, A. (1936). Anticipations and corroborations of the Freudian concepts from non-analytical sources. *American Journal of Psychiatry, 92,* 1127–1135.

Clymer, M. (1888). The stuff that dreams are made of. *Forum, 5,* 532–544.

Coomaraswamy, A. K. (1942). On being in one's right mind. *Review of Religion, 7,* 32–40.

Das, Bhagavan. (1953). *The science of emotion.* Adyar Madras, India: Theosophical Publishing House.

Delage, Y. (1891). Essay sur la theorie du reve. *Revue Scientifique, 48,* 40–48.

Delaney, G. (1979). *Living your dreams.* New York: Harper & Row.

Ellenberger, H. (1970). *The discovery of the unconscious.* New York: Basic Books.

Foulkes, D. (1978). *A grammar of dreams.* New York: Basic Books.

Freud, S. (1953). *The interpretation of dreams.* Translated by James Strachey. New York: Basic Books. (Originally published, 1900).

Freud, S. (1953a). The ego and the id. In J. Rickman (Ed.), *A general selection from the works of Sigmund Freud.* London: Hogarth Press. (Originally published, 1923).

Gomulicki, B. (1953). The development and the present status of the trace theory of memory. *British Journal of Psychology Monograph,* Supplement no. 29.

Hall, C. (1953). *The meaning of dreams.* New York: Harper & Row.

Hall, C. & Van de Castle, R. (1966). *The content analysis of dreams.* New York: Appleton-Century-Crofts.

Hervey de Saint-Denys, M. (1964). *Les reves et les moyens de les diriger.* Paris: Tchou. (Originally published, 1867).

Jones, E. (1953–1957). *The Life and Work of Sigmund Freud.* In 3 volumes. New York: Basic Books.

Jung, C. G. (1954). *The practice of Psychotherapy.* 2nd ed. Coll. Works, v. 16. Princeton: Princeton University Press.

Jung, C. G. (1961). Memories, Dreams, Reflections. Recorded & edited by Aniela Jaffe. New York: Vintage Books.

Jung, C. G. (1974). *Dreams.* Princeton: Princeton University Press.

La Rochefoucauld, F. (1665). *Reflexions ou sentences et Maximes Morales.* Many editions in the original French and translations. English version by G. H. Powell; Maximes, 1903.

Loemker, L. (1972). *Struggle for synthesis.* Cambridge, MA: Harvard University Press.

Mackenzie, N. (1965). *Dreams and dreaming.* New York: Vanguard Press.

Murphy, G. (1947). *Personality: A biosocial approach to origins and structure.* New York: Harper & Brothers.

Nietzsche, F. (1965). *Werke in drei Bänden.* Munich: Carl Hauser Verlag. (Originally published, 1871–1889).

Osgood, C. (1953). *Method and theory in experimental psychology.* New York: Oxford Press.

Osgood, C. E. (1961). Comments on Professor Bousfield's paper. In N. Cofer (Ed.), *Verbal learning and verbal behavior.* New York: McGraw Hill.

Paivio, A. (1979). *Imagery and verbal processes.* Hillsdale, NJ: Lawrence Erlbaum Associates.

Penfield, W. (1954). The permanent record of the stream of consciousness. *Proceedings 14th International Congress of Psychology,* 47–69.

Piaget, J. (1969). *The mechanisms of perception.* New York: Basic Books.

Piaget, J. (1971). *Biology and knowledge: An essay on the relations between organic regulations and cognitive processes.* Chicago: University of Chicago Press. (Originally published, 1967).

Piotrowski, Z. (1950). A new evaluation of the Thematic Apperception Test. *Psychoanalytic Review, 37,* 101–127.

Piotrowski, Z. (1952a). The Thematic Apperception Test of a schizophrenic interpreted according to new rules. *Psychoanalytic Review, 39,* 230–251.

Piotrowski, Z. (1952b). The T.A.T. Newsletter (Why traits which the T.A.T. subject attributes to figures unlike himself are the subject's own unacceptable traits as well as reflections of his opinions of others). *Journal of Projective Techniques, 16,* 512–514.

Piotrowski, Z. (1966). Theory of psychological tests and psychopathology. In J. Page (Ed.), *Approaches to psychopathology.* New York: Columbia University Press.

Piotrowski, Z. (1967). Inadequate heterosexuality. *Psychiatric Quarterly, 41,* 360–365.

Piotrowski, Z. (1968). Psychological test prediction of suicide. In H. L. P. Resnik (Ed.) *Suicidal behaviors* (pp. 198–208). Boston: Little, Brown & Co.

Piotrowski, Z. (1969). Long-term prognosis in schizophrenia based on Rorschach findings. In D. Siva Sankar (Ed.), *Schizophrenia: Current concepts and research.* Hicksville, NY: PDJ Publications.

Piotrowski, Z. (1971). A rational explanation of the irrational: Freud's and Jung's own dreams reinterpreted. *Journal of Personality Assessment, 35,* 505–518.

Piotrowski, Z. (1972). Psychological testing of intelligence and personality. In A. Freedman (Ed.), *Diagnosing mental illness.* New York: Atheneum.

Piotrowski, Z. (1972). From inkblots to dreams: Perceptanalysis generalized. *Rorschachiana Japonica, 14,* 1–10.

Piotrowski, Z. (1973). The Piotrowski dream system illustrated by the analysis of a specific dream (Freud's Irma Injection). *Psychiatric Quarterly, 47,* 609–622.

Piotrowski, Z. (1977). The M responses (movement). In M. Rickers-Ovsiankina (Ed.), *Rorschach Psychology*. Huntington, NY: R. Krieger Publisher.

Piotrowski, Z. (1979). *Perceptanalysis: The Rorschach method fundamentally reworked, expanded and synthesized*. Philadelphia: Ex Libris. (Originally Published 1957).

Piotrowski, Z. (1980). Computerized perceptanalytic Rorschach: The psychological X-ray in mental disorders. In J. Sidowski, J. Johnson & T. Williams (Eds.), *Technology in mental care delivery systems*. Norwood, NJ: Ablex.

Piotrowski, Z. (1982). Unsuspected and pertinent micro-facts in personology. *American Psychologist, 37,* 190–196.

Piotrowski, Z. & Biele, A. (1973). *Blind analysis of manifest dreams preceding death* (pp. 308–309). Scientific proceedings of the 176th annual meeting of American Psychiatric Association.

Piotrowski, Z. & Biele, A. (1983). The perceptanalytic dream system (PDS) as a tool in personality assessment. In J. Butcher & C. Spielberger (Eds.), *Advances in personality assessment*. Hillsdale, NJ: Lawrence Erlbaum Associates.

Piotrowski, Z. & Efron, H. (1966). Evaluation of outcome of schizophrenia: The long-term prognostic test index. In P. Hoch & J. Zubin (Eds.), *Psychopathology of schizophrenia*. New York: Grune & Stratton.

Prince, M. (1957). *The dissociation of personality*. New York: Meridian Books. (Originally published, 1906).

Schur, M. (1972). *Freud: Living and dying*. New York: International University Press.

Siebenthal, V. W. (1953). *Die Wissenschaft vom Traum*. Heidelberg, West Germany: Springer Verlag.

Ullman, M. & Zimmerman, N. (1979). *Working with Dreams*. New York: Delacorte Press/Eleanor Friede.

Vande Kemp, H. (1981). The dream in periodic literature, 1860–1910. *Journal of the History of Behavioral Sciences, 17,* 88–113.

Waelder, R. (1965). *Freud's main ideas and personality*. Lecture at Thomas Jefferson University, Philadelphia, PA.

Wallace, A. F. C. (1958). Dreams and the wishes of the soul: A type of psychoanalytic theory among the 17th C. Iroquois. *American Anthropologist, 60,* 234–248.

Wallace, A. F. C. (1972). *The death and rebirth of the Seneca*. New York: Vintage Books.

Woods, R. & Greenhouse, H. (Eds.). (1974). *The new world of dreams*. New York: Macmillan.

Author Index

Subject Index